GETTING IN!

GETTING IN!

The first comprehensive
step-by-step strategy guide
to acceptance at the
college of your choice.

Paulo de Oliveira
and
Steve Cohen

Workman Publishing, New York

DEDICATION

To B.J. Miller and Sarah Hill. They know why.

ACKNOWLEDGMENTS

Saying thank you to the many people who helped with this book reminded us how truly supportive, candid, and generous these people have been. This brief acknowledgment can barely convey our appreciation.

Our sincere thanks to:

Peter Workman, our publisher; Suzanne Rafer, our very talented and understanding editor; Wendy Palitz and Julienne McNeer, our book's designers; Joan Stewart, our agent and wonderful friend.

A number of admission professionals have been very generous with their help and encouragement. First among equals is James Rogers, Director of Admission at Brown University, who quite literally, in several ways, gave us our start. Jim, thank you.

In addition, we sincerely appreciate the assistance of Nancy Rhodes and Doug Langdon of Brown; Jim McMenamin, Director of Admission, Columbia College; Dick Steele, Dean of Admissions, Carleton College; Dr. Cliff Sjogren, Director of Admissions, the University of Michigan; Dr. Bob Bailey, Director of Admission, University of California at Berkeley; Ed Wall, Dean of Admission and Financial Aid, and Katherine Forte, Director of Admissions, University of Southern California; John Goldrick and Kevin Rooney of Notre Dame's Admission office; Richard Cashwell, Director of Undergraduate Admissions, the University of North Carolina at Chapel Hill; Fred Jewett, Dean of Admissions, Harvard; Margit Dahl, Director of Admissions, Yale; Roberto Noya, Director of Admission, New College of the University of South Florida; Dr. Stirling Huntley, Director of Admission, California Institute of Technology; R. Fred Zuker, Dean of Admission, Pomona College.

Among the many other professionals we worked with, we are especially grateful to Anne Thurber, the Buckley School; Patsy Carter and the rest of the staff at Beverly Hills High School; Dr. John Beyrer and the guidance staff of Lynbrook High School; Arthur Marmaduke of the California Student Aid Commission; Robert Seaver of the College Board; and Jonathan Wald, soon to be at Columbia.

For their typing, but more importantly their patience and good humor, we thank Marilyn Brown, Florante Sabado, Michelle Hale, and Tosca LaBoy.

For their encouragement and guidance, thanks to Bill Gladstone, Dick O'Reilly, Jordan Ringel, and Stan Moger.

And for having faith, thank you very, very much to John Sanzo, Chuck and Lane Consky, and Edna Lynn.

Library of Congress Cataloging in Publication Data de Oliveira, Paulo
   Getting in!
   1. Universities and colleges—United States—Admission. 2. Universities and colleges—United States—Entrance requirements. 3. College, Choice of.
I. Cohen, Steve   .II. Title.
LB2351.2.C63   1983   378′.1057′0973   83-1362
ISBN 0-89480-359-X
Cover design: Wendy Palitz
Book design: Wendy Palitz and Julienne McNeer

Workman Publishing Company, Inc.
708 Broadway
New York, NY 10003

Manufactured in the United States of America
First printing May 1983
10   9   8   7

CONTENTS

WHY THIS BOOK?

Miracles do happen. At least, one of us thinks so. Although both of us were admitted to and graduated from Brown University, one of us is convinced his own acceptance was an act of providence.

The "divine intervention" theory of college admission is probably as credible as most of the fantasies and myths that surround the subject. But it didn't sufficiently satisfy our curiosity about how and why we really were admitted to college. Nor did we think it would answer most high school students' questions, nor lessen their anxiety about the college admission process. Thus, this book was born.

Improving Your Odds

The purpose of this book is quite simple: to demystify college admissions and improve your chances of getting into the best school possible. It is not intended to help you decide whether college is right for you, nor which university you might be happiest attending; it cannot predict whether you will fit in, grow, or succeed there. It should, however, maximize your chances of acceptance at the college of your choice.

Exactly how this guide accomplishes that task is fairly simple:

1. It explains what colleges are looking for in prospective students. You will learn how admission policy reflects institutional needs—needs for football players, for alumni offspring whose parents can help build a new library, for cellists for the university orchestra, for classicists or chemists or aspiring historians to keep academic departments happy, for "nice kids" to maintain the school's social life. Once you can identify and analyze these needs, you will better understand what they mean in terms of *your* admission.

2. It explains the admission process: what the information in the application means, how it is evaluated, and how a decision is finally made. Most people—be they students, parents, or teachers—simply do not understand the realities of college admissions.

However, if you are aware of what colleges look for, and how the information you provide them in your application will be used, you *can* enhance your chances of admission.

3. It discusses ways to improve the quality of the information in your application, and how to communicate—or "package"—that information in order to increase your odds for acceptance. Your interview, your essay, your selection of an intended major, and a dozen other factors can make a difference. We will show you how to provide more useful information to the admission committee, thus improving your chances of admission.

4. It will help you to set yourself apart from the thousands of other applicants with whom you will be competing—to "position" yourself so that you stand out from the crowd.

5. It will provide information in applying for financial aid and making sense of recent changes in the college aid system.

While the purpose of this book is to enhance your chances of getting into the college of your choice, we will not claim—and you should not deceive yourself—that there is any instant formula for admission. Admissions are a complex business; there are no secret answers that will trigger an automatic acceptance. What we do offer you, however, are *tools:* tools to understand schools, their applications, and their admission committees.

PACKAGING
AND
POSITIONING

Throughout this book you will see the terms *packaging* and *positioning*. Although these concepts are described in some detail on page 87, it is useful to have a working understanding of them early on.

In the business world, *positioning* refers to a product's niche in the marketplace. The positioning of 7-Up has been the "Un-Cola"; Avis is positioned as the Number 2 car rental company (and thus they try harder). Positioning takes into account not only one's own strengths and weaknesses, but also the competition's.

Positioning can also be used to refer to students applying to college, where the "market" is the applicant pool. Since positioning—a product's or an individual's—can be influenced by the strengths one chooses to emphasize, students have a fairly open field in which to position themselves. For example, do you want to be thought of as a scholar? An athlete? A musician?

Packaging is one of the components of positioning and refers to a communications strategy. Packaging is *not* only a fancy binder containing your school newspaper articles, nor is it just the typeface in which your application is written. Rather it is *how* you go about telling the admission committee about your assets, about your positioning. The content of your package is far more important than the style in which it is presented.

As you learn about the college admission process, you will see that there is nothing sacrosanct about admission policies. *Who* gets into selective colleges depends largely on who applies in a given year. Admission criteria, particularly at private schools, are rarely set in concrete, and often change from year to year to reflect the quality of the applicant pool and the nature of the school's needs.

Finally, despite fantasies to the contrary, admission officers are *human*. They have biases, preferences, bad days, weak moments, flashes of insight, and more than occasional feelings of compassion. They recognize—and you should as well—that the admission process is imperfect. People make mistakes. Still, in general, the admission process *works*. And you can make it work for you.

Colleges and their admission staffs are looking for a wide range of students and if you provide them with useful information, think about setting yourself apart from the crowd, and target schools that may want someone with your attributes, you will have a pretty good chance of getting into a particular school or group of schools. Most admission officers agree that there are 6 to 10 colleges in this country that are so selective that it is virtually impossible to predict who will be accepted at any one of them. But they also agree that there are another 50 very selective institutions—where you will receive an excellent education and probably have a terrific time—for which you *can* predict admission outcomes. *If* you have the proper tools.

How to Use This Book

To take best advantage of this book, you should follow these six moderately easy steps:

1. Read it. You should really read the book from beginning to end at least once. Don't worry about details or specific recommendations, or how to apply them to your own situation. Reading the book from cover to cover—even very quickly—will give you an overview of the admission process, and what we mean by "packaging" and "positioning" yourself. This will prove invaluable when you get down to specifics.

2. Ask your parents to read it. Most parents know very little about the college admission process. It's important that *all* of you be liberated from the myths that surround college admissions.

3. Start early. Optimally you should read this book, and begin your college search, no later than the middle of your junior year. It may help to start earlier, but until your junior year you won't have a proper grasp of the record— grades and SATs—you'll be presenting to the colleges. If you start later than that, you will be scrambling.

4. Role play. The case studies we have included in Chapter Ten are designed to give you a feel for what various admission committees think of a particular applicant. If you consider the case studies from the perspective of an admission officer, you will be better prepared to evaluate your own application. Ask your parents to role play as well. The actual decisions made in each case, as well as explanations of those decisions, are provided. But don't peek at the "answers" until you've actually played admission officer

5. Reread the appropriate chapters. Your first reading should have given you an overview. As you prepare your application, return to the relevant chapters and *prepare*. Prepare for the interview; prepare for the essay; prepare for the campus visit. The chapters on these subjects contain specific recommendations that should make the whole process

less bewildering and alienating, and more manageable. The information they provide *can* make a difference.

6. Try working smarter, not harder. If you are serious about getting into a good school, you are probably already putting in a lot of effort. This book should not make you work *harder* at being admitted. Instead, it is designed to enable you to work *smarter*. Doing well in your courses, preparing for the SATs, and excelling at extracurriculars must remain your principal concerns. Your college application efforts should not interfere with them. This book will provide you with the information and tools to help you make the most of what you've got without taking too much of your time.

PART ONE

PREPARING
FOR
COLLEGE

YOUR HIGH SCHOOL CAREER

Admission officers at selective colleges are concerned with four elements of your high school career: courses and grades, SATs, extracurriculars, and work experience.

If you're already in your senior year, there's not much you can do to change your high school career—that combination of courses taken, grades received, test results, out-of-class activity, and the general impression you make on teachers and counselors. By this time, your record will be set in concrete. That's not to say that you can't better your midyear grade report, or use our suggestions to put your record in a more positive light. But basically, you will have control only over the application forms and interview.

If, on the other hand, you are one of the smart set who start thinking about college early, then you'll get a lot out of this chapter. And by early we mean your sophomore or junior year of high school—if not your freshman year. The earlier you begin thinking about how your high school efforts will affect your chances for admission, the better off you'll be.

The "Perfect" High School Career

There is no formula for the perfect high school profile. While there are general rules to follow, the "best" high school career is as much a reflection of your strengths and weaknesses as it is a reflection of those rules. Admission procedures and policies differ from college to college, and there is no such thing as a "perfect" applicant. There are many paths to the college of your choice, and it makes the most sense to maintain a strong sense of your own goals and interests, pursuing those rather than trying slavishly to meet the expectations of admission offices. This is especially true in extracurricular activity, where the nature of the pursuit isn't nearly as important as what you put into it and what you seem to get out of it. The "typical" minimum requirements for college admission are discussed later in this chapter, but you do have some latitude. Let the real person come out in those areas where you have some choices.

Grades versus Extracurriculars

Nothing can replace consistent hard work and discipline in bettering your chances for admission. No flurry of eleventh-hour activity can make up for years of neglect; nor will any application form glossing over overcome an essentially poor record. Most good colleges do not have cutoff points for grades and scores, but you can bet that the sheer number of applicants make it very hard for them to accept someone with mediocre grades and tests. The more selective the college, the more likely it is that someone with a mediocre academic record will be knocked into the "unlikely" category from the start. Only extraordinary background factors or extracurricular achievement will carry them into even the "possible" category. One of the few "universal truths" about admissions says: the essay, the interview, and your extracurriculars only have a positive effect on your

chances *if* you are already in that "possible" admission category— the result of decent grades.

Your Courses: The "Best" Schedule

If possible, start planning your course schedules in the ninth grade. Most schools do provide counseling sessions for incoming students. Listen to guidance counselors' advice about a "good" college preparatory program. Most have reasonable experience. And remember, any courses taken before the ninth grade are insignificant; it's the high school work that counts for colleges.

The junior year is pivotal. Your junior year grades are crucial to admission offices because they are sometimes the last representation of academic performance they'll see while evaluating your folder. If there is any time during which you should push yourself to get good grades, it is the junior year. But premature senioritis can be disastrous, since most schools request a midyear grade report featuring your senior year's first-semester grades. This is especially true for colleges that subscribe to the April 15 notification date. The midyear report is generally received by late January and can frequently be included in committee deliberations. For colleges that have a rolling admissions policy (see page 112), the midyear report is less crucial, because decisions are made on a "first folder complete, first served" basis. But even here the midyear grades will eventually be evaluated. In fact, virtually all colleges attach a rider to their acceptance packages indicating that admission is based on the continuation of a student's good record, and graduation from high school. Once you're admitted, of course, any college will be reluctant to deny you a place. But a disastrous drop in class performance or a serious breach of conduct leading to suspension or expulsion may result in an acceptance being revoked.

Valuable Courses

Whenever possible, enroll in the most rigorous levels of classes. Go for quality, not quantity. It's the *solid* courses that count. Colleges like to see students who try their best, and a B in an honors or Advanced Placement (A.P.) course is better than an A in a fluff course. This is especially true for courses in your potential major, if you've indicated that you're strongly channeled in a particular direction. Each year you should be taking at least four "major" courses in the liberal arts: English, mathematics, languages, history, and science. Avoid overloading your schedule with too many offerings like psychology or music, which aren't seen as good college prep subjects. There is a fine line, however, between a course load that is solid and demanding, and one that overextends your time and energy. Colleges want students who are realistic about their own limits. If you schedule a course load of five

honors subjects for yourself, and wind up getting C's or D's, you're telegraphing the fact that you don't know your strengths and weaknesses.

You should take the most rigorous classes in areas where you have the most strength. If you're a math-science whiz planning to study engineering, take advantage of your aptitude by opting for the toughest courses in mathematics and lab sciences. If your strengths are verbal, really explore English, history, or languages. If you're one of the rare people with equal strengths in both areas, appraise your own limits carefully. Then choose the toughest courses in fields you think you'll enjoy. You're bound to do better when the subject matter delights you.

At the same time you are developing your strengths, you should be dealing with your weaknesses. Show grit and follow through by consistently facing your weak points. You don't have to take courses in the most advanced tracks—A.P.'s or honors programs—but you should show that you're not shrinking from rounding out your education. For example, even if languages are your weakest area, you should still take at least three years of one language.

Show *depth, scope,* and *continuity* in your courses. Admission folk want to see a logical progression in your course work. They especially value follow-through.

Depth means taking courses that are progressively more difficult, enabling you to go into the material in detail. If you're a math wizard, this means that you will have taken every available course in your high school, really preparing for college math.

Scope means taking a variety of courses—not just those you're good at. That's all part of our "developing strengths, dealing with weaknesses" advice.

Continuity means following courses through to their conclusions, and not just stopping and starting subject areas irrationally. This is especially important in languages. It's better to have taken three years of one foreign language than two years of one and two of another. It also means trying to pursue that field you're really good at even if you don't have a course available at your high school. If you're a crack student of physics and can only take one course at your school, you may want to consider taking a local college course in the subject. Finally, it means taking courses in a logical progression: taking an A.P. course in mathematics only after you've completed the qualifying work in math.

Fulfill
Requirements

Be aware of both general college preparatory requirements *and* individual schools' requirements as you plan your schedule. It's like entering an amusement park; you need one ticket to be admitted to the park itself, and a number of other stubs to get onto particular rides. Make sure you've got all the tickets you need. This is especially crucial if you have definite plans for a specific major or academic program.

A good academic preparation would contain the following courses:

English: Four years, with emphasis on writing and composition.

Math: Three years college preparatory.

Languages: Three years, preferably of the *same* language.

History: Two years minimum, including one of United States.

Sciences: Two to three years of lab sciences: biology, chemistry, physics.

Electives: Two years, preferably in music, art, theater, journalism, etc.

As you begin to consider particular colleges, make sure you know those schools' specific requirements. In addition, if you are contemplating a particular program or division within a college, find out everything you can about it. You don't want your program to have any weak spots. Consult the college's most recent catalog as well as your counselor.

Electives:
Broadening Yourself

In addition to solid academic courses, like English, mathematics, languages, history, and sciences, you will probably have the opportunity to choose electives. Never try to replace your academic offerings with these electives, even if they are in areas like psychology or sociology. Colleges want to see evidence of work in the traditional liberal arts. Still, you should round out your profile by enrolling in music, theater, art, journalism, and the like.

These choices can be especially important if your extracurricular profile is tied into one of those areas. If you're selling yourself as a budding political journalist and have been appointed editor-in-chief of your school newspaper, a number of journalism courses fit right into your positioning. Draw judiciously from purely vocational courses like auto mechanics, shop, mechanical drawing, home economics, and drivers' education. There's nothing wrong with taking these courses, but you shouldn't consider them anything more than just a practical opportunity to learn a skill. The only way these courses can enhance your chances of admission is if you put to work what you've learned: if you start your own weekend car service business, or get a job in an architectural office using your mechanical drawing prowess. In sum, there's nothing wrong with broadening yourself, but it's a secondary consideration. Your core courses are the ones that count.

Advance Placement (A.P.) Courses

Advance Placement courses are college-level courses taught in high schools—for which you take national exams in the hope of getting college credit. A.P. courses can do three things for you. First, they provide you with in-depth, college-level course work. This has

intrinsic educational value. Second, they may enable you to get college credit if you do well on the A.P. exam. And even if you can't get credit, you may still "place out" (skip introductory courses) once at college. Third, a good score on the A.P. exam helps create a compelling picture of scholarliness, and demonstrates that you are disciplined, and serious about academics.

Not all colleges will grant credit for work done in A.P. courses, no matter how high a grade you get on the exam. (Test scores range from 1 to 5, 5 being tops.) Amherst College, for instance, will not grant credit toward its degree for work done in high school. Ed Wall, Amherst's former Dean of Admission, explained why in a publication called *How We Do It*, which examines Amherst's approach to admission. Mr. Wall says, "The Faculty feels strongly that a liberal arts education should be a cumulative four-year experience which they want to be as rich and varied as possible for the student involved. Three years is simply not enough time for a student to achieve that goal." Amherst will grant advanced standing in some courses, though, allowing freshmen to place out of introductory courses.

Other universities routinely offer advanced standing to entering students who have accumulated enough A.P. credits, allowing them to graduate in three or three and a half years—Harvard and Stanford among them. This approach saves you time and money: (We tend to agree with Mr. Wall, however, that you're probably better served by staying in college a full four years.) Some schools, like Brown, will make individual determinations on a case by case basis. They'll allow students to graduate early, but generally counsel against it.

As a general rule you should enroll in an A.P. course only if you feel you'll do well in it. If you're uncertain, examine your schedule to see how demanding it is, and whether you think you can handle the additional work load. It doesn't hurt to approach the teacher to obtain a course syllabus or description of what will be required of you, and an assessment of whether you are qualified to take the course based on your past history in the subject. Once again, you should play to your strengths, avoiding A.P.'s in areas that have traditionally bedeviled you. In keeping with our general advice, take the most advanced course wherever practical, but avoid overextension. For more information on the A.P. exams, write College Board Publications, Box 886, New York, NY 10101.

Courses at Local Colleges

If you're considering taking classes at a nearby college during your senior year, keep the following points in mind:

1. Make sure you've exhausted your high school curriculum in that subject. If you're a math whiz and have whipped through all your school's offerings, it might make sense to take calculus at a local college. But don't do it just to impress admission people. They might think you're avoiding your high school if you haven't exhausted all the courses it offers. And relatively unchallenging courses at a local junior college may not be thought of as very demanding, particularly when compared to A.P. courses in high school.

2. Make sure that the course work and reputation of the college itself make it worth your while. Any number of colleges open their courses to high school students. Some, like the UCLA Honors Program, uphold rigorous standards for admission. Others admit students on limited, "special student" basis with equally tough entrance criteria. But some places will open their doors to anyone who pays. The main criteria in selecting such a program should be its quality and reputation. Just taking courses at a third-rate community college does not place you ahead of students who have taken honors and A.P. courses at their secondary schools.

3. Make sure that you have a compelling reason for taking college courses. The most legitimate reasons are that you've exhausted your high school curriculum or that the subject is not offered in that curriculum. Before you enroll in such a program, consider whether you've fulfilled the requirements of your first-choice colleges. In other words, don't pass up your high school U.S. history course in favor of a college political science course because you think it will look better on your record.

Academic Programs
Outside High School

Many private colleges and some preparatory schools offer summer sessions, usually open to high school juniors. Among these are the Stanford Summer School, Harvard Summer Session, and Phillips Andover Academy Summer Session. The National Science Foundation also runs scholarship programs for outstanding science students at a variety of colleges around the country. For more information on these programs, see page 217.

If you have the resources and opportunity to attend one of these sessions, go for it. These programs allow you to live in residence with other students and get a taste for independent college life, as well as offer an exposure to rigorous academics. Most admission officers highly recommend such programs. They are essentially dress rehearsals for college living.

Testing:
The Second
Credential

Objective tests too often inspire sheer terror in prospective applicants. This is unfortunate because it's precisely this kind of anxiety that can trip you up when you're subjected to the Scholastic Aptitude Test (SAT), the American College Test (ACT), or Achievement Tests. There are many tales of students who bombed out because they partied too much the evening before their test, got choked with anxiety while actually taking it, or misnumbered their computer answer sheets in the rush to complete all the questions. As you approach your first objective tests, try to forget all those stories and relax! A positive attitude will probably do more for your scores than any amount of frantic preparation.

Keep these points in mind as you face these exams:

1. The SAT and ACT are not intelligence tests. If you get a low score on either, you're not a mental deficient. These tests measure verbal and mathematical reasoning abilities. Those reasoning abilities are developed over time and often predict academic performance in college, but have little to do with innate intelligence.

Some educators, in fact, maintain that a test score is only an indicator of how well you've done on the test. Keep in mind also that test scores have little to do with eventual success and happiness in life. If they did, a lot of professors, captains of industry, professionals, and authors would be out of business.

2. The SAT is not infallible. It has a built-in "error range" of 60 points in every score report. If your verbal score is 550, your actual score is between 520 and 580. The College Board has also been known to make mistakes in devising test answers. In more than one instance students have challenged the validity of an answer and won their cases by proving that more than one of the answers provided was correct. For most tests, you can obtain a copy of the actual test booklet and an answer sheet in order to make sure that the Educational Testing Service (ETS) made no mistake in grading your answers. Be forewarned, however, that the ETS is seldom wrong.

3. The SAT is not the most important credential.

Most prestige colleges put a greater emphasis on your grades and course work in predicting your academic potential, and most also consider a variety of other factors in their admission decisions. Admission officers know that objective tests alone cannot accurately predict academic performance in college. They also realize that SATs can't measure your drive, discipline, creativity, imagination, persistence, conceptualization, character, or dreams and goals. And these have a lot to do with success in college. So while objective tests play a significant part in admission decisions, every year selective colleges admit plenty of students who have scores in the 400s or 500s on either portion of the SAT, and deny many applicants with scores in the 700s. The higher the better, of course, but low tests mean little in and of themselves.

4. You can prepare for your exams.

And, probably do better on them than you would approaching them cold. This, like any other method of improving your chances of admission, takes some extra work. But it's worth your time.

The PSAT/NMSQT

1. What is this test all about?

PSAT/NMSQT stands for Preliminary Scholastic Aptitude Test/National Merit Scholarship Qualifying Test. It is important for a number of reasons. First, it's a rehearsal for later objective tests. It acquaints you with the format, approach, and thinking behind other such tests. Second, if you check a few boxes on the test form, you'll be considered for the National Merit Scholarship Program or the National Achievement Scholarship Program for Outstanding Negro Students. You *cannot* be considered for either program, which may lead to honors or scholarship money, without taking the test. Third, you can also indicate that you want your scores reported to colleges. If you do well, you'll be barraged with a great deal of informative material from all sorts of campuses. It's worthwhile to skim all the material you receive, and then read closely the literature that appeals to you.

The PSAT is a two-hour test, divided into two sections: verbal and mathematics. Each has a separate score ranging from 20 to 80, which with a 0 added corresponds roughly to SAT scoring. If you get a 50 Verbal, 60 Math, the SAT equivalent is 500 Verbal, 600 Math. Both the verbal portion and the math portion contain test questions roughly similar in approach to those used in the SAT. Both measure your reasoning ability, not your recall of facts or innate intelligence. But don't take all this too seriously; by the time you take the SAT you may well do better than your PSAT score would indicate.

2. How should you prepare for the PSAT/NMSQT?

There aren't too many study aids available for the PSAT. You may want to spend time with a preparation book to acquaint yourself with the logic of the tests. Then, get a good night's sleep (don't sleep more than you usually do—this might make you exhausted). Eat the sort of breakfast you usually eat. As you take the test, remember that it's really just a dry run—the big one is yet to come.

3. When should you take the PSAT? And how many times?

These two questions are tied together because of an increasing trend among high school students toward taking the PSAT/NMSQT twice. The conventional wisdom holds that you take the test once, usually in October of your junior year. You'll be more prepared than you would be in the spring of your sophomore year, and taking the test any later might disqualify you for the National Merit competition. (You'll probably be taking the SAT in the spring of your junior year, too.)

We don't advocate that you take the PSAT twice, mostly because in the scheme of college acceptance, the PSAT is a minor quantity, and taking the test even once is expensive. However, if you fear you'll do dismally, you may want to take the test first in your sophomore year. If you do as badly as you predicted, you can try again in your junior year. If, however, you've done satisfactorily the first time, then you should stay put and concentrate on preparing for the SAT. Keep in mind that you must score in the top half of the top 1 percent of test takers in your state in order to be a National Merit Semifinalist.

4. What do you do after you've gotten the score?

Relax. You have two shots at the SAT and Achievements, or the ACT. Your scores on the PSAT will be available to most colleges but they carry little weight. What you should really do is to analyze your mistakes in taking the test itself. Did you take too long to answer questions you weren't sure you could answer? Did you panic or let the clock get to you? Did you try to relax? Was there a particular section of the exam you flubbed? (The verbal section has four sections: antonyms, sentence completion, analogies, and reading comprehension.) If there's an area that gave you particular problems, practice before you go on to take the SAT.

The SAT

This, of course, is the biggie. Once again, you should *relax* when contemplating taking this test. Remember that good Achievement Test results can sometimes make up for sub-par SAT scores and that your grades are usually more important to colleges than is this three-hour ordeal.

1. What is this test all about?

The College Board itself says this about SATs:

"It is a test of developed ability, not of innate intelligence.

In a sense, it is a broad achievement test in which certain cognitive and analytical skills are tested. These are abilities that are related to academic success in college and that develop slowly, through both in-school and out-of-school experience. . . . An important difference between the SAT and the Achievement Tests is the limited dependence of the SAT on a specific curriculum."*

In format and approach the SAT is similar to the PSAT. A recent edition of the test consisted of six separate 30-minute sections: two verbal sections of 85 questions; two mathematical sections of 60 questions; the Test of Standard Written English (TSWE; 50 questions); and one experimental section that allows the ingenious testers to find better ways of mentally torturing generations of students to come. The TSWE is said to assist colleges in placing students in appropriate English courses. So what you should primarily concern yourself with is the verbal and math sections.

2. How should you prepare for the SAT? First and foremost, you should pay special attention to developing verbal and writing skills in English class, and to bettering your understanding of mathematics. Last-minute cramming will seldom have a significant effect on test scores, but an effort over even several months may help you to better your score. The key words here are *attitude*

Test and Technical Data for the SAT Administered in April, 1981, by the Admissions Testing Program of the College Board.

and *effort*. Guidance counselors have told us that among students who took the SAT, then a review course, and then the test again, the ones who showed a significant increase in their second exam scores were those who supplemented the course by doing practice exercises on a regular basis. Those who took the class but did no exercises fared no better the second time around. Beverly Hills High School has considerable experience in this field, and it is the opinion of its guidance department that steady preparation for the SAT can have an impact on one's score. Here are some of the methods people use to prepare:

▶ Working with vocabulary lists and grammar texts. This is probably something you can do on your own or with friends, and it's a good exercise even if you don't plan to use it for the SAT. But don't try doing this a week before the test; you're better off spending your time just getting acquainted with the SAT's format.

▶ Reviewing notes, and possibly working through the review sections of old textbooks. Again, these exercises should be started well before you take the test.

▶ Using preparation guides. Once again, you're best off starting early. There are a variety of such guides, ranging from those published by the College Board itself to those offered by educational publishers. Most of these contain sample tests with answers to help you to familiarize yourself with the test.

The advantage of using these guides is that they acquaint you with the format and procedure of the test itself. This will allow you more time to actually think about and answer questions: if you know what to expect, you won't waste time figuring out *how* to take the test. And you'll also be less anxious about the whole experience which means you're bound to do better—especially if you have a tendency to "clutch" in high-pressure exam situations.

You can overcome a lot of anxiety by practicing alone somewhere, in a quiet corner. Set a timer and pretend you're actually taking the test. Your parents might act as stern-faced test proctors, timing your performance and providing the proper atmosphere of stress to duplicate test conditions.

But however confident you may feel, you should unquestionably acquaint yourself with the format of the SAT and take a couple of practice exams before trying the real thing. Even if you're a natural at objective tests, and notwithstanding how brilliantly you may have done on the PSAT/NMSQT, you'll help yourself by being comfortable with the test format.

▶ Enrolling in special preparation programs. There is considerable debate over the value of in-depth test preparation programs. Before you sign up for one, consider its cost and the amount of time it will divert from other activities. If you really want to pay two or three hundred dollars for a commercial preparation course, it may help you. But make sure the course is run by professionals. More and more high schools are offering these courses; if your school has such a program, even better. Then you'll be sure that it's legitimate. The April 1982 *New York Times* Spring Survey of Education devoted a full article to the surge in test preparation programs and reported that a spot check of high schools in Connecticut or Westchester County, New York, showed that over 30 percent of college-bound students were enrolling in such courses.

The College Board claims that special preparation programs have little effect on SAT scores, with improvements in the 10 to 30 point range. The National Education Association, however, has released a study suggesting that healthy gains are derived from these courses. The NEA's July, 1980, study said that coaching programs that were offered in the months between the PSAT and the SAT could result in the average student's combined score being raised about 100 points (remember that the combined score ranges from 400 to 1,600 points). This is compared to the typical increase of only 40 points from the first test to the second. The average gain, therefore, is 60 points.

As with any other form of preparation, however, a special course will only be as effective as *you* want to make it. You won't improve your score by sitting like a lump in the class and never lifting a hand; you won't help yourself if you refuse to do outside exercises. You have to do the homework.

Is it worthwhile, then, to spend time on preparation, or in special coaching courses? That is a question that only you can answer. To some extent, the answer depends on your general aptitude for these tests as shown by the PSAT. If you've gotten a decent score—say, above 60 on each section—you might be better off just acquainting yourself with the SAT and spending more time on your classwork. If you really flub the PSATs, then you probably should take a course, or at the very least develop your own preparation program before taking the SAT.

Of course, the results of either commercial, school-sponsored, or personal coaching programs vary. You have to decide whether it's worth your time, effort, and money to prepare in this way. As in any other endeavor, moderation is advised—you should never let your coaching impinge on your schoolwork or activities. And be sure to check the program's reputation with your counselor or other students who have taken it before you sign up.

3. Taking the test. On the evening before you tackle the SAT, we don't advise that you necessarily cram or go to bed hours before your normal school bedtime. (Keep in mind that tests normally begin at 8:30 or 9:00 A.M.) Whatever it is you do that makes you feel alert and energetic the next morning, *do it*. Eat enough to sustain you for three hours of excruciating mental gymnastics, but not so much that your body will shout for sleep as it digests a feast. Some folks recommend bringing a piece of fruit or candy to munch on during the breaks for extra energy; if you think it'll help you, *do it*. And give yourself enough time

to get to the test center comfortably. During the test, stay alert—and follow directions!

4. When should you take the SAT? And how many times should you take the SAT? Most counselors suggest you take the SAT in the spring (March) of your junior year. This date will give you the maximum time to sharpen your skills for a first try, while still allowing you to schedule an additional SAT during the fall of your senior year, if necessary. The November test date is the last one that will get your test scores to colleges in time for most admission decisions. SATs are also administered in June and January, so you could pick either of these dates for your junior year SAT.

How many times should you take it? This really depends on how well you do on your first time out, and how confident you are that you'll improve on your second round. College Board statistics show this about the SAT:

▶ On the average, the lower your initial score, the better your chances are of improving the second time. Here's a chart of average increases:

INITIAL SCORE	AVERAGE SCORE CHANGE*
700	−7
600	+1
500	+7
400	+18
300	+36

*From *The SAT—A College Board Presentation* or *Taking the Scholastic Aptitude Test*, Princeton, NJ: College Entrance Examination Board, 1981.

Notice that those with test scores above 700 did worse, on the average, the second time around. Keep in mind that these are *average* increases—your case may be different.

▶ The average score increase overall is 15 points for a repeat of the SAT.

▶ Thirty-five percent of those taking the test have score decreases the second time around.

▶ One out of 20 increases on the second try will total more than 100 points.

▶ Only one second try in 100 will drop more than 100 points.

Now that you have some sense of the hazards involved in taking the test twice, think again. Our advice is that if your scores are above 700, there's no sense in taking the SAT again. According to the statistics it's likely you won't score as high. (This assumes that your 700 or better is on the portion of the test that relates to your interests and potential major—if you're planning on engineering, the 700 should be in math.)

If your scores are comfortably in the 600 range, you may want to consider a second round, if you have reason to think you'll do better: by having taken a coaching course, worked extra hard on vocabulary, preparation guides, or *something*. Most counselors routinely recommend taking the test twice in this situation, but they also recommend preparing for it.

If your scores are below 600, it's probably worthwhile to retake the test. Many colleges will accept either the high score or an average of the two as indicative of your potential, so it's better to try again. And it *is* a convention for most students to do so—especially at the better prep schools and public high schools. But you *must* have some program in mind for bettering your odds.

5. Should you take the SAT more than twice? Probably not, unless there were clear reasons for doing poorly on the first two go-arounds, and you assume you'll do better a third time. This is your decision, of course. But if you still scored poorly on your second attempt, you're probably better served by channeling your energies into your applications, your activities, and your courses. Admission officers may be tolerant of multiple attempts, but when considered with other signals in your application, this repetitive test-taking may project the image of a pushy, relentless, grade-grubber. It also may reinforce an impression that the applicant is a "plodder." It's best to leave well enough alone.

6. What should you do when you get the test results back? First of all, don't get cocky—or panic. The SAT is just one credential. Second, if you've done poorly, you can request from the College Board (for a price, naturally) a copy of your actual test booklet and answer sheet. These will be made available three months after the test date. You can then see for yourself which were your weak and strong areas, and reinforce your vulnerable spots before the next sitting.

In interpreting your score, remember that there's a difference between your national percentile (for all college-bound seniors) and your ranking in a particular college's applicant pool. For instance, the mean national SAT score for the April 1981 test was 426 verbal, 467 math. If you got these scores, you'd be smack in the middle of the national group. But if you were applying to Williams College, your showing would be well below the mean for the applicant group there.

In addition to these scores, you'll receive verbal subscores in reading and vocabulary ranging from 20 to 80, and a subscore on the Test of Standard Written English. (The reading subscore comes from sentence completion and reading passages; the vocabulary from antonym and analogy portions.) It's our experience that admission officers examine these subscores secondarily, giving more weight to overall scores. Look at these closely, however, because they will help you spot your weaknesses on the verbal part of the SAT. If your reading score is low, work on reading comprehension. If the vocabulary portion is low, use vocabulary lists for practice.

Achievement Tests

Many selective colleges require that you submit not only the SAT but also Achievement Test results. Some stipulate that you take one or two particular exams: Wellesley College, for instance, asks for three Achievements, including English and any other two from among language, social studies, or math/science groups. Keep these points in mind:

1. Achievements, in the College Boards' own words, "are curriculum based; they are designed to measure the results of study in particular subject matter areas." *Therefore, you can study for them, and should use materials reviewing the subject areas covered in the tests you want to take.*

2. Achievements should be taken in "terminal" course areas (those you'll only study for a semester or a year in all) *immediately after you have finished the relevant course.* If you take a chemistry course during your junior year, don't wait until fall of your senior year to brave the Chemistry Achievement. Sit for every test as soon as you've finished the necessary course work to be covered by that exam.

3. Each Achievement Test corresponds to a specified level of study in each subject area. For example, the Math Level I Achievement should be taken after two years of study that have included geometry, algebra, functions, and trigonometry. This test is more of a "survey," designed for the average mathematics student. Math Level II, on the other hand, requires you to have taken three years of math, including advanced algebra, plain and solid geometry, vectors, sequences, limits, and number theory. This is a more focused test covering material in greater depth than the Level I exam, and is recommended only for top students. Before you register for a particular Achievement Test, contact your teacher or counselor to determine whether your course work has prepared you for it.

4. High school curricula aren't necessarily geared to the Achievement Test program. For example, the Physics Achievement Test really covers a two-year college prep course—not an introductory class—and requires knowledge of mechanics, electricity, magnets, optics, waves, heat, and kinetic theory. You may find, too, that your high school history course covers less factual material than is quizzed in the U. S. History or European History/ World Cultures Achievement tests. So make sure you ascertain from your teachers whether on the basis of your classwork alone, you'll be properly prepared for the tests you're planning to take. For information on what is required for each Achievement Test, see the College Board publication *About the Achievements*, a copy of which should be in your high school guidance office.

5. At the same time that you're capitalizing on your strengths, don't overlook required Achievements at the colleges you're considering. You'll have to submit the English Composition test to Duke University, for example. And, if you're applying there as an engineer, you'll also have to take the Math Achievement. There's no getting around these requirements. Although some colleges are more liberal than others (Brown requires *any* three) and may be willing to overlook a requirement or two, you'll be making your ad-

mission that much more chancy by not following their instructions. Check your library's school guides for information on required Achievements. *Barron's Comparative Guide to American Colleges* contains this data, but it is best to check the college's most recent publication.

You can take an Achievement twice, and should if you believe that you'll do better the second time around by virtue of having prepared yourself better, or because you actually *know* more. Most language Achievements, for instance, are geared to students who have taken a minimum of two years of language, but you'll do better if you've completed three to four years of study in that area. It's up to you to decide whether it's worthwhile to put yourself through the experience twice. You might want to test later in your high school career to avoid this problem, but don't wait too long and then foreclose your option of taking a test again before an application deadline.

The ACT

The ACT is administered by the American College Testing Service in Iowa City, Iowa. Most private colleges prefer the SAT and Achievements to the ACT, but some (Stanford, Pomona, Oberlin, and Williams, for instance) will accept either test. The bulk of universities that require the ACT are land-grant institutions in the Midwest, South, and West. Check your college guide to determine which you might need, keeping in mind that the majority of selective colleges, be they public or private, rely on the SAT for most of their decisions. In the University of California system, for example, UCLA will accept either the SAT or the ACT; Berkeley will accept only the SAT. Both the University of Texas and the University of Michigan require the SAT.

The ACT is composed of four 35 to 50 minute sections, in English usage, mathematics usage, social studies reading, and natural sciences reading. The main difference between the ACT and the SAT is that the ACT is a yardstick of both reasoning ability and knowledge of specific subject matter covered in classes. The ACT is therefore considered a "complete" test. Because most of the colleges we're talking about in this book require the SAT, we don't want to belabor the ACT. If you need more information on it, we suggest you seek out guides on the subject.

The TOEFL

If English is not your native language (that is, if you spoke another language first, either because you lived abroad or your folks spoke it at home), you may want to take the Test of English as a Foreign Language. TOEFL is administered by the College Board. Geared to foreign students, the test measures the ability of non-native speakers to use English in a demanding college program. Most colleges require the test of foreign students as a supplement to the SAT. Clearly, if you didn't grow up speaking

English you may want to take the TOEFL, since your verbal SAT score may not reflect your true aptitude. Before you do this, we suggest you consult with your guidance counselor or admissions officers. Above all, you should be able to make a strong case for the validity of the TOEFL in measuring your aptitude. If you can only make a marginal case for taking the TOEFL forget it—admission officers will not be impressed by your high score.

Extracurricular Activities

Perhaps the greatest myth surrounding college admissions is that universities are looking for "well-rounded" students. In fact, they are looking for a well-rounded *class*. Their ideal is to assemble a student body of bright individuals, each of whom has a notable talent. Therefore admission officers like to see *mastery* of a particular field, not dabbling in a series of different and unconnected endeavors. Additionally, the admission officers want to see evidence of follow-through in that field—of perseverance and dedication over time. Quality, not quantity, is the key.

As you consider how much time to spend on any single activity, keep in mind that it's better to concentrate on one or two areas than to spread yourself thin. An admission officer will be much more impressed by a notable achievement or significant, long-term involvement in *one* area than by a laundry list of superficial activities. No college wants a "joiner"—someone who joins a club or team simply to say he is a part of it. Of course, there must be Indians as well as chiefs in every organization. But the applicant who will be noticed is the one who brings special skills, demonstrated leadership, or expertise to campus life—someone who will have an *impact* on the student body.

Remember, also: a good academic profile, as we keep repeating, is a *prerequisite* for admission to a good college. So academics should remain your top priority. Unfortunately, there is no perfect formula for the ratio of time you should spend on homework versus activities. There may be semesters when your courses are especially demanding, or others when your activities, whatever they are, start to take up an inordinate amount of time. The bottom line, however, is that you should spend more time on your school work than on all your activities combined. The admissions statistics just don't support the case for neglecting any of your studies.

Choosing the "Right" Activities

The whole business of extracurriculars is somewhat paradoxical. You're expected to choose your activities purely on the basis of what appeals to you. Yet at the same time, the prestige colleges keep sending signals that they want those student-council presidents, all-American athletes, and award-winning musicians. All this might infect you with doubts when you're unhappy with one of your out-of-class endeavors: "Am I really doing this for me, or for the admission office?"

Keep in mind that neither cold-blooded realism nor worldly cynicism will help you to succeed. You know how hard it is to excell at something you don't find enjoyable or challenging. If you're going out for track just because you think you might win a varsity letter and it will look good on your applications, you're fooling yourself. Some part of you has to savor running, competition, training. That doesn't mean you should ignore what might be impressive to an admission officer. But one activity does not look better than another in and of itself. Just because you've heard that Dartmouth College puts an unusual emphasis on athletics doesn't mean you should take up a sport and pursue it assiduously. Here's the basic rule: Do what interests *you* and do your *best*.

How to Stand Out

There are ways to highlight your own extracurricular experiences by putting in extra effort, and by carefully evaluating where you want to go with that effort. To do this, you must understand the difference between a cynical and an honest goal. A cynical goal sounds something like this: "I won't ever get into Harvard unless I become student body president, get my sculptures exhibited, or become editor of the paper." That's very different from

TYPICAL VERSUS
LESS COMMON ACTIVITIES

Here is a comparison of activities that tend to be listed very frequently by applicants versus those that are much less common and therefore more likely to catch the eye of an admission officer.

FIELD	TYPICAL	LESS COMMON
Athletics	Skiing Baseball Track and field Tennis	Wind-surfing Crew, water polo Rodeo Boxing, squash
Community Service	United Way Fund-raiser Hospital volunteer Student tutor	"Safe-Rides"—an organization of teenagers who drive kids home from parties on weekends, to cut down on teen drunk-driving accidents Teen paramedic Inner-city youth tutor
Extracurricular Organizations	Math club, chess team School newspaper Spanish club	Computer wargames team TV contest team Reporter for community newspaper Latino-Anglo friendship committee (or other interracial understanding group)
Leadership	Student Council President Drama Club President Political campaign volunteer	Organizer of town clean-up effort Founder of teen drama troupe Volunteer for environmental group
Creative	Painting Photography Drawing Woodworking Choir soloist School play actor Violinist in school orchestra	Electronic graphics Holography (laser photography) Designing boats Glass-blowing New Wave band lead singer Juggler Steel-string Hawaiian guitarist

setting an honest objective for yourself: "If I'm going to be on the school yearbook, as I want to be, it'll be my eventual goal to be made photography editor. And although I won't be devastated if I don't attain that objective, I'll strive for it with all the determination I have." Setting goals is a necessary part of achievement, and achievement is what the college admission process is all about.

If you do have a strong interest in a field, it's important to show your mastery or depth of commitment to it. There's no easy way to do this. It's mostly a matter of hard work and persistence, but it also involves planning. Here are two examples.

1. Creative activities. Let's say you're a painter. You could just go to your art classes, showing an occasional work in a departmental exhibit. You'd have a number of slides of your work to submit as supplementary application materials, and if you were lucky, your work would be judged by the college faculty or admission committee to be impressive. But this approach is passive and narrow.

A more active approach would involve your taking night or summer art classes at a local college or art institute. That way you'd begin to be involved with the local *adult* art community. You could contact a bank or movie theater to see whether they'd be interested in showing your work—even on a purely decorative basis. If they liked your paintings, they might even consider putting them up for sale.

You could also look into selling your canvases at local galleries. And if your first showings were successful, you could arrange monthly shows, not only of your paintings but also those of other high school artists. Your professors, teachers, and a local critic could judge the entries. In this way you would be rendering a service to the community by providing the public with an opportunity to see original local artwork. And you'd be doing fellow artists a service by giving them a forum in which to display their work.

Now let's compare these two approaches. The first, passive approach creates the profile of someone content to be alone with his paints and easel. You could enter your work in a state or regional contest, but if you didn't win, you'd be left with just the paintings themselves to show for your effort.

The second approach gives the impression of much greater commitment to the field of art. You've had your work exhibited locally. Maybe some of it was even bought on the open market. Most importantly, you've organized a regular showing of local art, to the benefit of your hometown. Regardless of the merit of your work—as judged by whomever rates supplementary materials at each college—you've shown a genuine commitment to the arts by pursuing them outside of your high school classes. This initiative and extra effort go a long way in setting you apart from the typical applicant.

2. Politics and civic affairs. Suppose that you're interested in politics and civic activities. If you were the typical high school politico, you'd run for student council in ninth grade. By lobbying and doing a good job, you'd then be in line for one of the council offices. If you were lucky, popular, and ran a good campaign, you might eventually win the election. But how many student council presidents can there be at one school? And if your opponent is more popular (and not necessarily better qualified), where does that leave you?

The alternate approach would have you ask yourself: What are the other avenues available to me, outside high school? You could:

▶ Lobby or run for the office of student representative to your local school board.

▶ Join a local political campaign and propose to your candidate that he or she run a student volunteer group from your high school.

▶ Volunteer as an intern to work in the mayor's office.

▶ Contact your local police department to see about setting up a weekly or bimonthly "rap session" between students (especially with those who are less civic-minded than you) and police.

Evaluating Activities

Almost anything is possible. Once again, some extra effort, initiative, and imagination can go a long way toward making you seem involved or a leader. And guess what—if you do any of the things mentioned above, you *will* be a leader. You could justifiably claim that you established a student volunteer program for State Senator Ward Heeler, or that you helped open up dialogue between students and law enforcement officers in your community. You could do all of these if you were student council president, but you don't have to be president to be a leader.

Whatever it is that interests you, try to figure out just how you can enhance and deepen your own involvement in it. Hard work and creativity can turn an ordinary situation into something special. As you go through your high school years, ask yourself the following questions about your extracurriculars:

1. Am I spending all the time I should on this activity?

2. Is there some way to make my work more efficient or productive?

3. Have I overlooked a talent or interest that I could put to use to enable me to deepen my involvement?

4. Are there other ways—through the community, friends, relatives, organizations, foundations—that I can be involved in this field, and show that I care about it?

5. Are there classes or groups outside my school that might provide another forum for my involvement, or improve my talent?

6. Can I organize a group to help me pursue my interests further? Can I enlist the help of a teacher or parent?

7. Is there a job or work experience out there that would be relevant to my interest or activity, and would deepen my commitment?

The Other Way to Stand Out

Consider yourself an admission officer for a moment. You've read hundreds, perhaps thousands of applications this season. You've seen countless student council members and officers, hundreds of varsity athletes, hospital volunteers, boy scouts, club members, debaters. Wouldn't you welcome the chance to read about someone different? (We're not being cynical here; quality and depth of involvement is just as important as uniqueness. But it is to your advantage to combine them.)

As you look at your various activities, consider whether there's something in your constellation of interests that's not just run-of-the-mill: being a breeder of roses; taking up the sport of parachuting—or spelunking; piloting super-light aircraft; weaving Navajo rugs. One applicant to an Ivy college listed on his application that he built sand castles. This sounded silly at first, until the admission office saw photos of his creations. They were spectacular, handcrafted miniatures of existing castles that he built of sand and glued on wooden platforms. His models were anything but weekend throw-aways: they were works of art. The young artist had won a number of prizes from a world organization devoted to building these castles.

Tied into his interests in art history and architecture, this activity not only showed mastery and depth of commitment, but also represented a first among applicants. No one had ever before listed sand-castle building as an extracurricular activity. Of course, this alone didn't guarantee his admission. But added to a well-rounded personal profile and a good, though not spectacular, academic profile, it got him in. In a sense, the sand-castle builder was "marketing" and positioning himself. One of the tenets of marketing is that to sell, a product must be differentiated from its competitors, even if it is a similar or identical product. This applicant wasn't that appreciably different from others in a general sense; but he positioned himself as an aspiring art historian/architect, and had an unusual activity to substantiate his positioning. This made him stand out.

Does this mean that you should necessarily choose an exotic or offbeat field of interest just so you stand out from the herd? Not necessarily. As we keep saying, it's neither the quantity nor the nature of the activity that is crucial; it's the extent of your mastery and the way you present it ("packaging") to the committee. But if you have a choice between two equally attractive activities, and one is significantly more unusual, opt for the exotic one.

Work Experience

ne factor that can mitigate a thin activities profile is evidence

AN "INTERESTING ACTIVITIES" DESCRIPTION

Here is an essay written by an applicant about the business she started. This is a particularly good example of an impressive work experience, demonstrating both leadership and entrepreneurial flair.

Conceiver, manager, and owner of "The Gingham Girls and Guys" party help service. In the eighth grade I decided to establish a party-help service in order to earn money. Originally the group was named the Gingham Girls. I employed five girls and we worked for $1.75 per hour. By the time I sold the business, the group had changed its name to the Gingham Girls & Guys and included twelve girls and three boys who worked for $3.50 an hour, and two bartenders, who charged a flat rate of $25 per job.

At parties, we arranged platters, passed hors d'oeuvres, had the dinner ready to serve at the time the hostess requested, served the dinner, cleared the table, and washed all the dishes. Basically, everything was done so that the host and hostess could enjoy their party. We did the work for them. I kept the master calendar and received all requests for help. I as-signed the jobs and took a percentage of the wages. I worked as often as I could myself, but we often found ourselves handling three or four parties a night. During the summers and on vacations we worked full time, but during the school year we worked only on the weekends.

We handled luncheons, open houses, teas, cocktail parties, dinner parties, baby showers, confirmation parties, wedding brunches and receptions, and charity benefits. As a sideline, we were also employed to check coats and hats at some of Cleveland's major fundraising functions such as the Bicentennial Historical Party at the Cleveland Western Reserve Historical Society, a benefit for the development of Public Square sponsored by the Garden Club of Cleveland, and the Decorator Showhouse, sponsored by the Cleveland Junior League.

Having this employment throughout my high school years, besides enabling me to earn money, has given me the responsibility of presiding over a business and the pleasure of making it a success.

of significant or extensive work experience. Colleges will overlook the sparse extracurricular career of a student who works after school to help support his disabled widowed father. What doesn't impress the Admission committee is the situation where a student works and has let his grades suffer; or has not been in-volved in extracurricular activities, but rather has worked simply for the sake of material acquisition—i.e., to buy a car, stereo, motorcycle. To help out in a financially constrained family situation is admirable. To show a bit of financial independence is good. To do so at the expense of learning is not particularly welcomed. And to work simply for some luxuries probably won't impress anyone. It is all a matter of degree and situation.

A heavy work schedule not dictated by financial necessity can have a positive impact on the committee's thinking, however, if the money earned supports other enriching endeavors; as in the case of a student who works long hours in a music store to save up enough money to buy a special cello or to help fund his choir's trip to Europe.

When evaluating work experience, admission officers also ask other questions. Is the work unusual or interesting? (If so, the student will stand out from the usual paper boys or fast-food cooks.) Does the student show signs of being a real leader or entrepreneur? Finally, does the work experience relate to academic or career plans? A student whose work experience relates to those plans is creating a stronger "handle" or positioning for himself in the applicant pool.

Here are some rules to follow when you're looking for work:

1. The work that pays best is not necessarily what will be most respected by admission officers. Working weekends at a nursing home for *no* money may be more impressive than mowing lawns, because it shows a true concern for the welfare of the elderly.

2. Try to tie your work experience into your application strategy. If you're building a picture of yourself in the application as a would-be social worker, being a youth counselor at an inner-city settlement house fits nicely into your strategy.

3. If you can find some job that is off-beat or exotic, all the better.

The Job Hunt

There are many ways to find work. The approach you choose will depend on your interests, goals, and financial situation. Your paramount objective may be to earn as much money as possible. That's fine, if you really *need* the cash. If you don't, you're lucky—you'll have that much more latitude in choosing from a variety of alternatives.

Here are some things to keep in mind as you look for work:

1. Start early. Don't expect to find a summer job as school is about to let out. Start making inquiries just after the first of the year.

2. Fill out applications even if there aren't any jobs available. You may get called eventually, and if you contact the firm later, you'll be high on their applicant priority list.

3. Talk to friends, teachers, parents—anybody who might know about job opportunities or give you ideas for work.

4. Check with your school board or local government. They may run a placement program or have job listings.

5. Use connections wherever possible, both to find out about work and to get it. It helps to

WORK EXPERIENCE

Just to give you an idea of what we mean, here is an example of some fairly typical work experience compared with less common work.

TYPICAL	UNUSUAL
Delivery boy, drugstore clerk	Organizer of a messenger service run and staffed by high school students
Moving company worker	"Poor students" home movers
Camera store clerk	Fashion photographer's assistant
Busboy at diner	Publicist for Beverly Hills eatery
Carwash dryer	"Detailing" service (shine and waxing)
Housepainter	Mailbox painting service for rural and suburban homes
Library, bookstore clerk	Writer's researcher
Waiter	Mime entertainer
Camp counselor	Animal trainer in pound
Appliance store stockroom clerk	Intern at local TV station
Campaign volunteer	Congressional page, youth adviser to Congressman
Messenger for law firm	Researcher in one-man law office; ranch hand; model; actor; wood-cutter

Now look at your own work profile to see what you've done and what *more* you can do in this area. Remember that you don't necessarily have to be *paid* to have had a worthwhile work experience. (In the part of the application that asks about the "benefits" of your employment, some applicants write "Personal growth," "Learned humility," or "Can grow my own garden." This might sound corny, but it is refreshing and at least as interesting as putting down "Earned $3.50 per hour.")

know someone, especially for jobs in business, professional offices, or at factories. Don't be ashamed to ask your pal's attorney father if his law firm is hiring any summer help.

6. Be imaginative when looking for work. And be prepared to look for some time before you find a job. It's tough going for teenagers in the job market, especially in the current economic climate. Persistence is crucial.

Starting Your Own Business

There are many ways you can put your skills to work running your own business. It takes initiative and hard work, but it can be done. If you can mow lawns, paint, serve food, or whatever—you can sell your work to others. This approach is especially advantageous for two reasons. First, your business will show admission people that you are responsible and imaginative. Second, you'll earn more money per hour than you would as someone else's employee.

Volunteer Work

You can also get practical experience and build your resume through volunteer work. Although you won't get paid, you will get valuable experience. Many nonprofit agencies, public and private, can use volunteer help. These outfits are usually understaffed and would welcome a bright high school kid to help out. Settlement houses, nonprofit summer camps, church or local nurseries, nursing homes, hospitals, and other organizations often have formal volunteer programs, such as "candy-stripers."

The nature of the work is less important than your commitment to it, what you can show that you learned from it, and how you tie it to your overall application strategy. In other words, make it part of your positioning. You needn't necessarily go through formal training programs; sometimes you can just approach the facility where you'd like to work and offer your services. Once again, take the initiative, and use your imagination.

Internships, Self-made and Institutional

Volunteer work is usually thought of in connection with non-profit agencies. It is generally easier to get volunteer work than paid employment. But more difficult than either is landing even a non-paying job in "glamour" fields like journalism, broadcasting, publishing, advertising, film production, government, foundations, or publicity. This is where the internship approach can help you.

A few companies run formal internship programs for high school students, but these are extremely competitive—it may be harder to land one of these jobs than to get into most prestigious colleges. What you will have to do is investigate companies in your area that might be interested in hiring a smart high school student at no pay.

One young lady we know engineered just such a summer internship at a major television production house in Hollywood. She got in the door through one of her father's friends, and so impressed her interviewer that he decided to take her on. She worked as "gofer" on a prime-time TV series. When she applied to colleges, she stressed the importance of her experience and tied it into her love for "communications." The internship became part of her positioning. With SAT scores in the mid-600s to low 700s and good rank at a small private girl's school, she got into every school she applied to except Brown, where she withdrew from the waiting list to go to Stanford.

Travel

Travel can also set you apart from the crowd. The more exotic the place the better, but even trips around the U.S. can be significant if you utilize them properly. You shouldn't assume, however, that listing 50 countries on your application will impress admission officers. More often, this will be read simply as a sign of affluence. The key to using travel to your advantage is, once again, extra effort and a consciousness of how to package yourself. Here are some things to keep in mind:

1. If you *do* travel somewhere unusual (or even not so unusual), *keep a journal of your experiences.* What were the people like? Did you get any insights into yourself and your own culture from examining others? Was there anything especially memorable that you did, or anyone especially memorable whom you met? What was your appraisal of the political situation? Do the country and its people correspond to their image in the United States, or are we misinformed? You can later resurrect your notes as raw material for a good essay, especially if you want to sell yourself as a world traveler.

2. Is there a way to work your travel into your positioning and packaging? If you're selling yourself as the country's next political whiz, you should do something with that junior year trip to Washington, D.C. Write about your reaction to the town that rules America and influences much of the globe. How did you feel about it personally? Put your travel experience to work and use it to fashion an overall picture of yourself for the admission committee.

Summer Abroad and Exchange Programs

Formal programs such as the American Field Service are also useful in setting you apart from others. Because selective colleges value diversity, anyone with out-of-the-ordinary experiences makes the admission committee sit up and take notice. Having been in such a program, you'll have an almost automatic advantage.

Once again, you'll do better if you can integrate your experience into your packaging and positioning. If you can convince the committee that you plan to study the language and politics of the region where you lived, or want to be in the Foreign Service, or long to study International Relations, then your travels mean more.

Summing Up

As we keep saying, academics are the first priority in admission to selective colleges. But other factors do make a difference—especially extracurriculars and employment. We've already talked about the importance of mastery and exoticism in setting yourself apart from the typical applicant. In addition, there also are ways of *building* your activities/work profile to your advantage, if you start early.

1. Integration. The idea of integrating your activities is to construct a profile that is so consistent, so directed, that it sets you

PROGRAMS FOR STUDY ABROAD

American Field Service (AFS), 313 East 43rd Street, New York, NY 10017. Through this nonprofit program a student will live with a host family abroad, attending a local school. Established in 1947, AFS is open (through a selection process) to high school juniors or seniors, ages 16 to 18. Applicants must have had at least two years of a foreign language. Scholarships are offered and a summer program is available.

American Institute for Foreign Studies (AIFS), 102 Greenwich Avenue, Greenwich, CT 06830. AIFS offers a variety of full-year, semester, and summer programs. It is open to high school seniors and recent high school graduates who have had two years of foreign language study.

The Council on International Educational Exchange, 205 East 42nd Street, New York, NY 10017, (212) 661-1414. The council is a nonprofit organization that serves as a sponsor and clearinghouse for students who are interested in studying abroad. Write or call for a copy of their guide, which is the most complete one available.

Experiment in International Living, Admissions Director, The Experiment in International Living, Brattleboro, VT 05301. Students on this program live with hosts abroad. It is open to high school and college students. A summer program is also available, as are partial scholarships and loans.

International Council of International Christian Youth Exchange, P.O. Box 66 CH-1211, Geneva 20, Switzerland. Nonprofit program for students ages 16 to 22. Apply to 55 Liberty Street, Room 1306, New York, NY 10005.

Youth for Understanding, 2015 Washtenaw Avenue, Ann Arbor, MI 48104. This is a nonprofit student exchange program, concentrating on Western Europe. Students live with a host family and attend local schools. Open to high school juniors and seniors with two to three years of a foreign language. Partial scholarships are available.

---

apart from others because of the extent and depth of your commitment to one field. Let's say, for example, that you have a great interest in psychology and plan to pursue it in college (you think). In the ninth grade, you could do considerable reading on the subject. If you were old enough by the summer after tenth grade, you could find work as a counselor at a neighborhood nursery or summer camp. In eleventh grade you might be a part-time teaching assistant for a teacher of emotionally disturbed or otherwise "special" children in your school system. The summer after eleventh grade you might apply for a National Science Foundation summer program, which would allow you to do independent research in some facet of psychology.

YOUR ADMISSION CALENDAR

NINTH GRADE

Introduce yourself to your counselor; begin planning a college preparatory course schedule.

Investigate activities you'd like to do; decide which you want to start pursuing in depth.

Keep your ears open for news about colleges and admissions.

Relax!

TENTH GRADE

Continue planning your course schedule. Play to your strengths, taking hardest courses in areas where you excel.

Possible first taking of PSAT/NMSQT as a dry-run.

Target activities to concentrate on.

Plan an interesting summer; possibly consider a reasonably challenging summer program somewhere.

Take Achievement tests in any terminal courses.

TENTH GRADE
Summer

Travel or summer programs.

Prepare for PSAT/NMSQT.

ELEVENTH GRADE
Fall

Take PSAT/NMSQT.

Go to as many college conferences as time allows.

Investigate A.P.s and honors courses for this and next year.

Winter

Start browsing through college guides.

Prepare for SAT.

Talk to seniors about their views on colleges.

Start thinking about summer job or activity.

Spring

Continue to take Achievements in terminal subjects.

Start positioning yourself for senior year activities.

Take late spring SAT.

Take Achievements in terminal subjects.

Plan summer program.

Write to colleges for summer interviews.

Summer

Summer jobs or activity program.

Start college visits and interviews, if you won't have time in the fall.

Write to colleges requesting interviews, catalogs, and/or applications.

Prepare for fall SAT, if necessary.

TWELFTH GRADE
Fall
More college visits and interviews. Talk to students.

Go to college conferences of schools that interest you.

Narrow the field—talk to people—develop a final list.

Concentrate on activities.

Take Achievements for last time.

Write applications.

Get references from teachers.

Submit supplementary application materials.

November 1–15: most early applications due.

Mid-December: decisions made by colleges on early applications.

Have alumni interviews.

Winter
Fill out financial aid applications, final applications.

January: application deadline for most colleges.

January–February: update applications.

February: check if applications are complete.

Spring
April: most colleges send out decision letters!

Make final decision on colleges to which you've been accepted. Visit those colleges, talk to students, parents, teachers.

The NSF summer might be parlayed into a job as a research assistant to a professor of psychology at a local university. Everything you've learned could then be used to do a science fair project in, say, attitudinal studies or behavior modification. In this way you'd create the picture of someone who is very interested in and *dedicated to* the subject.

You should be able to show in your essay and interview that this is a genuine interest and *not* an obsession.

2. Juxtaposition. By juxtaposition, we mean going beyond a stereotype: being a "jock-poet," for example—the boy who got laurels in long-distance running and at the same time won a Scholastic Award for his poetry, or got it published in *Seventeen* magazine. Or the pre-med who volunteers in a hospital and races dirt bikes on the side. Or the student-council officer who plays in a New Wave band that's written up in a local newspaper.

This sort of incongruity—a *positive* incongruity—catches the eye of admission officers because it is, quite simply, different. When you fall out of the mainstream, you become interesting. But juxtaposition is much more problematic than integration as part of your extracurricular application strategy, because it calls for you to have two major but disparate talents. Juxtaposition won't work if you don't achieve an impressive level of mastery or recognition in both of the fields you stress in your application. Therefore, we don't recommend it as an approach unless you're multitalented. Going for mastery and integration is a more solid approach.

Ultimately, remember our initial piece of advice: decide what you like to do and do it as well as you can. Gauge your own limits and be careful not to spread yourself too thin. At the same time, avoid appearing driven and narrow in your focus. Above all, don't underestimate the importance of classwork. And good luck!

SELECTIVE COLLEGES: AN OVERVIEW

Everyone has a story about a "name" school. We hear them ceaselessly, from grandparents, parents, uncles and aunts, sisters and brothers, friends, teachers, counselors, acquaintances, magazine articles, television, newspapers, films, even characters in novels. These tales attest to our obsession with prestige institutions. One by-product of that obsession is an assumption that all those ivy-covered communities are basically alike. We tend to lump Harvard, Yale, Stanford, Brown, Dartmouth, and about two dozen others in one batch, and assume their students are basically interchangeable.

But selective colleges are like people. They come in a variety of shapes, sizes, colors, and dispositions, with differing philosophies and directions. Like people, they also share common characteristics. We'll take a look at those distinctions and similarities in this chapter.

The Vast Field

As you look over lists of colleges in the United States, you'll see that many of them are clamoring for your application. There are 2,000 four-year colleges in the country. *Selective Guide to Colleges* identifies 265 of them, which author Edward Fiske says are among "the best and most interesting four-year institutions in the country—in other words, those which students should know about." Some of these institutions could hardly be called selective, as they accept over 90 percent of the applicants who send in an application.

Still, all of them qualify by virtue of their name recognition, prestige, faculty reputation, academic standards, athletic prowess, or high-powered student body. They range in size from the tiny College of the Atlantic, with a total student population of 180, to mighty Ohio State, with 59,450 students, 46,420 of them undergraduates. They range in location from small rural towns (Amherst) to huge urban centers (NYU). They differ in size and orientation from small, undergraduate, liberal-arts institutions to huge megaliths.

Some are educationally progessive; others have reinstated distribution requirements and offer few curricular options. And the field is split between state schools, with their legislative mandates to give preference to in-state residents, and private schools that can pretty much determine the kind of student body to admit.

Even institutions in the same general category, with common applications procedures, aren't exactly alike. The Ivy League, for example, is actually an *athletic* conference that was founded in 1956. It was essentially a gentleman's agreement limiting athletic recruitment and making financial aid available solely on the basis of need. Of course, it's no ordinary athletic conference, since it counts in its ranks the most selective colleges nationwide. Among its eight members (Brown, Columbia, Cornell, Dartmouth, Harvard, University of Pennsylvania, Princeton, and Yale), only seven are fully private. Cornell University is actually New York state's land-grant college; three of its colleges are actually state-supported. Only Cornell's College of Arts and Sciences subscribes to the Ivy Charter, which states that "in order to insure that financial awards to commonly admitted candidates are reasonably comparable, all of the Ivy Institutions will continue to share financial aid information concerning admitted candidates in an annual 'Ivy Overlap' meeting just prior to the mid-April Common Notification Date."

This alliance of highly selective colleges hardly agrees on admissions procedures. In 1982 Harvard admitted only 14.8 percent of the students pounding on its portals. By comparison Columbia admitted 46.2 percent of those who applied.

The institutions also differ in their ratio of undergraduate to graduate students. Brown, Yale, and Princeton are best known for their undergraduates, whereas Harvard and Columbia are world-class graduate factories where beleaguered undergraduates are outnumbered by those pursuing graduate degrees.

Obviously, in any grouping of supposedly similar schools there will always be distinctions. Still, the ways that these colleges cull and put together a freshman class can be quite similar.

The Myth of Selectivity

In evaluating selectivity, people tend to take a quick look at acceptance statistics and nothing else. The fewer people accepted, they think, the more competitive the admission process. This is true. But selectivity works both ways—first, on the part of the school, which only admits a certain number of students from the total group applying; and second, on the part of the student. Stu-

SELECTIVITY:
A COMPARATIVE CHART

College	Number of Applicants	Number Accepted	Number Who Enrolled	Percent Accepted	% Yield Rate
STANFORD	17,000	2,550	1,658	15	65
COOPER UNION	2,048	328	203	16	62
HARVARD	13,327	2,266	1,654	17	73
PRINCETON	12,720	2,162	1,168	17	54
YALE	13,030	2,476	1,461	19	59
BROWN	12,638	2,528	1,365	20	54
AMHERST	4,180	878	370	21	42
COLUMBIA	6,241	1,747	751	28	43
MIT	6,000	1,800	1,044	30	58
DUKE	10,300	3,296	1,384	32	42
MIDDLEBURY	3,430	1,098	461	32	42
CAL TECH	1,270	432	216	34	45
WESLEYAN	4,200	1,470	617	35	42
UVA	12,110	4,844	2,616	40	54
SWARTHMORE	2,210	972	399	44	41
NOTRE DAME	6,640	2,922	1,782	44	61
CARLETON	2,410	1,157	486	48	42
ROCHESTER POLYTECHNIC INSTITUTE (RPI)	7,150	3,600	1,200	50	33
UNC CHAPEL HILL	10,300	5,459	3,439	53	63
U.C.-BERKELEY	12,200	6,710	4,294	55	64
U. OF MICHIGAN	14,685	8,224	4,276	56	52
USC	10,084	7,160	2,935	71	41

Source: *The Selective Guide to Colleges,* 1986–87 by Edward B. Fiske, New York: Times Books, 1985.

dent selectivity can be assessed by looking at the college's *yield*—the number of those admitted who actually *choose to enroll* at the school in question.

The list on page 45 is prepared in descending order of selectivity (on the basis of acceptance only, not yield) of some of the more high-profile colleges in the country. Some interesting facts turn up: Stanford is the most selective in terms of how many applicants from the pool it actually accepts (15 percent), but Harvard has the highest yield rate—73 percent. Princeton isn't far behind on the first count, with an acceptance rate of 17 percent, but its yield rate is only 54 percent—which is about the norm for the rest of the selective colleges, most of which annually see about half of the prospects they admit.

Now look at yield. Which school has the third highest yield rate? The University of California at Berkeley, a state school that enrolls fully 64 percent of the students it admits. Berkeley gets this catch for two reasons. First, the University has an international reputation and first-rate faculty. Second, for in-state residents it costs one-third as much as the prestige colleges it increasingly competes with.

And look at Swarthmore. This liberal arts college, with its idyllic setting and good-natured student body, sports modestly good acceptance and yield figures of 44 and 41 percent, respectively. But its SAT composite (650 Verbal, 650 Math) is among the highest on the list. Even the University of Michigan, near the very bottom of this selectivity list, has SAT means well above the na-

tional norm. And its academic program, as well as its reputation, is first rate.

The point of this little exercise is to make you see that name and reputation aren't everything. Neither are acceptance statistics. As you begin your college search, you shouldn't rule out schools because they don't seem selective enough or you don't recognize their names. Nor should you dismiss a place because its statistics seem imposing.

You should also be skeptical of taking reputations at face value. Popular perceptions of schools are often based on past reputation and out-of-date information. One admission director recently acknowledged that the reputations that colleges enjoy today were often made a generation ago. Filtered through the media, alumni boosters, and educators, the "name" place enters the popular consciousness; but by the time it does, the very qualities that contributed to that image may have evaporated.

Schools quickly go in and out of vogue. At the height of the curricular liberalization of the late 1960s, one of the most selective schools in the country was newly-founded Hampshire College, in Massachusetts. Its lack of a traditional academic structure drew "progressive" students in droves. Today Hampshire accepts 75 percent of its applicants (a not very selective statistic).

Conversely, colleges' popularity can sometimes increase precipitately. For example, in 1981 Duke University received 8,100 applications, while four years later 10,300 freshman applied. Yet in 1981 Duke accepted only

2,810 applicants or 34.7 percent, while in 1985 it admitted 3,296, or 32 percent of the total. So, Duke is actually not much more selective now than it was before its popularity increased. The only way to determine just how selective and prestigious a school happens to be is by examining *all* the information available to you.

Admission Constituencies

Whether the school is Ohio Wesleyan University, which recently accepted 1,700 of 2,200 applicants, or Harvard, which enrolled roughly the same number from an application pool six times as large (13,327), admission offices exist to meet the needs of the institution. Colleges' institutional needs determine their goals, which in turn lead to their *admission policy*. Admission officers are then charged with fulfilling that policy.

How are those institutional needs determined? Largely by the administration's attention to various constituencies, on and off campus, beginning with:

1. The faculty. First and foremost, professors need students to teach. If the faculty had its way, the job of the admission office would be only to attract the most academically able, and admission decisions would be made just on the basis of SATs and class rank. Although they compose but one of a number of groups on campus, faculty members have tremendous influence. Most colleges have an *admission*

policy committee that guides the admission office in its decisions, and professors inevitably sit on these committees. The faculty also has constant contact with administrators, which means that not only are teachers highly influential, but highly vocal as well.

2. The students. Students also have something to say about admission policy, and administrators do listen to them. After all, they provide the bulk of operating revenues. No students, no college.

Many of the liberalizing reforms of the 1960s grew out of student protests. Similarly, affirmative action programs for minority students came about in response to student demands as well as federal legislation. As a result of these reforms, students sometimes sit on admission policy committees. They rarely, however, sit on the actual selection committee. Their primary impact is in the recruitment and admission of the underprivileged.

3. The coaches. Athletic staffers at most colleges are in a special position. While most are not faculty members, many earn salaries equal to or better than their professorial peers. And although they may teach no classes, their needs and goals are felt by college administrations to be almost as important as those of academic departments. A top-notch athletic program brings in revenues from happy alumni, who are more likely to donate if they read that "Old Swami" took the league title. The growth of multi-million-dollar TV sports contracts has also reinforced the great importance of college sports.

At some football schools with heavy television revenues, coaches are given virtual carte blanche to accept a limited number of very hot prospects. And even in the Ivy League, with its stress on "amateurism" in athletics, coaches provide detailed information to admission directors about their prospects, indicating on a "depth-chart" which players they need most to round out next year's team.

4. Alumni and friends of the college. This constituency is less important to the state schools, which get their operating revenues primarily from taxpayers, but it is essential to the privates. Especially with mounting cuts in federal aid to education, alumni and friends are a major source of funding for private colleges and universities. Keeping the loyal graduates happy is therefore an administrative priority.

In 1981 the University of Southern California, for example, received total revenues of $321,294,500. The single largest part of that budget, $131,392,168, came from student tuition and fees. A total of $16,971,662 came from endowment and investment income. And $54,541,416 came from private gifts, contracts, and grants. Endowment and private income thus paid for 22 percent of the school's budget. Some of that figure derives from corporate or institutional grants, but a significant portion was donated by alumni, honorary alumni, or powerful folks who believe in USC's value to the community.

When an alumni son or daugh-

CAL TECH—THE FACULTY DECIDES

The California Institute of Technology in Pasadena, California, is regarded as one of the best technical colleges in the country, rivaled only by the Massachusetts Institute of Technology. One look at its SAT medians confirms that it attracts some of the brightest students in the country. With its orientation toward the theoretical side of mathematics and science, you might expect that its admission procedure is somewhat different from the typical liberal arts college.

It is. How? All admission decisions are made by faculty members. The Director of Admission sits on the selection committee but does not have a vote. His role is advisory and administrative. As a result, admission criteria are primarily academic. Another difference is that very few interviews are given on campus. But several hundred applicants are interviewed yearly at their high schools. Once folders have been evaluated and the faculty has some sense of which candidates are "realistic" applicants, they fan out in late March to visit those applicants at their high schools. There, Cal Tech faculty members not only talk to the applicants, but frequently see the applicants' teachers and counselors. (Admission officers also take part in this interviewing.) The reason? So the college can be assured of admitting students committed to its high-powered, theory-oriented math and science curriculum.

ter, or even nephew or niece applies, the private college's admission office will do its best to admit that applicant. The decision is made both to keep the family tradition intact and also—more importantly—to encourage future financial support.

But keeping alumni happy is not only a matter of admitting their offspring. Colleges have whole departments devoted to alumni affairs. Old graduates take a fervent interest in their alma maters, and sometimes they gripe mightily about social or curricular changes that threaten their rosy memories of university life. Princeton University is a good case in point: following the admission of women in the early 1970s, the college was faced with a group of hoary old alumni who split off from the university-sponsored alumni organization and formed their own group to protest the new, "radical" policy.

5. The world outside. The press, the community, government. Colleges are very concerned about how they appear to the world outside their cloisters. Most institutions have a vice-president for "university relations," whose department is a combination press bureau and mini-diplomatic corps. It is responsible for interesting journalists in the college's accomplishments and activities and making sure that the resulting press coverage is positive.

Yet another concern is the school's relationship with the surrounding community. Administrators are forever trying to improve relations between town and

gown. In some cities, colleges will court local residents. Brown University, for example, has gone to great lengths to reassure residents of its surrounding Fox Point neighborhood (most of whom are working-class Portuguese) that it will continue to build housing and control off-campus student living, so that townspeople won't be displaced and housing prices will remain stable.

Certain administrators are responsible for government affairs—keeping abreast of and influencing local, state, and national legislation affecting education. For state colleges, this connection is direct. The cost of providing an education is virtually the same at public and private colleges. The difference in revenues (which is a result of lower tuition charges) is made up for by state subsidies. What this means for admission policy is that state governments usually dictate standards for admission, enrollment, and the ratio of in-state residents to out-of-staters. By law, for instance, 85 percent of the undergraduates at the University of North Carolina at Chapel Hill must be in-state residents.

6. The high school crowd. Educators, students, parents. This constituency is crucially important to private colleges. College admission staffs are usually sensitive to how they're perceived among students looking at colleges. But it's not only those high school prospects who matter; colleges need good on-going relationships with high schools and their communities. Admission officers know that if parents and students hear horror stories about a college's admission policy, they won't put it on their college list.

And if teachers and counselors are unhappy with admission decisions, they may discourage their top prospects from applying to the offending college. High school officials have long memories. More than one visiting college rep has gotten a hostile reception at secondary schools, finding himself forced to defend admission decisions of past years that may have been made before the rep even joined the admission office.

The Constituency Influence

Each year colleges examine their previous years' performance—and plot the next year's goals and needs.

Above all, every school needs a certain number of tuition-paying bodies. Projections of budget, faculty, enrollment, and dozens of other factors enable university planners to suggest various options. For example, the college's trustees may wish to keep the size of the student body fixed and increase the number of faculty members. To accomplish this, the school may have to raise tuition costs. Alternatively, the trustees may want to hold the tuition costs at current levels, increasing the number of freshmen admitted in order to bolster revenues.

These institutional needs and goals may translate into an admission policy that makes it (temporarily) easier to get into the school. Standards may not drop, but the number of students admitted may go up.

How Many Students Must be Admitted?

The following scenario is typical of many colleges. The administrators might say, "We project that we'll need 1,000 bodies to reach our trustee-mandated size of 4,000 undergraduates." Using statistics on the college's yield—the percentage of those admitted who actually enroll—the admission director will project the total number of applicants who must be admitted to yield that freshman class of 1,000.

Generally, the director will plan to admit a slightly smaller number than he actually requires to assemble the class, and then take the remainder from the waiting list. If the college needs a freshman class of 1,000 and its yield is 50 percent, the director may admit less than the required 2,000— say, 1,900 or 1,950. This way, if by some fluke the yield rate turns out to be higher than the usual 50 percent, the school won't wind up with a huge freshman class and overcrowding—a problem many schools experienced in the late sixties and early seventies. Admission statistics are usually stable from year to year, but the waiting list is the college's insurance.

In building the class, the college may shoot for some balance between the sexes. These days, with some notable exceptions, the figure is inching toward the fifty-fifty mark at most colleges. If the school wants to increase the total fraction of one sex, then more of that gender must be admitted. On the other hand, maybe the yield rate for women was higher than normal last year, so this year the college has to take fewer women.

Then come the more generalized requests from specific constituencies. The University Planning Committee and Mexican-American students feel more Mexican-Americans should be admitted. (Efforts will also be made to increase recruitment of these students.) The trustees are complaining that not enough "legacies" (alumni sons and daughters) were admitted. We seem to have too many Easterners in the student body. We should go for a more national profile. Recruit and admit more students from the South. The Music Department says it hasn't enough talent to put together a good school orchestra. The coaches are ready to revolt—be more sensitive to their needs.

We assume you're gathering from this that being an admission director isn't an easy task. And you're right. Admission people can never please every lobby. In fact, they seldom please *any* constituency fully. There just aren't enough places in the freshman class.

Admission policy is outlined in these general or detailed terms; it is then the admission office's duty to implement it. The admission director will usually give his opinion, make recommendations for change, protest unrealistic demands by the administration or constituencies, and warn about the inevitable limitations on his ability to deliver everything asked of him. The discussion will continue until goals are generally agreed upon, and a detailed policy is carved out.

An important part of this process is financial aid, and it will grow increasingly more important in the years to come. In order to attract a first-rate student body, the university will have to provide enough funding for financial aid. Policy decisions can enter here as well. Not too long ago, for example, the president of USC promised that all students meriting admission would get in regardless of their financial need. The college essentially decided to make a commitment to "aid-blind" admission, i.e., where financial need has no impact on admission decisions. Wesleyan University of Connecticut, on the other hand, announced publicly that it would scrap its formerly aid-blind policy—creating a stir that, ironically, was utterly unnecessary. The college later announced that it had enough funds to provide aid for all those students who needed it. But for a moment it had been thought that qualified applicants to Wesleyan might not get in solely because they needed financial aid.

The Well-Rounded Class

Forget everything you've heard about the prestige schools wanting well-rounded students. As we said earlier, what they want is a well-rounded class. As an individual, being *too* well-rounded can hurt your chances for admission. Colleges do want bright, versatile students. But in order to fulfill their goals they must have a student body that is diverse—religiously, ethnically, economically, geographically, and in interests, outlooks, and special talents.

This variety of types is required for two major reasons. First and foremost, it fulfills the demands of the constituencies involved in the admission procedure. Second, it creates a lively college community that will enhance students' learning.

A great part of the college experience happens outside lecture halls. In fact, if you really take advantage of your undergraduate days, you'll find you learn as much out of class as in it—through extracurriculars, late-night bull sessions, intellectual patter at dinner, and every other sort of shared activity. In a sense college is a rehearsal for life, providing the transition from childhood to the adult world. It weans students away from their families and gives them the social skills and open-mindedness necessary for success. And these objectives are as important to colleges as is book learning.

Of course, colleges view heterogeneity in many ways. One school's idea of diversity can be quite different from another's. Some places are more attuned to background and personal factors. They seek out students who will contribute to the quality of campus life. Carleton, for instance, looks for that special applicant with "pizazz." Brown values character and the potential to contribute to campus activities. Other universities emphasize scholarliness to a greater degree.

State institutions, on the other hand, are usually less concerned with variety. Operating under strict guidelines to admit a cer-

tain percentage of in-state students, they have little latitude in choosing applicants. Like the private colleges, state schools have obvious constituencies, the most active of which may be athletes and minorities. But their primary constituency is the state legislature, to whom they have a legal obligation. Generally this obligation causes state colleges to use specific admission formulas—which may take background characteristics into account only marginally, and extracurricular achievement not at all. But not all state schools use only academic credentials to make admission decisions. The key is to find out which use what criteria.

If you want to maximize your chances for admission, you must understand that not only is every admission process complex, but the admission process differs from campus to campus. It is essential to your application strategy that you begin to recognize these differences and put them to use for you. It is also important that you look beyond the college's buzzwords—those catch-all phrases that describe what a college supposedly wants to see—and try to understand what each really wants. We'll give you the tools to do this later on. And you have to be able to see recurring patterns in the schools' admissions policies, so as to sharpen your application strategy.

The Three Facts of Admission Life

Three basic facts apply to every lucky kid who gets into the college of his or her choice:

1. The applicant falls into a category of students that the college needs or wants on campus.

2. The applicant has credentials as good as or better than other kids who fulfill those needs. Those credentials can be SATs, grades, recommendations, essay, extracurriculars, or the interview, in various combinations, depending on the college. Whatever the factors considered, every applicant competes with those in his "category," and is admitted by presenting credentials equal to or better than those of others in that category. That's not to say that every applicant competes *only* in his category. Some people fall into more than one category of the admission pool, and the lines between categories of applicants are flexible. Someone may be admitted because he falls into more than one category, breaking stereotypes, or because he is very different from the norm.

3. The successful applicant who is generally "equal to" other applicants in one category is usually accepted because he communicates the information better than other students who are applying for the same admission place.

Categorizing the Applicants

Admission offices differentiate between applicants in two ways. First they evaluate background factors. Then they evaluate personal achievement, be it scholastic or extracurricular. The differences between these two categories should be clear to you. Having an Irish surname or being born in Kansas is pure background—you had nothing to do with it. Having won your high school basketball team's MVP award or being made editor of the school paper is achievement. You had a *lot* to do with those. In an ideal world it might seem that colleges would only look at your personal achievement. But would it really be ideal? Would you want to wind up at a school composed exclusively of grinds who are incapable of speaking in public? Or where extracurricular activity consists of studying in the library?

As we said earlier, colleges need balance to provide a good undergraduate experience. Consequently, they balance background factors—which contribute to campus diversity and satisfy constituents—and personal achievement, which contributes both to diversity and the quality of life on campus. First we'll discuss some of the background factors that influence admission decisions. These are factors over which you have no control as an applicant, although they may affect your choice of schools—you can find schools that respond favorably to your particular background.

Background Factors

1. Alumni parents or relatives. At some selective institutions, the percentage of "legacies," or alumni offspring, admitted is twice as high as the overall acceptance rate. Of course, just having a parent who is an alumnus may not be sufficient for admission, especially for a marginal candidate. But the more influence a parent has at the college, whether through donation of time or money, or because the parent lives reasonably close to the school, the better off the legacy applicant will be.

Having a brother or sister who is an alumnus or current undergraduate can also help. Colleges do want to keep the tradition in the family. The more recent an older brother or sister's association with the school, the more impact that association will have—especially if he or she is remembered on campus or by the admission staff. It is even better if he or she is still on campus, and can befriend an admission officer. Having a grandparent or uncle or aunt who is an alumnus barely qualifies as a school tie, unless of course the relative is an especially loyal or powerful alumnus. Additional advantages include having a parent on the faculty or staff of the college.

But a family tie can't overcome a hopeless set of credentials, no matter how powerful the alumnus relative may be: the admission office has to feel confident that the legacy won't be an embarrassment, and that his interests will be served by being at a high-powered school.

2. Diversity. Almost every college wants a heterogenous student body, unless the school is highly specialized or church-supported. Rooming with a farmer from Kansas, for example, will be an education in itself for a city kid. Moreover, when that farmer re-turns to his hometown and becomes a big fish in a small pond, he'll remember Old Swami and spread its fame far and wide on the prairies.

You may have a distinct advantage as a result of your geographic standing. If two students apply to the same prestigious private college, one from an area foreign to most of the college's applicants and the other from a high school that sends thirty yearly applicants to the college, the one from the unusual area will be in a better position. The selection process rarely incorporates this sort of choice—thankfully—but being a "geo," as some places call them, can give an applicant an edge over others.

But you don't have to live thousands of miles away from a college to be considered a geo applicant. Distance alone does not make for geographic diversity. Rather, it has more to do with the frequency and number of applications from a given high school or area.

Shaker Heights, Ohio, is quite a distance from either the West or East coasts, and yet it's generally not considered a geo area by most colleges: every year hundreds of its students throw their hats in the ring for Stanford, Wellesley, Princeton, Williams, or Duke.

A wealthy suburban community with a high percentage of professionals, it's not that different from Brookline, Massachusetts, Scarsdale, New York, Highland Park, Illinois, Beverly Hills, California, or Bloomfield Hills, Michigan. But just an hour by car from Shaker Heights is

Hudson, Ohio, a small town built like a New England village, with clapboard homes surrounding a commons area covered with grass and trees. Hudson High sends perhaps one applicant a year to each of the selective schools. Now *that's* geo status. Geos also come from local areas—the "boonies," as some admission folk call them. Applicants from rural areas of Rhode Island, for example, are seen as geos by Brown University.

The diversity category also includes cultural backgrounds that are exotic or rare in the applicant pool. Having lived abroad may qualify you for this group. Being the child of immigrant parents, while not as compelling to colleges as being a minority applicant, still carries some weight. This is especially true if there is clear evidence in the application of cultural differences in background. A kid who came to the United States from Italy at age eight, for example, probably has a perspective and history that is somewhat different from a typical American teenager, and will thus contribute to the mix on campus.

Finally, the diversity category can also include social, economic, or even sexual diversity—as in the case of a women's or men's college that has just gone coeducational.

3. "Feeder" schools. Until the mid-1960s, certain preparatory schools were considered virtual feeders into nearby Ivy colleges: Lawrenceville School for Princeton, Moses Brown for Brown, Phillips-Andover for Harvard, St.

Paul's for Dartmouth. Each year a good percentage of students who did not get into other selective institutions managed to make it into a neighboring prestige college.

Today these ties still exist, but only as shadows of once flourishing relationships. Lawrenceville still sends many graduates to Princeton, and Andover does to Harvard. But the local school tie isn't limited to private schools. Colleges are sensitive to their obligations to all "locals," as they're called. Whether this is because proximity allows instant complaints or because the college wants to serve the community really doesn't matter. The fact is that certain public schools send many of their graduates to nearby selective colleges. In his autobiography, *In Search of History*, Theodore White noted that most of the "townies" at Harvard in the 1930s came from Boston Latin School, a public school that's been around for ages. Others that fit this category include Bronx High School of Science to Columbia, Philadelphia's School for Girls to the University of Pennsylvania, and Ann Arbor's Hudson High to the University of Michigan.

Being a "local" isn't of massive significance to admission, but it can improve your chances.

4. Development. This category encompasses a handful of students every year—those whose families are wealthy enough to contribute significantly to the college, and who after graduation may donate a chunk of cash for a building or endowed faculty chair. There is an obvious lack of precision in this category, since no one

knows how much a development prospect may eventually donate. Every admission director has a story about being promised a substantial sum of money for the college by some wealthy parent if Junior is admitted. This tactic is counterproductive, since it usually rankles admission professionals.

5. Minority and disadvantaged.

Through affirmative action recruitment programs, colleges today have a fair number of minority students. The minority category includes Federally recognized minorities such as Native Americans, Blacks, Mexican-Americans, Asian-Americans, and Puerto-Ricans. Being identified as a member of one of these groups can have a very positive impact on admission.

Disadvantaged students may not be "official" minorities, but they may also receive favorable treatment in the admission process. While there is no vocal constituency on or off campus pushing for the admission of blue-collar or poor students, admission officers themselves are often receptive to these sorts of applicants. Most selective colleges have primarily middle or upper-middle-class student bodies; applicants from less affluent families are rare and sometimes seen as desirable for their contribution to the school's diversity.

Personal Achievement

Now that we have discussed background characteristics that interest prestige colleges, let's consider the categories of personal achievement that cause colleges to really sit up and take notice. These should be especially crucial to you as an applicant since you can't very well change your background, but you do have some influence over achievement.

1. Athletic talent.

We've all heard about the prep school quarterback who made it into Dartmouth or some other elite place, and wasn't skilled enough or interested enough to join the football squad. That's not the sort of athletic talent we're talking about, because there is a major distinction in admission between *recruited* athletes and *amateur* or unrecruited players. We have put recruited jocks at the top of the achievement categories because they are in a group by themselves. They have a very powerful lobby on campus—coaches. Coaches can't be ignored because they are very vocal and know what sort of players they need for a successful season. And there are always alumni who keep tabs on the teams' performances and grumble if they do miserably.

For a coach's top wide receiver, the issue is not whether his lower-than-average scores and grades are "outweighed" by his talent. The bottom line is whether the jock can survive academically and not embarrass himself or the university. Of course, the coach will present the admission committee with a number of wide receivers, in hopes of getting at least one admitted. A certain amount of bargaining goes on as the admission office decides whether to admit the top man, who has questionable credentials, or another, less impressive player with a better academic record.

Not all colleges give as much weight to coaches' recommendations as others. The extreme cases of great athletic sway are at the major football powers, like Michigan State. On the other end of the spectrum, the smaller "Little Ivies" athletic programs are sometimes just as oriented to "walk-ins" or amateurs as to recruited players.

2. Scholarly excellence. By this we mean unusually good scholastic ability, as evidenced by SAT scores in the 700s, very high grades, and teacher references that consistently extol curiosity and high intellectual acumen. The scholar is the classroom provocateur, goading others to think and work harder. He satisfies, for the most part, the faculty members—who, as we said before, grumble for more bright kids in their fields. The true scholar is rare, but when he appeaars, most colleges will grab him—unless his personality is so nerdy or driven and intense that his presence might be wearing on his peers. Most colleges find that true scholarship is an increasingly rare commodity, and essential to maintaining academic standards.

3. Special talent. Colleges have bands and orchestras, studio art classes, theaters, dance groups, and a host of other extracurricular efforts or courses which require a flow of participants to keep going. All sorts of kids have abilities which fall into this category: for example, the violinist who has won a state solo competition. He will be even better off if the school orchestra happens to need a first violinist and the faculty advisor takes notice of him, either through an audition or a tape of his music submitted as a supplement to the application. Art, music, athletics, debate, drama, and other fields of creative or physical endeavor fall into this category. The finer the applicant's ability in the field, the better off he or she is.

4. Extracurricular depth and community service. Colleges also have a variety of out-of-class activities that have to be manned by students: newspapers, yearbooks, radio stations, film societies, academic clubs, musical organizations, political groups, religious organizations, student government, and so on. Although many state colleges and some of the larger private institutions are unconcerned about attracting extracurricular whizzes, the smaller prestige schools are careful to admit a student body that will be "involved." A range of extracurriculars, they feel, not only rounds out students' educations, but gives them social and career skills as well as a sense of responsibility.

5. Leadership/entrepreneurial ability. We have all known a campus leader—the student who ran the student council on budget for the first time in a decade. Or the one who organized an annual school picnic to bring together faculty and students. Or the founder of a business that manufactures mailboxes and now grosses $15,000 a year. This is the applicant who colleges expect will shake things up on campus—perhaps even reorganize them. He or she has the combination of guts, charisma, and discipline to lead others and make things happen. Because campuses usually have a thousand or more students, real leaders are wanted to bring people together and provide a focus for student activity.

6. Personality. Some colleges look for a spark of humor or warmth or zest in their applicants—for the sort of student whose smile and verve will make the campus a special place. Part of this quality shows up in extracurricular activities and part in sheer character. It may not come up at all in the application. It is most clearly visible in the essay, teacher references, or interview. It is therefore elusive (especially at admission mills where interviews or recommendations are not requested or offered), and hasn't the same sort of impact on the admission committee as do easily measured variables.

Student versus Student

It's difficult for us to give you a blueprint showing exactly how students in each of the previous categories compete with each other within the applicant pools of various colleges. This is because every admission decision is predicated on a mix of factors. That mix of background and achievement—SATs, grades, rec-

ommendations, essays, and the like—will differ from school to school. Each college may give a different weight to each factor. And each may have a different mechanism for selecting.

To say that every applicant is categorized by admission offices and then competes only with others in his or her "category" is a grotesque oversimplification. Most admission offices don't have specific committees for athletes, minorities, leaders, locals, and so on. They consider the whole person. Besides, many applicants belong to more than one category. Yet thinking about admission categories is useful for two reasons. First, it provides a handle for you to categorize your own application, allowing you to "position" yourself within the applicant pool—by choosing which category you think you're in, or even would like to be in. Then you can "package" your application—present a stronger argument for admission than others in that category.

Second, it stresses that admission procedures aren't just formulated out of thin air: they stem from the college's various constituencies. Those constituencies determine institutional needs, which in turn prompt institutional goals. The admission office is then called upon to fulfill these goals.

Keeping this information in mind, you should begin thinking about how you can best fulfill their requirements to maximize your chances of admission.

PART TWO

THE
APPLICATION
PROCESS

CHOOSING THE RIGHT COLLEGES FOR YOU

Choosing the right schools for you is a two-part process. First, you must generate a list of the ones which you think you might like to attend. Second, you must develop another—and not necessarily identical—list of colleges that might be receptive to your candidacy.

The schools to which you finally apply will probably include places that appear on both lists, but one or two may appear only on one. You will find as you explore your options that differences between schools are usually more subtle than you imagined, and that your chances of getting into a particular place may be better than you would have thought. It is crucial that you undertake a thorough college search, for in the process you may decide to apply to schools that you had never thought of before—schools that are more selective than those you think will admit you, but that may welcome your application because you have a background or achievement they want. For instance, if you're from the West Coast, you may want to consider some selective East Coast schools that look for a geographically diverse student body, where your chances might be better than at a comparable West Coast college.

Where to Begin

Most high school students begin to think seriously about college near the middle of their junior year. True, just about everyone you know has told you that it is never too early to start "preparing" for college—not *worrying* about it necessarily, but certainly preparing: taking the right courses, getting good grades, and participating in extracurricular activities.

But sometime around the middle of your junior year, you will be thrust into the neurotic world of college admission. For one thing, you will take the PSATs. Also, the seniors just ahead of you will be totally obsessed with the subject. Suddenly they will forego the latest reruns of *Star Trek* in order to write their last college essay or take one last SAT review course. Welcome to the loony bin.

As soon as you receive your PSAT scores, you too should start thinking seriously about college. If you want to improve your chances of getting into the school of your choice, you should *start early*. Your junior year is just about the right time to begin, although you should have already been working hard at courses and activities.

The most critical element in maximizing your chances of admission involves objectively assessing your own record. You *must* be willing to recognize your own strengths and weaknesses. That doesn't mean you have to resign yourself to being rejected at Harvard if you're not an A + student. But you may have to "sell" yourself as something other than a scholar to get a nod of approval from Harvard's admission committee.

Fourteen Steps to a Good College List

Step 1. List your grades, PSAT scores, awards, extracurricular activities, interests, personal strengths and weaknesses—anything that will be of interest to an admission officer.

Step 2. List all the colleges and universities that you have heard of, and that, for whatever reason, you might be interested in. If your Dad went to Penn and your mother has always been enamored of Yale, write them both down. If your older sister's best friend went off to Smith and loved it, put it on the list. If you once wanted to be a physicist and followed Oppenheimer's work at Berkeley, list it.

Step 3. Start a filing system for college. Organize it any way you wish, but make it work for you. The material you receive from colleges will begin to fill up your room, and with about a dozen forms in each application, you'll soon have enough sheets to wallpaper the kitchen. Too many students hurt their chances of admission because they lose a form, forget to send something in, or miss a deadline. So get organized!

Step 4. Prepare a second list of colleges for which your credentials make you particularly well-suited. These should be your most obvious alternatives if you don't get into more selective colleges. Some high schools organize their college catalogs into groups based on selectivity; you can browse through those groupings and pick schools of interest to you. You can also use college guides. One that is useful for the purpose of this exercise is *Barron's Guide to the*

Most Prestigious Colleges, Woodbury, NY: Barron's Educational Services, Inc., 1981, which ranks good colleges into three groupings of selectivity.

Keep in mind that if a college guide lists *median* SAT scores, fully one-half of its freshman class will have scores *below* that figure. You shouldn't rule out Stanford, for instance, because you assume its freshman medians of 625 Verbal, 675 Math are an admission cutoff. They aren't; many students walking around Palo Alto have scores well below those. The idea is to gauge selectivity, and pinpoint those schools that would seem to welcome your application based on rough statistics. Also include on your list those schools that seem like obvious "safeties." These are colleges to which you're 99 percent certain you'll be admitted on the strength of your board scores and grades.

Step 5. Talk to people. You should meet with a member of your high school's guidance staff. Your counselor will probably ask you where you might be interested in applying. While you don't want uncertainty to set the tone for your college search, if you're unsure, say so. You should ask your guidance counselor which schools he or she might think appropriate *at this time*. You are not wedded to these choices.

Now talk to your parents, a teacher you particularly respect, an older friend or relative whom you like, and recent graduates from your high school. Ask for their suggestions. Make a list or lists of all these suggestions, and file them away.

Step 6. Using all your lists, look for patterns. Are there colleges that show up more than once? Do state schools keep coming up? Ivy league schools? Combine these multiple lists into a single listing containing those schools that appear repeatedly.

Up to this point, you have been collecting other people's opinions, compiling *their* choices. Now it is time to start compiling your *own* list of "serious contenders." This process is particularly difficult because the assumptions you hold may be totally erroneous. For example, you may come from a small private school, and feel you'd like the change of pace that a large cosmopolitan campus might offer. (Or you may be graduating from a single-sex high school and are now certain you'd like to be on a coed campus.) But you won't have any way of testing your gut instincts until you begin visiting campuses and gauging your reaction to the real thing.

It can be useful to begin your college search with assumptions about the types or sizes or locations of schools you think you would like to attend. In fact, most of the people you talk to will ask you, "Are you thinking about a small school or large one?" "Do you want the East Coast or the West?" But the answers you give will direct and limit the suggestions they offer. So *be careful about your assumptions* when you make your initial selection. Keep an open mind, and don't automatically rule out colleges that may not exactly match your notion of the ideal campus. With more research, you may find those schools are more appealing than they first appeared to be.

You will no doubt also make assumptions in your college search about your intended field of study. You are expected to list a probable area of study on your applications, and you may even need to apply for a particular degree program or school within the college. You probably should have an intended major in mind for purposes of the applications, so as to better focus your strategy and "positioning." But you are not wedded to that choice throughout your college experience, nor should you view it as a critical choice that will affect you forever.

Do be aware that this assumption may influence *and limit* your college search more than any other factor. Let's assume you have done better in your high school math and science courses than in English or history courses. Consequently, you think you might like to study engineering in college— a perfectly reasonable assumption. But many sorts of colleges offer excellent engineering programs: large universities, midsized "university colleges," smaller liberal arts institutions, and, of course, specialized technical colleges like MIT and the California Institute of Technology. Choosing from among these many alternatives requires that you think about your own needs and desires (Do I want to go to school with only math-science students at Cal Tech, or do I want a university setting?) and then test them by doing research and visiting the college.

You should always start however, by considering many campuses and then refining your choices. Ironically, most of us are more certain of our "perfect major" as high school juniors or seniors than as college students. Often during our second or third year of college, we may suddenly find ourselves wanting to switch majors or experiment in new areas. This is perfectly normal. In fact, if you anticipate the *possibility* of broadening your interests, you will be better prepared for a truly productive college experience.

Each year as alumni representatives, we interview high school students who say they are determined to become doctors. Frequently they say they want to study "pre-med." Many apply to special six- or seven-year programs that combine undergraduate and medical school educations. Of course, theirs may be a logical and heartfelt choice. And then again, it may result from parental pressure, a desire for prestige and money, or a simple need to start *somewhere*. It is *very* important to recognize for your own sake that your interests may change once you get to college. One of our friends studied engineering for two years, switched to history and political science (which he had hated and done very poorly in during high school) and wound up as a journalist. Educational and career paths change for many people, some of whom, years later, shudder at the thought of careers they seriously considered as high school students. Just be aware that this can happen to you too.

Step 7. For purposes of your college search and application strategy, list the academic areas that you might be interested in pursuing. Keep these areas in mind as you read college catalogs and guidebooks. If you decide that you are interested in business, make sure business courses are offered to undergraduates at the schools you are considering. If oceanography holds a particular appeal to you, make sure there are more than two or three courses available. A number of reference guides provide this information, listing each major and the colleges that offer it. Two of them are: *What's Where: The Official Guide to College Majors* by Joyce Slayton Mitchell, New York: Avon Books, 1979, and *Index of Majors*, 1982–83 Fifth Edition, Princeton, New Jersey: College Examination Board, 1982.

Step 8. In Step 6 you compiled a master list of the colleges you might be interested in. Now it's time to start reading about them.

Consult *several* college directories. Dozens of guides to colleges and universities are published each year. Some are quite good. We recommend you consider several of the more useful books: *The Selective Guide to Colleges*, 1982–83 by Edward H. Fiske, New York: Times Books, 1982; *The Insider's Guide to Colleges* by the staff of the Yale Daily News; *Barron's Guide to Colleges*; and the *Comparative Guide to American Colleges* by James Cass and Max Birnbaum, New York: Harper and Row, 1981.

Each of these books takes a very different approach to examining colleges. *The Selective Guide* evaluates more than 265 compet-

itive schools on three scales, based on interviews with students, faculty, and administrators. These scales are academic, social, and quality of life. Each school is awarded from one to five stars in each of the three catagories. Lengthy, subjective comments are provided, and the book is generally quite insightful. In addition, the guide lists costs, average freshman SAT scores, type of location, total size, male/female ratio, and acceptance statistics.

The *Yale Insider's Guide* is written by Yale undergraduates and gives an unabashedly subjective and useful perspective on a number of colleges.

The *Barron's Guide* is statistically exhaustive. It tells you about programs offered, costs, freshman profile, admission, and limits itself to objective information.

The *Comparative Guide* is similar to *Barron's*. Each of these books provides a separate piece of the admission puzzle and is therefore worth examining. We recommend that you consult at least one "objective" and one "subjective" guide—and particularly the latter, since their assessments, though open to debate, will give you much more insight.

Step 9. Get the literature. After you have examined each of the colleges on your "pattern" list (Step 6) in college guides and through further conversation, you can determine which of those schools still interests you. You are now ready to write to these to request information and an application. (Just because you request an application, incidentally, does not mean you have to apply. Carleton College, for example, annually sends out information to some 25,000 students. Only about 2,500 of them, or 10 percent, actually file applications.)

Send each college a letter or postcard requesting a bulletin, application, and information on any specific programs that may interest you. Tell the college when you'll be graduating from high school, and be sure to include your name and return address. If you are in doubt about a given college contact it anyway. Read its bulletin before eliminating it from consideration.

When you ask for information from a college you will generally receive a bulletin or "viewbook" along with the application. Rarely will they send a catalog with a complete list of courses.

The viewbook is very much a marketing device. It is part of the college's effort to sell itself to you. Usually it will describe the college's philosophy and history, its curriculum, the student body, and offer lovely pictures of happy students, hardworking faculty, impressive campus buildings, and pastoral settings.

Viewbooks are useful because they leave few doubts about how each school sees itself and wants you to perceive it. They also provide you with important information on degrees and courses offered, special programs (interdisciplinary or foreign study, for example), distribution requirements, prerequisites for admission, and the like. *You should read this information carefully*. Be a bit of a skeptic—don't take the book's word until you've verified it through other sources or your own research.

Step 10. If a particular program or department intrigues you, ask for more information. Many colleges prepare in-depth brochures about specific areas of study, sports programs, and extracurricular activities. Write and describe your interest as best you can. If you have further general questions, you can ask those as well. Each piece of information you receive helps you get a better feel for the college, enabling you to make better-informed choices.

In addition to the formal information usually sent to students, there are several informal items you can request. Not all schools will send them to you, but it is worth asking. These include college newspapers, student magazine, the school literary magazine or humor magazine, and various guides to the campus and town.

Step 11. See as many college reps as you can. Each year thousands of admission officers visit high schools all across the country. Their visits are intended to give high school juniors and seniors information about their colleges, and to attract prospects who might otherwise not apply. These are "selling" efforts by the colleges: getting the word out and triggering interest among the most desirable students to ensure that the admission office will have a good group of students from which to select a freshman class.

A second objective of these visits is to enable admission officers to meet high school guidance counselors, students, and faculty. Remember that most admission offices are organized so that individual admission staffers have geographic responsibilities. They try to get to know not only the academic reputations of "their" high schools, but also the social and economic qualities of those schools and their communities, along with any attributes that make them different or special. This knowledge puts a student's academic performance into proper perspective. Two high schools may be only a few miles apart, yet represent two very different worlds. And by visiting schools and meeting the people behind the recommendations, the admission officers can better determine the value of the information they receive.

Admission officers like to meet students because they too provide a "feel" for the high school. Rarely do individual students stand out to such a degree that their chances for admission are affected. But they do provide a subjective impression of the high school's student body. See as many of these visiting admission officers as you can. Usually your guidance office will post a notice of admission officers' visits, or place the schedule in the school newspaper. (If a college intrigues you and will not be sending an admission officer to your high school, ask your counselor whether perhaps the college could be contacted and urged to send someone out.)

These sessions can be very useful to you for a number of reasons. First, they allow you to hear a general presentation on the college, from the admission representative himself. This will help you decide just how interested you really are in that school based on the details you get. Listen to anything substantive that the admission officer says, don't make judgments about the college based on how handsome (or pretty), articulate, warm, or ingratiating he or she is. Admission officers come in many sizes and dispositions, and your final judgment about the desirability of a college should be made on the basis of firsthand observation, research, and the opinions of peers and adults whom you trust—not because you loved a college rep. Still, the information you receive *will* help you to narrow your choices.

These visits also allow you to ask specific questions you may have about the school, and have them answered by an expert. If you have particular questions about academics, housing, student life, location, costs and financial aid, the application process, or even what kind of students the college is looking for, *ask them*. That's why the admission officer is there. Don't be brash or pushy and don't monopolize the session. Put your concerns forward in a smooth, easy-going way. Try not to be nervous—nine out of ten times the admission person won't remember you if you apply later on. But be sure to address any concerns you have. If you don't, you're wasting your time.

This presupposes that you've done some research already, and you should have researched those schools that really intrigue you. Still, don't be afraid to go into these meetings cold. The admission officer's presentation may raise some questions for you to ask. If you don't have any, sit back, relax, and soak up the information.

With some luck, you may make a favorable impression on the admission person, who will then remember you and perhaps act as your advocate before the admission committee. This is a tricky thing, however. You don't want to register a negative impression on the rep, and in a large group you may look obnoxious if you're trying too hard to make yourself heard. From personal experience we can say that the kids who stand out in groups are those who ask *incisive, challenging* questions, and who do so without appearing arrogant or prickly. Only you can judge how effective you might be at impressing an admission officer. Some students engage in personal conversations after the group session. If you have questions you want to ask afterward, keep in mind that the representative may have to race off to an appointment at another high school. Don't be too demanding of his or her time. Above all, be yourself, and don't think too much about impressing admission officers. When it happens, it usually happens naturally; and it's better to leave no impression at all than a negative one.

Step 12. Prepare the "first cut." Obviously you will not be able to apply to an unlimited number of colleges. Most high schools limit applications to between six and ten per student. Therefore, you should choose the schools you finally apply to very carefully—not

only in terms of your concerns about where you'll be happiest, *but also as a means of maximizing your chances of admission.* Keep in mind that this process should be seen as fluid and changeable. As you develop a better sense of your own strengths and weaknesses, an understanding of the various schools that you might consider, and decide on your admission strategy, your final selection of colleges may change.

Based on your grades and SATs (ignore all but the most outstanding extracurricular achievements), roughly determine your "marketability." Are your grades and boards going to place you in the top ranks of people applying to Dartmouth? Or the top third of those applying to Syracuse? Are you an obvious choice for the most competitive, highly competitive, competitive, or somewhat competitive colleges? Keep in mind that the SAT scores listed in most college guides are medians: at least half the freshmen had scores *below* those scores.

Step 13. Using all your college lists and sources of information—talks with counselors, teachers, friends, family, and college reps; bulletins, etc.—begin to group the colleges on your lists into three clusters: *reaches, possibles,* and *sure admits.* Without question, these categories are only a very rough approximation of your desirability to certain schools. As we have said before in this book and will continue to say throughout, there are very few certain acceptances or rejections, and decisions are based on criteria other than grades or board scores. But

THE THREE CLUSTERS—
EXAMPLES

Several examples of college clusters are represented below. Each individual has listed several schools in each of the three clusters—reaches, possibles, and sure admits—based on grades and board scores alone.

Michele Miller
Manhasset High School
Manhasset, New York
Average grades: 88
 Top ¼ of class
SATs: 630v/540m

REACHES:	Cornell
	University of
	Pennsylvania
	Wesleyan
POSSIBLES:	Union
	SUNY Stony
	Brook
	Carleton
	SUNY
	Binghamton
	University of
	Michigan
	Georgetown
	Boston University
SURE ADMITS:	SUNY Albany
	Ohio University
	Hofstra

John McLoughlin
St. Xavier High School
Cincinnati, Ohio
Average grades: 94
 Top 2% of class
SATs: 660v/710m

REACHES:	Stanford
	Brown
	Yale
	Princeton
	Williams
	Dartmouth

POSSIBLES:	Duke
	Columbia
	Notre Dame
	Colgate
SURE ADMITS:	University of
	Cincinnati
	Georgetown
	University of
	Michigan

Mark Robbins
Winchester High School
Winchester, Mass.
Average grades: B+
 Top ⅕ of class
SATs: 540v/530m

REACHES:	Dartmouth
	Duke
	Colgate
	University of
	Virginia
	Tufts
POSSIBLES:	Brandeis
	University of
	Vermont
	Bowdoin
	Lehigh
	Bucknell
	Washington
	University
	Rice
	UCLA
SURE ADMITS:	University of
	Massachusetts
	Suffolk University

to begin the process of selection and to maximize your chances of admission, you must start with a realistic perception of the *objective* credentials you will be presenting to the admission committee. Based on your grades and boards scores alone, how are schools likely to react to your candidacy?

The *reaches* are those schools that admit students with grades and board scores substantially above your own. "Substantially" may mean 100 to 150 points on each of the SAT sections; and a full grade point average above your own. Certain colleges—usually those who accept only one-fourth to one-fifth of their applicants—will be reaches even if you meet their median statistics.

The *possibles* are those colleges that admit students with grades and SATs near or slightly above your own. If your SATs are zero to seventy-five points below the college's average scores, and your grades similar to most entering freshmen, then the school is probably a possible.

The *sure admits* are not *certain* admits. If your application makes you appear arrogant or obnoxious, your grades and board scores might not be enough to ensure your admission. But for the purpose of preparing clusters, let's assume you don't flub the application or interview, and don't alienate people you've asked to write recommendations for you. The sure admit cluster should include those schools that accept students with grades and board scores notably below your own. "Notably" means 75 points below your own on each section of the

SATs, and a grade point average a half point/grade level below your own. Sure admits may also include state colleges that guarantee admission to residents who meet certain test and GPA standards.

The bulk of the colleges you are considering should fall into the possible category, with fewer in the reaches and still fewer in the sure admits. Here are the percentages of schools on your list that should fall into each category: reaches—25 percent; possibles—55 percent; and sure admits—20 percent. If your first cut of colleges does not roughly correspond to this distribution, you should ask yourself why. Are you being unrealistic about your credentials? Are you setting your goals too high or too low? (Even if you have attributes outside of grades and boards scores that are incredibly impressive, you shouldn't be figuring them into estimates of your marketability.) Think about considering schools that give you a better distribution among the three clusters.

Step 14. Try to limit your first cut to a total of twenty schools. Your list should include about five reaches, eleven possibles, and four sure admits. Remember that you will wind up applying only to about half this number. The important thing is to know *which* half.

"Targeting" Colleges

If your objective is to get into the best colleges possible, then targeting should be part of your strategy. As you assemble your list of colleges, you should keep in mind which schools might be most receptive to your candidacy. Of course, you want to stand out from among the other students applying, but you also don't want to overlook any schools that might be looking for someone like you. In other words, you can improve your admission odds by applying to those schools that are looking for people with qualities or background or achievement that resemble yours. These schools may be every bit as selective or attractive as other colleges that you are considering. But because their institutional needs happen to correspond to some of your qualities, your chances of admission are enhanced. Here are some criteria you should be thinking about, and the questions you should ask yourself as you target schools.

1. Geographic diversity. Are you applying only to colleges in your region? These are likely to get hundreds of applications from your home town or high school. Are there colleges located some distance from you that have good reputations, but that do not receive many applications from your region or school? Since they don't see many students with your geographic background, you may fare better than the typical student applying there because you are geographically "different."

2. Local ties. On the other hand, are you avoiding applying to that respected college in your own backyard because it seems so familiar and unglamorous? Is the college one for which your high school has been a traditional feeder? Are there good ties between your counselors and the college's admission officers? Does the college acknowledge an obligation to local applicants? If so, your chances as a local will be better there than at a comparable institution farther away, where you are one of many similar applicants. (Yes, we know you want to get away from Mom and Dad, but you can still live in a dormitory on the far side of campus. This won't get you away from your parents totally, but you'll be able to live your own life.)

3. Ethnic, religious, or economic diversity. Are you overlooking a college that may be seeking students with your background? Brown University, for instance, has a special interest in attracting Portuguese-American students, who belong to a distinct and sizable ethnic group in Providence. Dartmouth feels a special kinship with Native Americans; Notre Dame sees few Jewish applicants and would respond positively to more. You don't have to be a member of a federally-recognized minority group to get special consideration.

4. Sex. No, it's not what you're thinking. Is there a good single-sex college out there that recently went coeducational, and is looking for good prospects of your gender? Do you know of a co-ed college that is trying to change its ratio of males to females, and for which you fit the bill? Whereas you might just be average at a co-ed college, a school looking specifically for men or women would be more favorably disposed toward your application.

5. Family ties. When you reject Dad or Mom's suggestion that you apply to their illustrious alma mater, are you just trying to be different or difficult? Does one of your parents or relatives have a close association with, or work at, a selective college? If you don't take advantage of these ties, you may be cutting off your nose to spite your face. Think about it. We know you may want to "do it on your own," but you will anyway; legacy status only goes so far in improving your chances for admission. We're just suggesting that you keep an open mind.

6. Special achievements, talents, or life experiences. Not every college reacts to your achievements in the same way. Some colleges want oboe players; others need linebackers. Is there any prestige school out there looking for someone with your talent, achievements, or life experience? A drama department may be looking for gifted actors. Maybe the college has a first-class debating team and gives special consideration to hot-shot high school orators. Or a school may want world travelers, or leaders, or students with personal sparkle. Think about it; when you find a school that is looking for you, target it for an application.

7. Academic interest. Do you have a *demonstrable* interest in a special subject, and the tests and grades to prove that you're good at it? If so, there may be a college out there looking for you. Whether you are a genuine theoretical physicist or a true classicist (or at least can sell yourself as one), a certain department may be searching for students with your academic bent.

How do you find out about all these variables? Well, the only category that gets special consideration across the board is family ties. Even so, technical or art schools requiring very specific skills are loathe to admit marginal applicants just because they are legacies. So, the only sure way to know is through investigation. Talk to your counselor, teachers, parents, and other students. Read college literature. And keep your ears open when you're making campus visits.

Once you have limited yourself to about 20 colleges, you must begin serious investigation. This exploration includes visits to campuses, interviews, and strategic analyses. (Chapter Four discusses college visits and interviews, while Chapter Five explains how you should go about making your "final cut.")

CAMPUS VISITS AND INTERVIEWS

There are many reasons for visiting colleges, and most of them are far more compelling than just the desire for an inspiring stroll among Frisbees and ivy. Campus visits are essential to a smart application strategy because they help you "get a feel" for college; enable you to narrow your choices; and provide a focus for your application. Equally important, a campus visit and interview can help the admission committee understand you, thereby improving your chances of acceptance.

Who Should Visit College Campuses?

If you are seriously considering applying to a school, you should examine it personally. Even if you have "known" since you were seven that Wellesley is the only place in the world for you and are certain that your credentials are impeccable, you should *still* get a firsthand look. Your perceptions of an institution may be very different from reality, and you don't want to be unpleasantly surprised by your freshman experience. For example, every year dozens of incoming cadets drop out of West Point, Annapolis, and the Air Force Academy within their first week. These students knew about the glory and the traditions of the academies, but weren't the least bit prepared for the realities of freshman hazing, the rigidity of the military, and the difficulties in adhering to the cadet honor code. Had they investigated beforehand, they might have decided to attend a more relaxed civilian college.

The second half of the who-should-visit question really has to do with parents. We will probably be criticized by Mom and Dad for this, but we suggest that you visit colleges alone or with friends, *not* with your family. Encourage your folks to visit on their own, but do your reconnaissance without them. If you show up on campus with your parents at your side, your impressions will be different than they would be if you were on your own. Undergraduates' perceptions and descriptions of their colleges will be "filtered" differently if they are talking to you alone, as opposed to you and your parents.

There *are* valid arguments for your parents accompanying you, or at least touring the campus on their own. Your college search is bound to be heavily influenced by other members of the family. Their insights and reactions can help you make a wise choice. And, after all, they'll be footing the bill. But ultimately you, not your mother or father, have to live with your decision. You don't want your parents to choose your college for you, nor do you want to be too heavily influenced by them. You also don't want to be overwhelmed by your parents' information. If they know more about a school than you do and are obsessed with your going there, you may not have a fighting chance in making your own decision.

But most important, you should visit colleges alone to get a better feel for what it's like to be on your own in a college environment.

Most kids don't really know if they prefer a large campus or a small one, a coed institution or a single-sex school. It is foolish to make your selection based on uninformed assumptions. If your parents do accompany you, spend as much time as possible touring the campus without them. Let them wander about as you explore on your own.

When to Visit

It is best to visit colleges in the beginning of your senior year. By then, you will have three years of grades and at least one SAT score to compare against the college's requirements. And, more significantly, you will be in the applicant pool then under consideration by the admission staff.

Call or write the colleges you may be interested in during the spring of your junior year to determine the best dates to visit, and to secure an appointment for an interview. Give the Admission Office at least six weeks notice before you visit. But keep in mind that many colleges have booked *all* fall and winter interviews by late summer.

Obviously, you will want to time your trip to a campus so that it does you the most good. Showing up unannounced and hoping to get an interview is foolish, as is planning a trip when interviews are not being conducted.

When a fall-of-senior-year visit is not possible, two less desirable alternatives come to mind: the summer before your senior year, and the winter of your senior year. At first glance, the summer before your senior year may seem the best time to visit colleges. But unfortunately you are not the only one taking a vacation.

Admissions officers and college undergraduates are also off during the summer. Before you plan your campus tour, make sure that the admission office is conducting interviews during June, July, and August. Most do, but there may be exceptions.

During the summer, students may also not be on campus. Many schools have no summer sessions and few job opportunities for undergrads who remain in town. Find out if there will be anyone around to talk to. Even if the admission office offers guided tours with undergraduates during the summer—and most do—there may be few students on campus to approach on your own. Time your visit accordingly.

The other "logical" time to visit colleges is during the winter of your senior year. Let's assume you play soccer in the fall, have decided to really improve your grades for one last semester, and honestly haven't decided where to apply until late November (not a terribly uncommon scenario). Now what do you do? Do you still have the opportunity to show the admission office how wonderful you really are?

Maybe. But you might be too late. *Telephone* the college to find out if interviews are still being conducted. By November most colleges have filled all their appointments through the deadline period. And interviews that are conducted at the last minute or during a particularly hectic time in the admission office may not be to your advantage.

Remember that you have two objectives in visiting colleges. The interview is only one of them. The other is to get an accurate impression of the place. If you visit during exams you'll get a sense of the campus, but it could be a rather jaundiced one. Undergraduates may not have time to talk with you at length, and you probably won't get an accurate impression of the campus. Even at the most marvelous schools, life is a bit crazy and students a bit restrained during exam time.

The bottom line? Plan ahead! *Well* ahead!

College: The Decision Is Yours

We recently met a girl whom we'll call Polly. She was interested in Princeton, but admitted that she wasn't entirely sure black and orange tigers were for her. She also wasn't sure if she could get in. Her mother, however, was absolutely certain that Princeton was the *only* place in the world for her daughter. Mom had visited the campus, read the catalog, bulletin, school newspaper, and bathroom graffiti. She met with professors, students, janitors—just about everyone. She was a walking encyclopedia of Princetoniana. In short, it had become Mom's principal mission in life to see her daughter at Princeton. Whether Polly would be happy there was a totally different matter. It is unclear who would be more disappointed if she doesn't get in: Polly or Mom.

Polly's situation is extreme, but instructive. Because Mom knows so much about Princeton, it is terribly hard for Polly to express her reservations about its suitability or her chances of getting in. Mom simply has more ammunition. If Polly knew more about Princeton, she could explain to Mom why Princeton might not be for her, thus countering this motherly obsession.

Whom to Visit

The very best way to visit a school is to spend several days on campus. Try to include at least one weekday, when classes are in session, and a weekend day and evening. Take the official campus tour; it's a good way to start. And you should *try to stay overnight on campus*. The most important people for any high school senior to meet are current undergraduates. They know the strengths and weaknesses of their institution, and are the most likely to be candid. Students are not only the best sources of information, but will give you the best sense of whether you will fit in or be happy at a particular school.

Some colleges have programs that house interested high school students with undergraduates on campus visits. Ask the admission office about this possibility. If you know undergraduates at the school, you should of course try to stay with them. In either case, try to spend at least one night on campus.

The second most important individual to meet on campus is the admission officer. *But not everyone should have an interview.* Make an appointment only if you believe it can help you! (More on this later in this chapter.)

The third group of people to consider seeing on campus are faculty, coaches, and extracurricular advisors in areas of particular interest to you. The purpose here is twofold: first, to learn more about a program; and second, to try to gain an advocate on your behalf. The first objective makes

sense for almost everyone; the second does not. If you are sincerely interested in learning more about a college's history program, this is a perfectly valid reason to seek out the department's chairman. If you think you can honestly impress him with your current reserch project, that too is reasonable. But if your grasp of the professor's field is a bit shaky, you probably won't win many points and had best not waste anyone's time. Similarly, if you're the high school basketball team's most popular bench warmer, you shouldn't expect to win over the college coach.

Finally, if you expect to apply for financial aid, you should try to see a financial aid officer. He or she will be able to give you the specifics of the college's aid program (see page 139 for more information).

How to Cut Through the Bull

If you spend time on campus talking and listening to people, you will begin to develop what Hemingway called "an effective crap-detector." Honing this rather important tool won't be accomplished overnight, but if you don't roam the campus with glazed eyes dreaming of frat parties, you'll probably start to learn how to read between the lines. Spend time where students spend time, read what the students read.

One way you can strengthen

your crap-detector is by focusing your questions. You could begin by asking students, faculty, even admission people, if they think their evaluation in *The Selective Guide to Colleges* was accurate. Was it fair? Did it miss hidden qualities or ignore recent changes?

Another way to cut through is to find out what the most common gripes are on campus. Do students resent the distribution requirements? Do they go out of their way to take "gut" courses in order to get around the distribution requirements? How do students react to the academic program? Do they think the course load is too heavy? Too light? Are professors available to see undergraduates during visiting hours? Are most courses taught by professors or graduate assistants? Does the library have open stacks so you can browse? Do faculty members share students' perceptions? Do students publish a course and teacher evaluation guidebook? Are the majority of senior faculty (or teaching assistants) praised or panned? How do students rate the social life on campus? Do they leave on weekends? Do campus parties lead to serious drunkenness or drug use? If a student isn't a member of a fraternity on a "Greek-oriented" campus, will he be a social outcast? The quality of the questions you ask will dictate the quality of the information you gather.

In assessing the quality of life at a college, listen for griping by students. If complaints about the administration are a common topic of conversation at the dinner table or in the student pub, you should begin to wonder. Is this attitude pervasive? (If so, find out *why* it is.) Some campuses just aren't happy places. If students complain about the cafeteria food and it seems perfectly acceptable to you, perhaps the complaints are really directed at something else.

Your crap-detector can be used very effectively during your interview. Admission officers usually are rather knowledgeable about their college. While dedicated to selling the place and finding the best students they can, they're often quite cognizant of an institution's shortcomings.

But you must be diplomatic. The last thing you want to do while face to face with an admission officer is to appear arrogant. If you have read the college bulletin and newspaper, talked to students, and think you really have a sense of what the college is all about, it could be to your advantage to ask some hard-nosed questions.

For example, you could ask the admission officer to talk about the college's strengths *and* weaknesses. Ask about the students' or faculty's principal gripes. Inquire about the college's main competitors and how the experience at one school might differ from that at another. This approach differs from the standard interview because you are seeking a subjective assessment of the college from the admission interviewers. This subjective information can prove invaluable.

The Interview

Some colleges recommend interviews; few actually require them. But the vast majority of admissions people admit that interviews can and do make a difference in admission decisions. In fact, the interview is one of the few segments of the application process that you can "control"; your grades and SATs are engraved in stone.

There are several types of interviews: the on-campus one-on-one interview; the on-campus group interview; the alumni interview; and the college rep high school visit. Clearly, the most important, both for the selectors and the selected, is the on-campus one-on-one interview. Typically it is conducted by an admission officer, and the interviewer's reaction to the thirty- to sixty-minute dialogue is included in the applicant's folder. This interview is the most useful to the admission committee, because the source of the judgment is known and the basis for comparison is rather broad. Most admission officers have conducted hundreds of interviews, often with other students from the applicant's high school.

Two other types of interviews—the group and the alumni—do occasionally provide critical information to the committee. Alumni interviews, however, are becoming more valuable to admission offices as participating graduates become increasingly sensitive to the qualities that make interview reports useful.

Group interviews, usually conducted at the college with anywhere from a handful to a dozen students (and sometimes their parents), rarely provide admission committees with significant insights into candidates. They exist primarily to provide the appli-

cant with information about the school. Exceptions to this rule do occur, however. They usually involve a student who manages to distinguish himself or herself, *not* by talking boastfully but rather by asking terrific questions. These students are impressively prepared for their campus visit; their inquiries are insightful, interesting, subjective, and tough. In addition, they accomplish all this without alienating their peers at the session or appearing to dominate the conversation. Admission officers may make notes about these students and include them in the applicant's folder.

A similar but even less common scenario can develop during a college rep's visit to your high school. These visits provide students with basic information, and are also designed to interest or recruit the most promising high school prospects. Occasionally, a student will so impress a visiting rep by his questions that the admission officer will make a mental or written note that is later included in the student's application folder. Remember, a visit by an admission officer to your high school is not an *interview* unless you specifically meet in a one-on-one format. Just because you meet with a campus rep does not mean you shouldn't seek a personal interview on campus, and/or an alumni interview.

Who Should Interview

It is important to understand that virtually no one is a sure admit or sure deny at most selective colleges. If the straight-A, 800-

board-score applicant writes an incoherent essay or has recommendations that suggest he is an egotistical intellectual bully, he may not get a nod from the Dukes or Stanfords or Carletons. Conversely, the B student with 550 SATs who is incredibly dynamic and writes a wonderful essay may just get accepted. And in each of these cases, the interview can weigh heavily in the decision. (One admission dean suggests that if you live within two hundred miles of a college that recommends interviews, you should make every effort to have one. If you don't, the committee may feel that the school is not your top choice.)

People who are terribly shy, who crack under pressure, or who come across as arrogant probably should avoid interviews. But if you don't fall into one of these categories, you should strongly consider the experience. As we have said before, and as we will continue to stress, interviews can improve your odds for admission—*if* you are prepared.

Objectives of the Interview

Cloaked in the college's rhetoric about wanting to answer students' questions is another objective of the interview: to find and attract the "right" and the "very best" prospects. You, in turn, are seeking the right college for you and want to maximize your chances of admission. These objectives are not mutually exclusive. You can, therefore, use the interview (along with the rest of your application) to convince the college that it is perfect for you

and you are perfect for it.

Sounds obvious, right? Maybe so; but you'd be amazed at how many students blow it. Very few actually destroy their chances by saying something offensive or witless. But many do little in the interview to *enhance* their chances of admission, which is just as foolish. If you fail to take advantage of as big an opportunity as the interview, the sheer odds can beat you.

Too often during interviews, students forget their goals or, in the adrenalin-rush of the moment, lose direction or momentum. All that many applicants hope for is to limp through without embarrassing themselves. That's not enough. You must want to *achieve* something. The key is to establish specific objectives for your interview.

Setting Your Objectives

As we mentioned earlier, all schools have institutional objectives that guide their admission policy. Most look for the well-rounded class; others want the "best" as defined primarily by academic achievement. As we will discuss later in this book, you need to develop a personal strategy for admission. That strategy requires that you first position yourself—set yourself apart from the rest of the applicant pool—and then package yourself and your application accordingly.

Let's assume you have finished reading this book, have begun to develop your application strategy, and have now returned to this chapter to prepare for your interviews. Based on your strengths and weaknesses—both in your high school record and in your personality—you can develop your interview objectives. These interview objectives are essential elements of your overall admission strategy and must be consistent with the rest of your application:

▶ How do you want the interviewer (and thus the admissions committee) to remember you? How do you want the admission officer to describe your case?

▶ How, in 30 minutes to an hour, can you communicate to the interviewer that you are special, interesting, warm, intelligent, and perfect for his or her college?

▶ How, in that same period, can you dispel doubts the admission officer might have about a weakness in your record? For example, how are you going to explain those D's in Spanish?

▶ How can you find out whether the college is right for you, and determine your chances for admission?

How to Prepare for the Interview

There are three general areas for which you can prepare before your interview: the college, yourself, and interview questions.

The first area—the college—is as simple as it is obvious. And yet an incredible number of students appear for their interview surprisingly ill-prepared. *Read* the literature sent to you by the college. It is chockfull of information—most of it rather interest-ing—about the place where you might spend the next four years. In addition, you really should talk to graduates, students, faculty, and others on campus. Take the time to do it right. If possible, spend time investigating life on campus *before* you interview. This will give you more fodder for questions that will keep the session flowing and at the same time answer your own concerns about the place. You should know that Yale has distribution requirements and Columbia a freshman core curriculum. If you ask your Brown interviewer about its business degree, you've had it: there are no business courses offered at Brown, and if you had read the catalog or bulletin you would have known that.

Almost inevitably, admission officers will ask you for your questions. Be prepared by having at least several intelligent questions ready *in your head*. It's best not to show up with a written laundry list of questions. Try to appear spontaneous.

The second area—yourself—refers to personal objectives. Have clearly established in your own mind what you are trying to achieve in the interview, and how you are going to go about accomplishing it. Once you have identified your admission strategy and interview objectives, decide if your approach will work. Will you have to depend on the interviewer to ask questions or will you be able subtly to point the discussion in the direction you want it to go? Some colleges recommend that you bring a grade transcript for evaluation by the interviewer. Others don't, but their interviewer may still ask you about your grades. If this happens, remember that the interviewer is not "out to get you," but is interested in forming the most complete picture possible of you. Be prepared to explain without complaining, making excuses, or putting the blame on others. Candor and maturity will work in your favor. Griping, immaturity, and reticence will not.

The Interview Questions

The interview questions people talk about and sometimes dread— philosophical or off-the-wall—are the exception rather than the rule. True, a friend of ours who has served brilliantly on the staffs of two Ivy League universities did sometimes ask, "If you could be any vegetable, which would you be and why?" But such questions are not terribly common, and usually are injected when the interviewer feels the talk is unenlightening or boring.

You can expect the admissions officer to ask questions about various aspects of your personality or high school career. These questions have no "right" or "wrong" answers, but do help to create a picture of you that will be condensed to a few paragraphs for inclusion in your folder.

Here are some of the more typical questions you can expect to be asked. You don't have to prepare a "briefing book" of preferred responses—as the president of the United States does before each press conference—but you do want to have given each some thought *in light of your interview objectives*. If you are

trying to position yourself as the ultimate student politico and are asked a question about defense spending versus social spending, don't give the interviewer a moonfaced "Huh?" in response. You'll be much better served if you can discuss government deficits and then ask about the college's problems with government aid.

1. Why are you considering this college?

2. How did you come to include us among your choices?

3. What makes you think this college and you are right for each other?

4. Where else are you applying and why?

5. Which is your first choice? (See The Right Answer, page 82)

6. What do you hope to major in? Why?

7. What are your plans for the future? What do you expect to be doing ten years from now?

8. What have you liked or disliked about your high school?

9. If you were the principal of your school, what would you change?

10. What would you like to tell us about yourself?

11. What newspapers and magazines do you read? How often? (See The Right Answer)

12. What books *not* required by

your courses have you read recently? (See The Right Answer)

13. What television shows do you watch? (See The Right Answer)

14. Tell us about your family.

15. How do you spend a typical afternoon after school? Evening? Weekend?

16. What extracurricular activities have you found most satisfying?

17. What are your strengths? Weaknesses?

18. Do you have any heroes, contemporary or historical?

19. How would your best friend describe you?

20. If you could talk with any one living person, whom would it be and why?

21. How do you feel about:
The nuclear freeze
Nuclear power
The use of drugs and alcohol
Advertising
Gun control

22. What events have been crucial in your life?

23. What is the most significant contribution you've made to your school or community?

24. What is the most important thing you've learned in high school?

25. What historical event do you

The Right Answer

Some interview questions have "right" answers.

▶If the interview is at Penn and the admission officer notes you are applying to Brown, Harvard, and Stanford, you've somehow got to convince the admission officer that Penn really is your first choice, or at least that you are really gung ho about the place. You should be honest and candid but not too naive. Admission officers know that over 70 percent of those who get into Harvard go there.

▶Don't try to impress an interviewer by pretending you've read books still sitting untouched on your shelf. Similarly, don't profess to be addicted to *The New York Times* if you're not prepared to discuss the philosophical differences between Anthony Lewis and William Safire.

▶If science fiction is your favorite escape, admit it. (But if shoddy romance novels are your idea of serious literature, you may want to temper your response.) Reading is imperative to success in college; you should get used to it in high school.

▶If you are asked to discuss your favorite films and television shows, don't fake it. If only half the people who claim to watch *The MacNeil/Lehrer Report* actually even turned it on, its audience Nielsen ratings would match those of *Dallas*. Admission officers don't award extra points to students who say they love the films of Ingmar Bergman, nor do they subtract points for those who admit to crying during *E.T.* Be yourself!

feel has had the most impact on the twentieth century?

26. Tell me about your innermost fears.

27. What do you want to get out of your college experience?

Preparing Through Practice

Now that you understand the need to establish personal objectives for the interview and recognize the types of questions you will probably be asked, you can do even more to improve your interview. You can practice: engage in mock interviews with your guidance counselor, your parents, your best friend.

Role-playing is a very useful tool. We recommend that you first play yourself in an interview situation, and ask a friend or a parent to role-play as the interviewer. Then you should reverse roles so that you get to share the admission officer's perspective. Seek advice from your counselor and teachers on a particular college's interviews, and from friends on how you sound.

One of the most important and most difficult lessons you must learn is that *it is not what you say that counts, but what the other person hears*. It is one thing for you to say, "I'm terrific." It's quite another for the admission officer to hear you talk about your work in a tutoring program and have him say to *himself*, "This kid is terrific."

By engaging in practice interviews you will improve the quality of what you are trying to com-municate. You will learn which phrases work and which simply confuse people. You will learn which activities truly appear impressive and which are merely run-of-the-mill. And you will learn which explanations evoke sympathy and which sound like bull.

Preparation versus Spontaneity

If you sound like a robot during your interview, you'll trigger a negative assessment. The same is true if you respond to the admission officer's questions with a pseudointellectual rap filled with "Uhs", you will also get "dinged." But if you engage the interviewer in 30 to 60 minutes of intelligent dialogue, show that you are prepared, have specific things to say, and plan to make it an interesting session for both of you, then you'll improve your chances of admission.

No interviewer enjoys a session with a kid whose responses have been so rehearsed that he sounds programed. Nor will he warm to a student who doesn't listen to him and cannot respond intelligently. Your preparation for the interview should not detract from your spontaneity or flexibility. The very best actors and actresses make each performance seem natural, as if each is the very first; you should try to do the same. You can have a rough spiel planned in your head, but be prepared to abandon it if necessary.

Some high schools video-tape practice interviews and then analyze them with the student. If you have the opportunity to do so, we recommend it. It's good practice, and it's fun. If your school has the equipment but has no formal program, get one of your friends on the audio-visual squad to set it up for you. If you have never seen yourself on the tube, however, don't be too distraught by the outcome of this little exercise. Most of us look and sound rather silly on camera. We're usually not as obnoxious as we appear; nervousness and self-consciousness caused by the camera's presence can exaggerate our flaws. If, however, you seem brilliant, calm, convincing, and gorgeous on the television, don't get too cocky. Your composure can fly out the window in the face of a *real* interview.

The "For Real" Practice Interview

Some students we know used a questionable technique to help them with their interviews. Several weeks prior to interviews at the schools they cared about, they scheduled one or two additional interviews at colleges they were not interested in as a means of refining their pitch and getting over the jitters. We have mixed feelings about this technique. On the one hand, admission staffs are usually overworked, and insincere or "practice" applicants place additional burdens on them. On the other hand, these sessions can help you. So use your own judgment.

There's another less questionable way to capitalize on interviews. If possible, schedule interviews at your "sure admit" schools first, so that by the time you get to your "reaches," you'll be prac-

ticed in the art of genteel conversation. Travel logistics may not allow this, but see if it can be done. Afterward, analyze just what mistakes you made and how you can improve your performance.

How to Dress for the Interview

Dress in a manner that is typically yours unless you're a slob. If so, ignore the above advice and do your best to appear neatly attired. But dress comfortably. If you're going to be tugging on your tie because you are unaccustomed to wearing one, then don't wear one. If you're going to be self-conscious about your legs, don't wear a dress.

The interviewer will probably wear a tie, or a skirt and sweater. Remember, you are trying to make a favorable impression on someone who is trying to decide whether you will fit into his or her community. Fitting into a "preppy" campus, however, doesn't mean you *have* to dress like a prep. Use your head.

Above all, don't let your dress be distracting. You don't want to be remembered for what you wear, but rather for who you are and how you communicate it. Try to look as if you realize it's an important occasion, but not as if you've just stepped out of a wedding party.

Several More Rules for the Interview

1. Listen. You shouldn't do all the talking. If you ask the interviewer a question, listen to the answer, and if possible, ask a follow-up question to show that you were listening and know how to probe deeper.

2. Be positive. Stress your strengths and explain your weaknesses, but don't dwell on the negative. And don't complain.

3. Don't fight with the interviewer. It is one thing to be feisty, and another to be acrimonious. If you are discussing something about which you feel strongly and the interviewer disagrees with you, stick to your position but don't berate or condemn his. You might humorously suggest a future conversation in which you can try to convert the interviewer to your position. Remember, the interviewer may be seeking to determine your flexibility and ability to think on your feet.

4. Answer all questions. Try to respond to all the interviewer's concerns. If you are confused, ask for clarification.

5. Keep the conversation going. Don't be afraid of a few pauses, but be sure you're not taxing the admission officer by making him call all the shots: you can ask questions, too!

6. Ask questions about what concerns you. The interview is a two-way process; take advantage of it. And don't be afraid of appearing stupid! Admission officers are tolerant. If you want to know something about the application, for instance, ask!

7. Try not to lead the conversation into a "trouble" **area.** If you know little about current events, don't direct the talk to that area.

8. Be honest. Always. And don't try to kid anyone. You can't win. If you don't know the answer to a question, say so.

9. Enjoy yourself. You'll survive the interview and many more. Turn the session to your advantage. Don't get psyched out and don't worry too much. If you try to do your best, you probably will be successful.

10. Send a thank-you note. A personalized thank-you note to your interviewer never hurts. Just make sure you spell the admission officer's name correctly.

Multiple Interviews

If you determine that interviews generally work in your favor, you can and probably should seek an on-campus admission officer interview *and* an alumni interview. If your on-campus interview goes poorly and you think you can improve your performance with a second chance, seek out the alumni representative in your area. It may counterbalance your on-campus showing. Also, alumni interviews are required by some colleges, and the alumnus may wonder why you didn't respond to a request for an interview, even if you had one on campus. This is another opportunity to win an advocate for your application.

Stress Interviews

Be wary of the "stress" interview, which is thought by advocates to reveal the true personality of the applicant under pressure. There aren't very many stress aficionados left these days. (Even the Rhodes Scholarship Committees have toned down their former Draconian method of confronting candidates, we're told.) But you should know when you're confronting them, and treat them accordingly. Under no circumstances should you attempt to outdo the stress interviewer in cleverness or aggressiveness. *Smoothness* is the key to response to any stress interview, the whole point of which is to unsettle, befuddle, and upset the interviewee. The more unruffled you appear to be, the more highly the inquisitor will think of you. Most of all, keep in mind that the presumptuousness and arrogance of the stress interview have nothing to do with you. (In fact, they reveal much more about the inadequacies of the interviewer's personality.) Don't take anything personally, keep cool, and view it as a game to be played properly.

THE FINAL CUT

The first step in your final college selection is a realistic appraisal of what you really want. Your parents may constantly remind you that you want to be a doctor, but unless you are truly intrigued by the thought of studying, talking, and breathing medicine every waking moment for the next ten years, you probably won't have the self-discipline to get a medical degree. Or if you do, you'll probably be very unhappy. Likewise, if Daddy went to Yale and is absolutely certain you'll love it while you've had your heart set on the palm trees and idyllic lifestyle of Santa Cruz, you had better be objective enough to acknowledge that they are worlds apart. You'll be asking yourself many questions about what you really want as you consider various schools. Make sure *you* answer them.

The second part of your strategy involves the often unspoken factor of competition. While your application is evaluated on its own merits, you will still be considered in the context of others in the applicant pool.

Finally, your strategy must acknowledge colleges' needs and objectives. Each college seeks certain characteristics in its students; each has institutional objectives. You should include these factors in your "final cut." In other words, you will be targeting certain colleges that should respond positively to your attributes—in essence, trying to match your profile to a college's needs so as to better your chances of admission.

Positioning

Positioning is a marketing term that refers to a product's niche in the marketplace. Positioning takes into account the product's strengths and weaknesses, the competition's assets and liabilities, and the nature, history, and probable future of the marketplace. Positioning includes not only an analysis of a product's place within a market, but also incorporates a strategy for highlighting and improving that place. A product's positioning is intended to improve its sales, and involves advertising, packaging, pricing, and promotions.

To give an example in a real market, a BMW is positioned differently from a Volvo. Whereas the BMW is the "ultimate driving machine," a glamorous refinement of the art of driving, the Volvo is "the car for people who think," a durable automobile that is well-constructed and well-engineered. The BMW is positioned to appeal to driving enthusiasts who will pay for good handling and performance; the Volvo to "smart folks" who will pay for quality, durability, and engineering.

A person, like a product, can also be positioned to compete in specific marketplaces. An individual can position himself for a specific job. A baseball player, for example, can sell himself as a reliable singles hitter as opposed to a home-run king. If the team is looking for a good, consistent base-hit swatter, he'll get the job.

In the same way, a student can position himself for a college. If you apply to a college and make the admission committee remember you as the kid who trekked across Nepal, you are positioning yourself. If you are categorized by the committee as a scholar, that too is a positioning.

The problem is that most students have an indistinct or inappropriate positioning. If it is indistinct, that is usually the fault of a boring, unmemorable application. If the positioning is inappropriate, it is usually the result of an inadequate assessment of personal strengths and weaknesses, the competition's assets and liabilities, or a misreading of the marketplace.

Go back to that sheet of paper from Step 1, on page 62, on which you listed your grades, board scores, and significant extracurricular activities. Now pretend you are an admission officer. Review the sheet quickly and complete the following sentence as if you were making a brief presentation to the other members of the committee. Remember, you're role-playing, and have to be objective about the real you. Keep your answer short and pithy:

"This is _____ ,
(your name)
who _____ ."

How is the admission officer going to describe you based on the most fundamental facts? Are you a "nice kid"? A scholar with great grades and boards? Are you another suburban prelaw/premed with a respectable 90 average? Are you a star athlete or science fair winner? Be honest. How are you going to be perceived, and where does that position you?

Now go back to that list. Add *all* of your activities and interests. Add your hobbies, your potential field of study, how your friends or teachers think of you. Using this additional information, decide if there is anything *of substance* on that list that could sustain an alternative positioning (especially if you planted the idea of that positioning in an admission officer's mind).

List each of the alternative positionings that are possible, and can be justified by your record: "This is the kid who . . ."

Each of us has several possible positionings based on geographic origin, academic performance, extracurricular interests, abilities, and the like. You don't have to settle on *the* positioning, at least not yet. Just list them all, making sure each is credible.

The Three College Categories: Refining the List

Go back to the list of colleges you prepared in Step 13, on page 68. It is now time to whittle down that list to a manageable number; to include only the schools to which you will actually apply. We recommend you do this by preparing a chart that compares schools' requirements, selectivity, and objectives with your own assets, goals, and possible positionings. Some people prefer to incorporate all the data on one large sheet of paper. Others swear by separate pages for each college. It's your choice.

Whatever format you decide to use, the important thing to remember is that the purpose of this exercise is to help you to make *intelligent* choices. The analysis that will result is neither scientific nor foolproof. But like a compass or guide, it should steer you more accurately in your college quest.

Step 1. Ask the following questions for each of the colleges on your list.

▶How selective is the school? How many people apply and how many are accepted?

▶What are the average SAT scores of entering freshmen?

▶Is the applicant pool self-selecting that is, are only certain types of students applying to the school?

▶How does the school see itself? Progressive? Traditional? Religious? Offbeat?

▶What types of students is it looking for?

▶Do most of the students come from particular states or regions?

▶Does the school have any particular needs? An outstanding debating reputation to maintain? An academic department or program that is well-funded but underenrolled?

▶What criteria does the school use in evaluating applicants? (Very often the application itself is a good clue in answering this.)

Step 2. Play admission officer. For each of the schools on your list, pretend you are on the admission committee. Based *solely* on your grades and SAT scores, give yourself an academic potential rating on a scale of one to five (with five being a super-scholar.) Remember that your ratings should differ according to selectivity: a "five" at Clark might only be a "three" at Harvard.

Step 3. Continue playing admission officer, but this time focus on your possible positionings. Again, for each of the colleges on your list, evaluate those positionings on a one to five scale and in the context of the college's needs. For example, let's say you are a good high school football player who has a reasonable chance to play at a small college, but wouldn't even be allowed into the stadium of a Big Ten school. Don't give yourself a four or five rating as a jock when you're applying to the University of Michigan; that rating would only make sense for small private places such as Wesleyan or Trinity. Remember that you may have more than one way to position yourself. If you are first flutist on the school orchestra and also have been a summer ranch hand, you could use either of those positionings within the applicant pool—or even combine them.

As you assign yourself a rating, take into consideration how many other students with similar credentials might try to position themselves in the same way. Remember, positioning takes into account your competition's assets as well as your own. So if you're editor of your high school newspaper, and you're considering positioning yourself as a crack investigative journalist, keep in mind that *other* newspaper editors will be applying also.

It is critical in this exercise that you be honest with yourself. Many students (and especially their parents) tend to be unrealistic about the value or marketability of their credentials. If you are critical about your record, you will have a better sense of how you should position yourself and where you should apply.

Now you are ready to put together the ratings you have made. For each of the schools you have listed, you have put yourself in the admission officer's shoes. You should have first evaluated your academic potential on a five-point scale from each school's perspective. Second, you should have rated each of your personal positionings (flutist, ranch hand, football jock) for each college on the one to five scale.

Step 4. For each of the schools on your list, add three more columns. The first should be a ranking of how much *you* want to attend that school. The second should reflect your parents' desires. The third includes other peoples' recommendations: those of teachers, guidance counselors, and other authority figures. You've got to deal with all of these people. While the choice should be yours alone, most parents will want to have their say and often teachers and counselors like to be heard, especially those who are interested in your college career and are willing to write your recommendations.

Use a 1-to-10-point scale to measure your own interest. A "1" means no interest; a "10" represents a willingness to sell a younger sibling into slavery for an accceptance. Your parents' and others' interest in each college should be on a 1 to 5 scale. Now total your scores.

Step 5. Any school that receives a "10" in terms of your interest, or "5" by your parents or teachers should be included *automatically* on your final list. Even if you give Princeton a "1" while Dad ranks it a "5", you should apply. We realize this is a controversial suggestion. But we have included it because if your parents or teachers feel *that* strongly about a college, they may make your life *very* difficult if you don't file at least a perfunctory application there. If you're admitted, you may then have to use some of the "coping with parents and others" strategies included on page 124. You can also use your applications to these places as bargaining chips: "Okay, Dad, if you want me to apply to Princeton . . ." Don't substitute one of these colleges for your own choices; find the extra thirty dollars for the application fee and add it to your list of choices.

Conversely, if Mom is against your going to a "party" school and you've had your heart set on the University of Miami, then apply. You'll never forgive yourself if you don't at least try to get in.

Step 6. Now, for each of the remaining schools, total up the three "interest" ratings: yours, your parents, and others. The highest potential score is twenty. Write the appropriate cumulative score next to each school, and list the schools (highest to lowest interest scores) within each category (reach, possible, sure admit).

Step 7. The tough part has arrived. After each school and the score representing "your" (your own, your parents, others) interest in it, list the probable interest the school will have *in you*, based on your academic potential. You calculated this ranking in Step 2. Add it to the list.

Step 8. Now go back to your list of possible personal positionings for each college from Step 3. Take the highest positioning rating for each school, and enter *it* after your academic rating. (Remember that some schools may be more intrigued by your geographic origin than by your prowess as a musician. If Penn is going to be more impressed by the fact that you're a geo hailing from Wyoming than

by your ability as a debater, don't let your ego get in the way. Penn sees scores of good debaters, but very few ranch hands.) On your final selection sheet, write down whichever positioning nets you the highest score for each of the colleges. If your academic and personal ratings are the same for each of the colleges, you probably haven't done your homework. You haven't researched carefully enough what the schools want. The University of Michigan cares almost exclusively about grades and board scores, but doesn't use a statistical formula for the bulk of its decisions, whereas University of California schools do. Brown places almost as much emphasis on personal qualities as academic performance. Your research may not give you the definitive answer to what a school is looking for, but it should give you clues. If your ratings show few subtleties or variations, start over.

As you stare at your list of colleges and numbers, several obvious choices should begin to appear. You will find some schools are more receptive to your personal positionings than others. Some may reject you solely because they care only about grades or SAT scores.

For each school you now have these numerical scores:

1. Your interest in the college (on a 10-point scale).

2. Your parents' and teachers' interest (on a 5-point scale).

3. The college's interest in you as a scholar (the 1-to-5-point academic rating).

4. The college's interest in you as a person and as a member of the school community (the 1-to-5-point personal positioning rating).

Step 9. Circle the schools that will (probably) award you the highest academic and personal positioning scores. Within each category (reaches, possibles, sure-admits), which schools will probably have the greatest interest in you? Usually the reach schools will have a lower set of ratings for you. Conversely, your interest ratings will probably be higher for the reaches than for the possibles or sure-admits. Remember, though that you may actually have more interest in a possible than a reach for a variety of reasons.

Which schools are more likely to be receptive to your candidacy?

Step 10. Correlate those schools that will have the greatest interest in you with those you are truly excited about attending. Place a star next to the half dozen or so places to which you think you should finally apply. The list should include one or two reaches, three or four possibles, and one sure admit.

Step 11. Show the complete list, with all the numbers, and the starred final cut, to your parents, guidance counselor, friends, and teachers. See if there are any major errors. What assumptions have you made about a place or about your own record? Are they reasonable? Discuss your choices, and if necessary amend the list.

How One Student Did It

The following section takes you, with student "Jim Peters," through the steps of making the final cut. Jim Peters is from an upper-middle-class professional family living in Palo Alto, California. He is a B+ student at a good public high school, which puts him in the top quarter of the class. His SAT board scores are 630 Verbal, 680 Math. He is captain of the wrestling team, but has more impact as team leader than as an athlete. He is vice-president of the senior class, and student coordinator of his local congressman's most recent campaign.

His positioning statements include: Jim is the applicant who

1. comes from the West Coast and can't wait to live in the Midwest, the South, New England. (Geo)
2. is the ultimate student politico and leader. (Politico)
3. is the solid West-Coast athlete who has focused on wrestling. (Athlete)
4. is the all-around California kid who is both jock and leader. (All-around)

Jim Peters' initial list of colleges, compiled from his own knowledge and parents', friends', and counselors' recommendations can be grouped into three categories—reaches, possibles, and sure admits:

Reaches: Yale, Stanford, Amherst, Dartmouth.
Possibles: Bucknell, Georgetown, Duke, University of Michi-

gan, Pomona, Carleton, University of Virginia, Northwestern, Notre Dame, Rice.

Sure Admits: Berkeley, George Washington, Washington University, USC, Kenyon.

Steps 1, 2. Jim's Academic Rating

Jim investigates each of the schools and determines its selectivity. He does this by listing the average SAT scores of the school's freshman class.

Jim plays admission officer and ranks his own chances solely on the basis of grades and SAT scores (on a 1 to 5 scale, with 5 high).

School	School's Average SAT Score V/M	Academic Potential Rating (630/680/B+)
Reaches		
Yale	675/675	2
Stanford	625/675	3
Amherst	650/675	2
Dartmouth	625/675	3
Possibles		
Bucknell	550/625	4
Georgetown	625/600	4
Duke	625/675	3
University of Michigan	525/600	4
Pomona	600/625	4
Carleton	600/625	4
University of Virginia	575/600	4
Northwestern	575/625	4
Notre Dame	575/650	4
Rice	625/675	3
Sure Admits		
Berkeley	525/625	4
George Washington	525/550	4
Washington University	575/600	4
USC	475/550	5
Kenyon	550/550	4

Step 3. Jim's Positioning Ratings

Jim plays admission officer once more, this time using his four alternate positionings, and again ranking them on a 1 to 5 scale, with 5 high.

School	#1 Geo	#2 Politico	#3 Athlete	#4 Jock/Leader
Reaches				
Yale	3	2	2	3
Stanford	3	2	2	3
Amherst	4	3	3	4
Dartmouth	4	3	1	4
Possibles				
Bucknell	4	4	3	4
Georgetown	4	1	3	3
Duke	4	3	2	4
University of Michigan	4	–	–	–
Pomona	1	3	3	3
Carleton	4	4	3	4
University of Virginia	4	3	2	3
Northwestern	4	3	2	3
Notre Dame	4	3	1	3
Rice	4	3	2	3
Sure Admits				
Berkeley	–	–	–	–
George Washington	4	3	3	4
Washington University	4	4	3	4
USC	1	4	1	3
Kenyon	4	4	3	4

Step 4. Interest in the Schools

Jim rates his interest in each school on a 1 to 10 point scale. Then he has his parents rate their interest in the same schools on a 1 to 5 scale, and his guidance counselors /teachers rate their interest on a 1 to 5 scale as well. Then he totals the scores for each school.

School	Jim's Interest 1–10 Scale	Parents' Interest 1–5 Scale	Teacher/ Counselor Interest 1–5 Scale	Total Score
Reaches				
Yale	4	4	3	11
Stanford	8	4	4	16
Amherst	2	5	3	10
Dartmouth	6	3	4	13
Possibles				
Bucknell	5	2	2	9
Georgetown	8	4	4	16
Duke	5	4	4	13
University of Michigan	7	4	4	15
Pomona	1	5	4	10
Carleton	4	4	3	11
University of Virginia	8	4	3	15
Northwestern	5	2	3	10
Notre Dame	9	1	3	13
Rice	3	2	2	7
Sure Admits				
Berkeley	5	4	5	14
George Washington	6	4	3	13
Washington University	2	3	3	8
USC	5	4	4	13
Kenyon	2	2	2	6

Step 5. Refining the List

Those schools that should automatically be included in the final application list include:

Based on Jim's ratings: Stanford, Notre Dame

Based on Mom and Dad's ratings: Amherst, Pomona

Based on guidance counselor's ratings: Berkeley

Schools that should automatically be excluded:

Based on Jim's ratings: Pomona

Based on Mom and Dad's ratings: Notre Dame

Based on guidance counselor's ratings: None

Problems. Jim has given Pomona his "absolute no" rating while his parents include it in their "absolute yes" group. Similarly, Jim is very keen on Notre Dame while his parents don't want him to go there. This provides the basis for a compromise. Jim includes Amherst (which he has little interest in attending) *or* Pomona to his application list in exchange for Notre Dame. Because his guidance counselor is rather adamant about Berkeley, that too will be included in the final application list.

Step 6. Refining the List Further

Listing the schools in order of interest:

School	Total interest rating	School	Total interest rating
Reaches			
Stanford	16	Pomona	10
Dartmouth	13	Bucknell	9
Yale	11	Rice	7
Amherst	10*		
		Sure Admits	
Possibles		Berkeley	14*
Georgetown	16	George Washington	13
Univ. of Michigan	15	USC	13
Univ. of Virginia	15	Washington Univ.	8
Notre Dame	13*	Kenyon	6
Duke	13		
Carleton	11		
Northwestern	10	*Automatic inclusions (and compromises)	

Steps 7, 8, 9, 10. The Final Cut

With the schools listed in order of their interest, Jim can see which ones may be most excited in his candidacy by placing the appropriate academic and positioning scores on the same sheet. The circled schools would be most interested in him. The schools with asterisks (*) are those automatically on his list. The final list is indicated by ●'s.

School	Interest rating	Academic rating	Highest positioning rating
Reaches			
●Stanford	16	3	3 (Geo, all-around)
●Dartmouth	13	3	4 (Geo-local, all-around)
Yale	11	2	3 (Geo, all-around)
●Amherst	10*	2	4 (Geo, all-around)
Possibles			
●Georgetown	16	3	4 (Geo)
Univ. of Michigan	15	4	4 (Geo)
●Univ. of Virginia	15	4	4 (Geo)
●Notre Dame	13*	4	3 (Geo, politico)
Duke	13	3	4 (Geo, all-around)
Carleton	11	4	4 (Geo, politico)
Northwestern	10	4	3 (Geo, politico, all-around)
●Pomona	10*	4	3 (Politico, athlete)
Bucknell	9	4	4 (Geo, politico, all-around)
Rice	7	3	4 (Geo)
Sure Admits			
●Berkeley	14*	4	—
George Washington	13	4	4 (Geo, all-around)
USC	13	5	4 (Politico)
Washington Univ.	8	4	4 (Geo, politico)
Kenyon	6	4	4 (Geo, politico)

Step 11. The Final List

Jim's final list of colleges should include one or two reaches, one or two sure-admits, and four or five possibles. He has choosen:

Reaches: Stanford
Dartmouth
Amherst

Possibles: Georgetown
University of
Virginia
Notre Dame
Pomona

Sure Admits: Berkeley

Stanford is included because Jim, his parents, and his teachers awarded it their highest cumulative interest rating. His chances are slim but not hopeless because he is a "local geo."

Amherst is included, as is Pomona, because Jim's parents want him to apply there. Dartmouth is included because Jim has more interest in it than in Amherst.

Berkeley is a good "safety" or sure admit. The possibles include Georgetown, because it was top in the interest ratings, and Notre Dame, because it was part of the Pomona-Amherst compromise. The University of Virginia may be interested in Jim and it's included over Michigan because Jim is slightly more interested in the University of Virginia than in Michigan.

Although Carleton and Bucknell are circled, Jim has little interest in them. He would rather go to Berkeley, which is very likely to admit him.

If more schools were to be added to the final application list— or if a school dropped off and a replacement were needed—the schools, in order of priority, would be:

University of Michigan
Duke
USC
George Washington

YOUR APPLICATION

Imagine that it is 1960, and you work for a small foreign car manufacturer that is trying to sell its automobiles in the United States. American car makers are producing large, fast models with sweeping tail fins, giant engines, and enough chrome to blind you. And the American styles are selling well.

Unfortunately, your model is, to put it gently, ugly. It's small, unusually shaped, underpowered. How are you going to convince the American car buyer to even consider your automobile, much less buy it?

Well, if you're Volkswagen, you establish a positioning for yourself in the marketplace, and then package your communications (principally through your advertising) to reinforce that positioning niche.

Positioning requires you to take into consideration not only your own assets and weaknesses, but the competitions' as well. If you're Volkswagen, you realize that your design might be out of vogue, but you do have attributes. In fact, your strengths are directly related to your size and shape. For example, your cars are much more economical than Detroit's gas guzzlers.

How do you convince the public of this? By packaging your communications believably and memorably. You run ads with unusual headlines, like "Think small", "Lemon", and "Ugly". When we say "Think small," for example, we are suddenly making a credible argument for economy. Wouldn't it be nice to get 30 miles to the gallon instead of eight? We are now the economical and reliable automobile. So what if we're ugly; we've positioned and packaged ourselves in such a way as to turn our weaknesses into strengths.

Seventeen Rules to a Better Application

Rule 1. Don't Lie, Exaggerate, or Make Things Up! Volkswagen recognized the most important rules of positioning and packaging. Don't pretend to be something or someone you are not. Not only is such deception wrong, but it is dangerous. For one thing, you almost certainly will be found out. We're not offering you a morality lesson. But we are offering some pretty sound advice to anyone who is "thinking" about tinkering with their records, or inflating their awards or sweetening their extracurricular record. Don't! You will get caught.

Prepare your application yourself. Discuss it, argue about it, ask for feedback. But do it yourself! It's just not worth improving your chances of admission at highly selective schools only to find you are disqualified from applying at all. There's nothing unethical about seeking advice from others, nor even asking that they read your essay for feedback. But ultimately, *you* have to present yourself as you are, and only you can do that in the best and most authentic way.

Rule 2. You do want to be remembered for something. Consequently, the more pieces of your application that reinforce this "something" about you, the better!

Consider another example: in the 1960s Avis Rent-a-Car was struggling. Hertz was the dominant company in the field and Avis was neck-and-neck with National Car Rental for the number two slot. Suddenly Avis recognized that it could improve its competitive position by establishing a unique positioning. It would call itself number two to Hertz's number one; it would position itself as the company that "tries harder."

Avis packaged its communication of this positioning by saying, "We have to try harder, we're number two." Suddenly it was perceived as being in competition with Hertz, whereas before it was really in competition with National. The result? Avis grew and prospered, not really at Hertz's expense but at National's.

What the Avis example shows us is that you can *define* the arena you want to compete in, at least to a certain extent. If you have the credentials, you can influence the way people perceive you.

Rule 3. Give the admission committee a reason to vote for you. This rule is not always easily followed, and not because applicants don't have qualities or a record of some virtue. Most people have *something:* some attribute that, if communicated well, can be a solid reason for admission. More often than not, the problem is that students don't emphasize or package this asset. Think about your own assets, and how to present them in your application so as to give the committee a reason to accept your application.

Rule 4. Give the admission committee a reason to remember you. The vast majority of students fail at this—but you should not. Imagine yourself as an admission officer reading *fifty* complete folders each day. Certainly you can understand how one applicant's record begins to look very much like the next. It is all too easy for your application to get lost in the shuffle. So *don't be boring!*

That's not to suggest that your application should be snide, or sarcastic, or arrogant, or come right out and say, "Remember me!" But somehow you've got to present something in your application that triggers a clear and positive response from the committee.

Rule 5. It is not what you say, but what the committee "hears" that counts. As you write your application, test it on yourself occasionally, trying to react the way an admission officer might. Are you being repetitive? Tedious? Do you sound snobbish? Don't be afraid to ask friends, family, and teachers to react to what you've written. Put your application away for a while, and come back to it for a fresh evaluation.

Rule 6. You do not have to use one positioning for all of the colleges to which you apply, but each alternative positioning must be fully supportable. There is nothing wrong with positioning yourself as a science whiz to a school seeking engineers, and as a "geo" to a different school outside your locale. Just make sure that your record bolsters your contention by *fine tuning* your applications to reflect each of your positionings. You won't be telling a different story to every college, but simply highlighting alternative aspects of your record and personality— matching your assets with each college's needs.

Rule 7. Packaging means communicating effectively. Communicating effectively requires hard work and a critical eye. Never accept your first draft as your final effort.

The process of packaging your application can be divided into two elements: the substance, and the presentation. The *substance* of your application is clearly the more important element. What you say in your essay and what you list as your most important activities *can make a critical difference* in the admission committee's decision. *How* you say what you want to say is also very important. You don't want to raise doubts about your literacy because you can't write a complete sentence.

Less important but not to be ignored is the *presentation* of the application. Make sure it is neat, legible, and follows instructions. Don't attempt to cram too much information into too small a space. If you are allowed an extra sheet to explain your answer to a question, don't submit two or three additional pages.

Unless you print very neatly, type the application. Of course, if the application asks you to write in your own handwriting, do so. But if "your own handwriting" is illegible, provide a typed transcript of the handwritten material.

And type your own essay. Although you want your application to look good, most admission officers do not appreciate your having Mom or Dad's secretary typing it for you. When admission officers see a "too perfect" application, they may wonder how much other parental or professional help the student has received. Has a parent written the essay?

Rule 8. Never use your essay to repeat information that appears elsewhere in the application. Expound on it, explain it, draw lessons from it, but don't repeat it! If in your list of extracurricular activities you explain that you were youth coordinator of your local Congressman's campaign, don't include that fact in your essay. For example, if you want to discuss a particular aspect of the campaign and what it meant to you, that's fine. But don't be trivial and don't be repetitious. We stress this point because many students are guilty of violating this rule.

The essay is the single most important element of the application that you can use to influence directly the committee's perception of you. If you position yourself as an aspiring journalist, you can use the essay to accomplish that goal. If your positioning involves your being perceived as a sensitive, reflective type, your essay's topic (and mechanics) should reflect that.

Most applicants misuse the essay. Not only are their essays boring—they usually don't tell the committee anything of value. Too many students try to appear intellectual and wind up sounding like shallow pseudointellectuals. Or they write about an extracurricular activity (or summer job) and what they learned from it. This is tame, forgettable stuff. Occasionally they try to be witty, and emerge sounding hopelessly sophomoric. True, the best way to be remembered through the essay is to be amusing. But, most of us aren't very funny when we write.

If you have to choose a topic, what should you write about?

Anything that is important to you, that you know something about, and that can be made interesting to someone else.

As you consider your essay topic, ask yourself the following questions:

▶ Will this topic enhance my desired positioning?

▶ Do I know enough about the subject to make a credible argument?

▶ Is the essay interesting to other people, or mainly of interest to me?

▶ Is the subject covered elsewhere in the application, and if so, have I added anything new in this essay?

▶ How many other applicants will write about the same subject?

▶ Do I sound like I'm whining or complaining?

▶ Will an admission officer say to his colleague, "Hey Jane, you've got to read this one?" And will he be saying it admiringly or critically?

▶ Have you addressed issues that the committee wants answered?

If you had a problem—a suspension, a failing grade—find a place in the application to explain it, but don't sacrifice your essay as a defensive maneuver. The essay should be offensive, to bring out what you want to emphasize, to enhance your positioning. There are usually other places in the application—or on an attached sheet—to explain suspensions, failing grades and aberrations in your record.

Once you have completed a first draft of an essay, go back and ask the same questions again. Be critical! You can ask your folks, or your teachers, or your friends to critique your essay; just make sure the work is your own.

Rule 9. If you have the time, put your completed essay away for a few days, then read it once again with a fresh, objective eye. As you write an essay, you may find that you are too close to what you've written to evaluate it properly. The opinions of others may be valuable in helping you to polish your final draft, but *you* are probably your own best critic. Once you have completed a first draft, go on to some other part of the application process, then return at least a few days later to what you've written. Imagine you're an admission officer burning the midnight oil to complete your daily folder-reading assignment. How will you react to that essay? Will it catch your eye? Is it dull? Is it well-constructed and thoughtful, with proper punctuation and spelling? Does it have a premise, direction, and conclusion, or does it wander from topic to topic? You can then complete your final draft of the essay. (This means, of course, that you should *never* write on the actual application pages until your essay is truly completed.

Rule 10. Make sure that the people you have asked to write recommendations know you and like you. Most colleges require two recommendations from teachers, and a third from the guidance counselor or principal. The easiest way to determine if teachers will write a good recommendation is to ask them (not if they'll write you a "good one,"—just if they'll write one at all!). If the teacher seems flattered by your request, it's a safe bet you'll get glowing reports. If the teacher is reluctant—says she has too much work, and hems and haws—look elsewhere for your recommendation.

Not only should a possible recommender like you; he or she should really know you. It is not a good idea to enlist someone who has only taught you for one semester. Nor is it wise to approach a teacher who has known you only in an extracurricular setting, or even in a minor subject. And it is best to seek the assistance of teachers in whose classes you have done very well. When you give them your forms, include a list of your extracurricular activities and any other notable facts about yourself (maybe even a short biography) so that they are aware of and can write about what you do outside of class.

Rule 11. Seek recommendations from people whose comments will enhance your positioning. If you are trying to sell yourself as a math-science whiz, your recommendations should be from math and science teachers, and they had better be glowing. If you want to position yourself as the next Woodward or Bernstein, your English or journalism teacher is a fairly logical choice.

You can, and usually should, explain to your recommenders what it is that you are trying to communicate in your application.

You may even want to explain your positioning. Any reinforcement your positioning receives from recommendations enhances its credibility.

Rule 12. Make things as painless and convenient for your recommenders as possible. Be thoughtful when you ask teachers or others for references. Remember that you're probably not the only student asking for their help. A little bit of consideration can go a long way in securing a recommender's good will. Here are some suggestions to that end:

▶ Give each teacher the proper forms, along with a stamped envelope addressed to the college.

▶ If you give one teacher a number of references to fill out, suggest that she could type up a letter of reference and attach a Xerox copy to each form, filling out the "objective grid" by hand. This approach is acceptable to most colleges, and certainly preferable (from both your standpoint and that of the college) to a scrawled, terse comment.

▶ Start early! Give your teachers enough time to compose lucid, thoughtful letters. Don't force them to resent you by asking them to recommend you one week before the application deadline.

▶ A few weeks after you've given a teacher his forms, politely ask how he is doing on them, and whether he needs any more information. If the recommender has completely forgotten about your references, this question will jog his memory, saving him from embarrassment.

Rule 13. Do not seek an outside recommendation unless the writer knows you very well, and then only if you have worked for that individual, or if there is a compelling reason for the writer to support your candidacy.

Outside recommendations are letters of support written by employers, clergymen, politicians, and any others who are not teachers or counselors. In the majority of cases these recommendations do little good, and unless handled sparingly and carefully could actually harm you. There is an old admission office adage that sums up the committee's feelings about outside recommendations: "The thicker the [application] folder, the thicker the kid."

Many of the weakest students pad their application with outside references. Usually these are letters written by famous or "connected" individuals—those with close ties to the college. But typically these recommenders have little knowledge of the applicant, and write perfunctory comments that can antagonize or annoy admission people. The most effective recommendations are those that are *substantive and detailed*.

If you are still intent on an outside recommendation, be very choosy about whom you ask. Perhaps outside work is a significant part of your positioning, and your employer was impressed by your efforts. If so, solicit a recommendation. For instance, your reorganization of the summer camp boating department led to a more profitable program—and that fits into your positioning as a budding entrepreneur—get a reference. If your research for a state senator led to her giving testimony before the Special Committee on Teenage Drug Abuse, then seek her support.

Rule 14. If you have achieved considerable distinction in a particular activity—and it is really quite impressive or important to you—make sure that it is explained fully somewhere in the application. Admission officers recognize that extracurricular activities are an important part of the high school experience. They also know which activities are substantive and which are largely for show. Because committees are generally more impressed by depth than they are by breadth, an applicant who has been involved in a few areas and reached a position of responsibility or leadership is preferred to the student who has dabbled in numerous, diverse activities.

Remember: you do not have to list every activity you tried throughout your high school career. If you attended four meeting of the Spanish Club as a sophomore, don't bother to include that fact. Avoid creating a "laundry list" of superficial activities, and instead concentrate on out-of-class work that really means something to you or admission officers.

How you portray your extracurricular involvement can affect the credibility of your positioning. Because some applications ask you to list your extracurricular activities "in the order of their importance to you," it is important to assess that ranking in light of your positioning. Be careful to be consistent throughout your application. Are your answers likely to confuse admission officers? Are you trying to position yourself as a "student leader"—someone who has brought opposing cliques together or organized the first effective citywide student congress—only to list individual, solitary pursuits as your most important activities?

If you have any doubts whether an admission office will recognize an activity, organization, or award, add a few words of explanation.

If your direction of the school play got you a summer job at a regional theater or if your work in the hospital emergency room landed you a mayor's recommendation, tell the committee. *Don't be shy.* But don't be arrogant, either. Many admissions directors have complained to us that too many applicants don't tell the committee enough about themselves. The opportunity to sell yourself exists principally in the application. Don't sell yourself short!

Even if your activities are not extraordinary, you can help yourself by explaining fully what they involved. Look at the difference between listing the name of your activity and explaining fully what you do for it:

Literary Magazine vs.
Literary Magazine—6½ hours weekly.
Collect and read sophomore submissions; write poetry column.

As we keep stressing, leadership, commitment, and expertise are important characteristics that colleges seek. Have you explained fully any unusual distinctions or achievements or have you just *assumed* that the admission staff is familiar with them? Is a particular club unique in your school or your part of the country? Are you involved with any novel groups or activities?

Rule 15. Choose a major that truly interests you and fits your positioning—or don't choose one at all. Sometimes your choice of academic major will affect your chances of admission. Whether it does or not, you can be sure that your "probable major" will help the committee form a picture of you.

Most high school students don't really know what they want to study. There may be several areas that interest you, and most admission people don't expect you to be absolutely sure. So if you're undecided or uncertain about your major, say so. Most colleges expect a majority of students to change their area of study anyway.

If you do select an intended major, however, you should be aware of how it may affect your application strategy. If you are trying to sell yourself as an historian, and designate mathematics as your major, you'll confuse and vex the committee. At the same time, you should avoid appearing narrow. Recently, a "science-nerd" applicant to an Ivy League college told his interviewer that he really wanted to explore subjects outside of his intended major of biology. When the excited admission staffer asked what that included, the high school senior beamed, "Biomedical en-

gineering." The interviewer was not impressed.

One of the riskier application strategies involves positioning yourself as aspiring to an unusual academic major. By suggesting that you want to study classics, or Egyptology, or psycholinguistics, you do set yourself apart from most other students in the applicant pool. But unless you're sincere, you'll find it tough to convince the admission committee that your interest is genuine, and to substantiate your ability in that field. Admission officers are not very tolerant of students whom they think are trying to "pull a fast one" on the committee.

Rule 16. Don't submit unusual materials just to be remembered. Supplementary information should be substantive and tied into your positioning. Don't try to be too cute! Many students feel that applications alone do not afford sufficient opportunity to present themselves or their best work to admission committees. Fortunately, most colleges agree, and encourage applicants to submit additional materials such as artwork, musical tapes, or published articles to the admission office. This is an important opportunity for many students, and one that is often abused.

Too many students send admission committees term papers, book reports, or research projects for which they received high grades. *Don't!* Unless your history paper of Franklin D. Roosevelt's vice-presidential campaign was so impressive that it was reprinted in a professional journal, let it lie in your files. The fact that

EXTRACURRICULAR ACTIVITIES:
A CASE STUDY

Very often, an application asks for extracurricular activities to be listed "in order of their interest or importance to you." The choices you make can create decidedly different pictures of you in the minds of the admission committee. For example, consider the case below. The same activities are listed in both columns, but they are arranged differently:

Jessie Hunter
Great Neck North H.S.
Great Neck, New York

VERSION A
National Honor Society 3, 4
Varsity Soccer 2, 3, 4
Student Council 3, 4
Key Club 3, 4
Literary Magazine 2, 3, 4
  Associate Editor 4
Band 2, 3, 4
School Newspaper Staff Writer
  2, 3, 4

VERSION B
Associate Editor, Literary Magazine 4
Literary Magazine 2, 3, 4
Staff Writer, School Newspaper
  2, 3, 4
Varsity Soccer 2, 3, 4
Student Council 3, 4
Key Club 3, 4
Band 2, 3, 4
National Honor Society 3, 4

Jessie Hunter's alternative lists present two very different portraits. The first, Version A, suggests that Jessie may be a little preoccupied with what she thinks the admission committee will consider an impressive list of credentials. She ranks National Honor Society first—despite the fact that it is little more than an honorary organization, a recognition of good grades and no felony convictions. Similarly, Jessie probably thinks Key Club will be viewed favorably because it is a service organization.

Continuing on down the list are activities that touch on the full range of the high school experience. The overall impression, however, may be one of "breadth without depth," or even of an individual who is a bit unfocused. Of course, this single piece of information will be fit into the rest of the puzzle to form the complete picture of Jessie Hunter. But the initial reaction to this element may not trigger a notably positive or memorable impression.

Version B of Jessie's extracurricular activities list creates a rather different impression. Jessie is now someone who is very interested in writing. She may not be a star reporter or editor, but she shows perseverance and consistency. She downplays the National Honor Society and the Key Club, and may even add credibility to her application because of this.

Remember: as the admission officer reads the application, each piece of information contributes to the total picture of the applicant. Contradictions tend to form a negative image, while consistent elements reinforce a positive impression.

you got an A+ or even knew that FDR ever ran for vice-president (and lost) isn't enough to impress admission staffers.

Supplementary materials that can help your chances of admission include work that is truly impressive—as judged by outsiders. This can include an article published by a "real" (not school) magazine or newspaper; a recording of a musical performance that won you an award; an article written about you describing an unusual accomplishment; photographs or slides of your artwork that appeared in a gallery.

Submissions that reinforce your positioning and that are clearly interesting can also help you. Consider, for instance, the catalog of the company you started; the advertising you developed for your friend's student council campaign; the calendar of church activities before and after you took over as program chairperson.

Supplementary materials can hurt an individual's chances when the submission conveys arrogance, plagiarism, or instability. Another negative situation can arise when an applicant submits mediocre work and positions himself in a way that inextricably ties him to this material. The problem here is less the submission itself than the lack of judgment that it conveys.

Rule 17. Consider applying to special divisions or schools within selective colleges, especially if they accommodate your academic interests and positioning strategy.

Within selective universities there are specialized colleges and programs whose standards are less stringent than the "name" programs. Sometimes these are technical departments like the School of Education or the College of Agriculture. Without naming names and thereby generating an avalanche of applications, suffice it to say that these programs/schools do exist at some of the better large universities in the country, and that their admission standards are typically lower than those of the arts and science or engineering schools.

If you consider applying to these schools, you should be sincere in your desire to pursue these specialized avenues of study. Be aware that opportunities to take courses outside the special college, or your ability to transfer into the "name" division, might be restricted. And keep in mind that at some schools, it may actually be more difficult to be admitted to certain of these colleges. Do proper research before considering this gambit.

Application Dos and Don'ts

Dos

1. Do find a "handle" (or a positioning) for yourself, something the admission committee can remember you by, and do be consistent in your presentation of yourself.

2. Do try to set yourself off from other students applying from your high school, and from the applicant pool in general.

3. Do find out everything you can about a school. Make sure that the program or major you're applying for is actually offered.

4. Do show interest in the school to which you're applying and emphasize the positive reasons for your application to that school.

5. Do provide your guidance counselor and teachers with sufficient information about your reasons for applying to each school and your intended positioning. Do they know about all your awards, activities and interests? Have you chosen recommendation writers wisely?·

6. Do try to establish a personal relationship with an individual admission officer. That person can act as your advocate before the committee. At the very least, establish a relationship with an alumnus who can lobby on your behalf.

7. Do schedule your interviews so the least important come first. (Remember, you want to give yourself some practice and build your self-confidence for the schools that you really want.)

8. Do write your essays early to allow time to put them away for a week and rewrite them if neccessary.

9. Do show your essay to an amenable teacher or counselor who will give you critical, objective comments.

10. Do ask admission people about specific programs and require-ments—or even whether to include something in your folder.

11. Do send supplementary application materials if they are relevant to your positioning and if they show genuine ability.

12. Do feel free to ask your admissions interviewer (politely) about the committee's composition. (Traditionally, the more faculty involvement, the greater the emphasis on scholarliness.)

13. Do Xerox *everything* you submit. There's always the possibility that a form will be lost in the mail or in the admission office itself. Then if you need to resubmit a form, you can do so quickly and efficiently. This is *especially* crucial for your essays.

Don'ts

1. Don't ever be be boring! Never repeat information already in your folder—in your essay, your list of activities, your recommendations — unless you are adding something important. Entertain the committee. Make sure that your application is a pleasure to read.

2. Don't ever try to put one over on the admission committee. Don't exaggerate or take credit for things that are not yours.

3. Don't be arrogant or pushy or driven. Show grace and charm in your writing and personal dealings. Be assertive but not aggressive.

4. Don't overload your folder. Send only the best examples of your work if you're including supplementary materials; and ask for the best, most in-depth recommendations. Remember, what counts is quality, not quantity.

5. Don't ask to have access to your recommendations. (You have this right under the Buckley Amendment, but we suggest you waive it.) Admission officers will take your teachers' comments more seriously, and your teachers will write more candidly. Comments that stress both your strengths and weaknesses work more for you than colorless, guarded references.

6. Don't read from a list of questions during your interview. And don't come out with a memorized speech. Spontaneity is important.

7. Don't telephone the admission office between January and April unless you have an urgent problem or something crucial to determine (e.g., has a missing form arrived?) Admission officers are very busy during this period, and resent unnecessary intrusions.

8. Don't telephone with new information. If you want to include something about your latest achievement in your folder, write a letter. (Keep it entertaining.) In this way, the update will go right into your folder—which is essentially *you* to the admission committee.

9. Don't forget to write a thank-you note after each interview, whether conducted by alumni or admission officers. You want to show interest, exhibit class, and reinforce their impression of you.

10. Don't pretend you're superhuman. You're an individual with feelings, fears, and subtleties of character. But don't dwell on your problems. Be positive!

11. Don't assume all colleges are alike in their approach and admission standards. They are different. Research them as best you can.

12. Don't write superficially. Explain in detail what various experiences meant to you.

13. Don't seem driven. Admission officers seek students with a desire to learn and internal drive, not neurotic determination.

Sorting Out Your Admission Options

These days, students applying to colleges are faced with a bewildering variety of options. As you look over application materials you will encounter a host of application programs: rolling admissions, early decision, early action, advanced standing, visiting student status, midyear or summer entrance. This range of possibilities has sprung up in response to both students' and colleges' needs.

Early Decision

This is one of the oldest of options, and exists at many good private colleges across the nation. As an early decision applicant, you can apply in the fall of your senior year, well before the typical deadline of mid-January—usually around November 1 or 15. The college will generally render a decision by mid- or late December.

There are two types of early decision plans: a "single-choice" approach whereby you may not apply to other colleges until the early decision college decides on your application; and a "first choice" approach that allows you to apply to other colleges, but still requires you to withdraw these applications if accepted by the early decision college.

Because colleges have nothing but historical experience to help them assess the limited group of students who apply through early decision, and no sense of how the applicant pool will look in the spring, their standards are very high. In most cases, colleges receive no more than 10 or 15 percent of their applicants through early decision plans, and admit no more than 5 percent. What you must also remember about early decision is that if you are admitted in the fall of your senior year, *you are officially obligated to enroll at that college the next fall, and must withdraw your applications from other schools.* So while there can be a great advantage in applying through early decision—if you are accepted, you won't have to worry about other applications—it also leaves you no flexibility. While you may withdraw from that college, you may not file applications elsewhere that school year. This rule is strictly upheld by colleges that subscribe to College Board guidelines—including virtually every selective college you'd want to consider. Keep these points in mind, then, regarding early decision.

1. Do not apply under this program unless you're *absolutely certain* the college is the perfect one for you. If you have doubts or want to do some further investigating, give yourself the luxury of time. Once accepted, you have no other options. On the other hand, if the college is definitely your first choice, you will be expressing the depth of your interest by applying this way. That sentiment, whether it's "B for B" (burning for Brown) or "Y for Y" (yelling for Yale) can work to your favor with admission committees, who love to admit applicants who love their school.

2. Check to see what the early decision procedure will be at the college of your choice. Generally, colleges will either accept or defer applications under early decision. If deferred, your application will be considered in the regular spring applicant pool. If the options are either defer or accept, your credentials shouldn't influence your decision. If, however, the school can also *deny* your application under its E.D. plan, think about whether your credentials are strong enough to compete against the tough standards imposed. If your credentials appear borderline for that college, you may want to wait to be considered with the overall applicant group—when they will seem more impressive in relation to others.

Once your application has been denied, it cannot be resurrected.

3. If your application can be denied under the early decision plan you're considering, think about whether your credentials will look stronger in the spring. Are there potential prizes, honors, or awards in the offing? Are you taking your SATs and Achievements again? Do you anticipate that your grades will be going up? Will you be able to report on an extraordinary extracurricular activity? If so, we recommend you apply under the regular decision plan, when you'll have more with which to impress the committee.

4. Under no circumstances should you apply to more than one college under this plan. If found out (and the odds are you would) your applications might be automatically withdrawn by the colleges involved.

Early Action

Early Action is a fairly recent innovation in the admissions game. Offered by four colleges in the Ivy Group (Brown, Harvard, Princeton, and Yale), originally it allowed students to apply in November to any *one* of the four colleges. That college evaluated the student's application and rendered an "accept," "deny," or "defer" decision. If accepted, under Early Action, an applicant was *not* obligated to attend the college. Furthermore, he or she could apply to other colleges under regular admission, and did not have to reply to the Early Action offer of admission until the College

Board standard reply date of May 1. This plan was conceived to allow good students the luxury of making college plans early, but unlike early decision, gave them the freedom to go elsewhere if they so desired. Like early decision, it was a subtle recruiting device to attract the best prospects, but didn't "lock" them into one alternative.

The program offered today is similar, except that an applicant may only apply to *one* of the four Ivy colleges. He or she may still have his or her application accepted, denied, or deferred, and does not have to reply to the offer of admission until May 1.

If you are interested in a college that offers early action admission, you will have the advantages of early decision without its disadvantages: you will communicate your interest in the college to the admission committee, may enjoy the luxury of making college plans early, and won't be locked into attending a school if accepted. Once again, however, your application may be denied; standards are unusually high for early action admission. This calls for caution on your part.

Rolling Admissions

Many colleges and universities don't wait until they have assembled a huge group of folders before they make comparisons between them and send their letters out. Instead, they use rolling admissions, which essentially means that they will render a decision as soon as a folder becomes complete. Rather than waiting until

April 15 to post thousands of letters, as the Ivies do, these schools will send them out in small groups, until they have received enough enrollment deposits to fill their class. At that point, the application process is closed.

Any time you encounter a school that uses rolling admissions, keep these points in mind.

1. Get your application in as soon as possible. The longer you wait, the worse your chances of admission, as places in the class may already be taken by other students.

2. If you think that later you can produce a credential that might make a significant difference to your odds for admission, you may want to hold off a bit. But unless you anticipate being able to mail it within a reasonable period of time, you're better off submitting your application and sending the new credential in when it becomes available—if a decision has not been made already. You may want to contact the admission office directly to get some sense of whether this anticipated new honor or grade will really help you.

3. Be aware of deadlines. Some schools, like U.S.C., have two filing periods: those applications submitted before November 15, the "first priority filing period," are considered in one group. Those received after that date are still considered, but only after applications from the first priority period have been acted upon. Obviously, your chances will be better if you apply under the first filing date.

Advanced Standing

Many prestige colleges offer advanced standing to entering freshmen with a sufficient number of A.P. credits. This means you might actually enter with sophomore status, and be allowed to graduate after only three years of study. Because requirements for advanced standing admission are so varied, if you are considering it, consult a college catalog or other publication to find out what it takes to qualify. This sort of program can have a great financial advantage because you will only pay for three years of college and still get a degree. But our advice is to spend the full four years in college. Sit back and enjoy the experience.

Early Admission

Early admission refers to the admission of high school students to college after their junior year. Most private colleges and a few public ones offer this alternative, but standards for admission are extremely high. It's not enough simply to have exhausted the high school curriculum, although this is usually a prerequisite for serious consideration. Students must be able to demonstrate that they will gain by leaving high school after three years and will be "academically stifled" if they remain.

And one doesn't just have to be brilliant to be admitted to college as a high school junior; admission offices are even more concerned with the applicant's emotional maturity, and his or her reasons for leaving high school early. Will the student be able to handle the sometimes emotionally disorienting and draining freshman year? Will he or she run amok once freed from parental restraints? And will he or she really be stifled intellectually by staying in high school for another year?

Most admission people counsel against applying for early admission, unless you are an exceptional student and demonstrably mature. If you feel you're really wasting your time at high school, you could consider working out a program of study at a local college with the help of your counselor. This would allow you to ease into college without being exposed to it full force when you're still unprepared. In any event, you *can* apply for early admission and, if denied, reapply the next year when you are a high school senior. In most cases, this will not work against you; in fact, many students denied at selective colleges as juniors will be admitted a year later as seniors.

Above all, *think carefully* if you are considering leaving high school early! It's better to stick out high school for one more year than to rush into college and wind up at a mediocre campus—especially if you have a chance to get into a more selective college a year later.

Deferred Admission

Under this program a student applies to a college in his senior year. If accepted, the student can spend the next year pursuing work, travel or extracurricular activi-

ties full-time, and start at the college the following year. Plans vary from informal to structured, but colleges almost always want to know what you have in mind for your year off. The advantage of this program is that it allows you to take time off from school while still providing the security of knowing that you have a college to go to at the end of your year away.

Midyear or Summer Entrance

Not all colleges admit students only for the fall semester. Increasingly, institutions find themselves having to open their doors to students between semesters or quarters. You may be able to apply for entrance during the spring or summer, particularly to state universities. In many cases your chances of admission may be better at these times of year, although the situation will vary from year to year and from college to college. Check into the specific situation, not only by inquiring at the admission office, but also by talking to undergraduates and others, and, of course, by carefully reading the literature you receive.

Special and Transfer Student Applications

We will discuss these approaches to admission in Chapter Seven.

THE LONG WAIT

Okay. You've worked hard to put together the best application strategy possible. You've targeted schools that might be looking for someone like you. You've slaved over your applications, taking pains to properly position yourself and package the presentation of your credentials. The forms are in the mail. It's February, and life seems comparatively easy after autumn's application frenzy. Now you can relax, right?

Not exactly. Even after you have mailed your forms, you shouldn't become complacent about your applications. In order to maximize your chances of admission—as well as deal with the anxiety—you still have work to do, even after your application forms are submitted. That work involves not only keeping up with courses and extracurriculars, but also taking the final steps to better your odds for acceptance. Finally, when the decisions arrive, and you (we hope) have some choices to make, there'll be more work. So be prepared.

Updating Information

Remember that the selection process at most selective schools is in full swing from February through April. Under no circumstances should you let deadlines slip by. At the same time, you shouldn't interpret the passing of deadlines to mean that colleges don't want to hear from you. They expect to receive additional materials from applicants and high schools during the decision-making period. These updates are welcome if they are presented in a way that doesn't inconvenience the admission staff. This means that you should never telephone the admission office with news of your latest accomplishment. Unless the news is earth-shattering and the mails don't allow enough time to get it to colleges, *write a letter*. It will go into your folder or to the area admission officer. Here is a list of updates you may want to submit:

1. Midyear grade reports. Some colleges, particularly those with admission notification dates in April, require your high school to submit a midyear grade report. This notes which courses you've taken during the first semester, their level, and your first semester grades. Deadlines for submission of midyear grades vary: Brown asks that they be sent by February 15 while Pomona requests that the whole secondary school report be sent by February 1.

If you are applying to a school that does not require this kind of grade bulletin, or to a school with rolling admissions that hasn't decided on your application, think about asking your guidance counselor to submit an informal midyear report—assuming, of course, that your courses and grades are pretty good. If they're mediocre, you should seriously consider whether this bit of initiative will work against you.

2. Additional recommendations. If you've become better acquainted with an employer or a teacher in the last few months, and he or she can write you a terrific supplementary recommendation, go ahead. It may help you.

3. Updates of special achievements, additional credentials. Let's say you're a hockey goalie who has just been selected as the league MVP. Or an actress who has just won one of the lead roles in the school play (or even better, one in a local or semiprofessional production). By all means, let admission committees know about your newly-won award, honor, or achievement. You can write to admission offices yourself, or enlist the help of your counselor, advisor, or some other authority to make the new piece of information even more official. Coming from a counselor, an announcement that your latest drawing won a Scholastic Art Award has more clout. Moreover, the committee will be impressed that the counselor took the time to write on your behalf.

4. "Disasters" and negative updates: how to approach them. Not every update is a positive one. Your midyear report may contain a disastrous grade. Through a misunderstanding or because of some silliness on your part, you may have been suspended from school. What do you do if you know that a letter is on its way from your high school notifying the admission office of your problem?

You must first decide whether it's worth explaining what happened. If the offense is a minor one (or if you have no good explanation for, say, a flunking grade), it may be better to keep quiet. In most instances, however, you will be better served by addressing the issue than by pretending it doesn't exist.

If you're faced with this kind of unfortunate situation, *it is imperative* that you convince the committee that the incident was an isolated one, that it won't happen again, and that you've learned something from it—thereby making you a better person and, of course, a better applicant than you were before. Here are our suggestions for handling this situation:

▶ Be honest. Explain as best you can what happened and why. If there is no good reason for it, but you were just being juvenile, say so. Admit your mistake, then go on to *show* how it won't happen again. Avoid sounding too defensive, and don't put the blame on others. Colleges will respect you for taking responsibility. And don't make up stories. The area admission officer is only a telephone call away from school officials, who will be happy to provide their own version of events.

▶ Offer to provide further information or cooperate with the admission office in any way you can. If you are truly embarrassed or ashamed, provide the whole story. Your explanation will be kept confidential. More importantly, make clear how much you want to get past the "problem." Offer to come to campus for an interview, or to speak on the telephone at greater length about the incident if that would help your case.

▶ Be contrite. And if you can't be, make a good case for why you are not. This is a tough one. Maybe you've done something you honestly feel wasn't wrong.

In most instances, however, the admission committee will side with the secondary school. But whatever the college's attitude, you must decide your own. If, in good conscience, you cannot claim to recognize the error of what you did, then you should say so. But be prepared to make a compelling, logical argument for your case. (Drafting this letter should probably occupy more of your time than any essay.) Once again, avoid sounding defensive. Be humble

but sure of yourself. Above all, appear flexible, sensitive, and thoughtful, if you're not sorry. Don't sound arrogant.

▶ Try to arrange a note from a school official. If, for example, you were caught hiding a remote control camera in the locker room, and you've finally done your penance through service to the school (perhaps through special grounds-keeping work), ask your counselor to write another letter on your behalf to colleges. You should do this only if you feel your relationship with your school has been sufficiently repaired so that the reference will be positive.

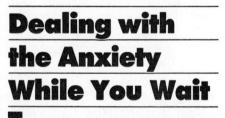

Dealing with the Anxiety While You Wait

There's no anodyne for the anxiousness you'll feel as you await your decision letters. Your mailbox will become a kind of shrine, your postman (depending on the thickness of the letter he carries) an angel of light or messenger of doom. And you'll go through a daily ritual of rushing home to see if you've gotten the word from your first choice.

It is important to keep things in perspective as you await the outcome of your years of effort. One admission director we know has a favorite saying: "We're not denying this applicant an education by not admitting him." If you have followed our advice, have been realistic about your odds for admission, and have taken pains to include a couple of sure-admits among your college choices, you *should* have somewhere to go after high school. And that campus should appeal to you and meet your basic requirements for a fulfilling college experience. Moreover there will be alternatives open to you, even if you don't get in where you've applied (we'll discuss them later in this chapter).

During this excruciating period, try to concentrate on your other activities and your schoolwork. Get everything you can out of your high school experience. Remember that you'll soon be leaving it—the victories, the disasters, friends, teachers, and in most cases, your parents and family. Since there's usually nothing more you can do about your applications, you might as well sit back, relax, and enjoy your last few months as a high school senior.

Sure, you say. How can I relax when I don't know if my file is complete? What if there's a credential missing, and I don't know about it?! Our answer to that: Relax! Most colleges run checks on all applications to ascertain whether or not they are complete. They'll notify you if something is missing. This is particularly true of smaller, private colleges. One word of caution: some larger and state institutions may not make the same effort. But if you've followed our advice, you've probably been pretty organized, and your fears are most likely groundless.

Above all, never, ever telephone the admission office before a college's notification date to ask whether you've been admitted.

Admission officers at schools with one-shot admission dates have heard every excuse ever conceived by teenagers or anxious parents. At Brown, for instance, every spring could be counted upon to bring a number of lines— at least two or three typical— about why someone needed a decision early:

▶ "My family is leaving for a vacation in the Bahamas and I'm going with them. Can't you give me the decision on my application so I can enjoy the sun and surf?"

▶ "My grandmother is on her deathbed and just wanted to be assured, before she expired, that her granddaughter would be enrolled at Brown. . . ."

▶ "Someone else in my class already got his admission letter. Where's mine?"

This sort of gambit will give the admission office an impression of you as nervous and pushy—no matter how clever your excuse may be. Remember once again how busy admission people are in the spring. They have better things to do than listening to fables concocted by hypertense applicants.

Dealing with Early Acceptances

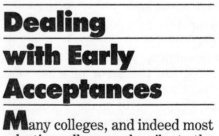

Many colleges, and indeed most selective colleges, subscribe to the College Board Candidates Reply Date Agreement. The CRDA ensures that even under rolling admission plans, participating colleges will not require you to reply to an offer of admission before May 1. This means that you will not have to make your decision until you've heard from all the colleges to which you've applied. However, you may find you have been accepted by a "possible" or "sure admit" college, before you have heard from your "reaches." In rare cases the college, not subscribing to the CRDA, may ask you to respond to its offer of admission before you are slated to hear from the others. What then?

1. Let your guidance or college counselor know immediately. He or she can help you in contacting the colleges to plead your case.

2. If the college requires a deposit, have your counselor ask whether you can obtain an extension. He or she should explain your situation, saying that you haven't heard from other colleges and want to make an informed choice. With luck, the "early" college will give you some time.

3. If the college does not give you more time to respond, you have a choice. First, you can send in the deposit, knowing you may lose it if you are admitted and enroll elsewhere. This is perfectly normal operating procedure. The college admitting you will already have figured a certain number of no-shows among its "firm" enrollees. And if you still feel uneasy about doing this, keep in mind that the college is unfairly putting you in the position of having to decide *before* you have heard from others. That's not quite cricket.

Second, if you cannot afford the deposit and you're unable to get an extension, plead the case for your limited financial resources, asking that the deposit be waived. If the college still insists on the deposit, scrape it up somehow.

4. Under no circumstances should you turn down an early offer of admission under pressure, assuming that you will be admitted elsewhere. That first acceptance, even if it's only to a sure admit college, may conceivably be the only one you get. There's no way of knowing. Therefore, do everything in your power to hold your place at that college. Beg, borrow, but get the deposit money. You should, of course, try every means to get an extension. But if you can't get one, make sure you respond to the offer of admission with a deposit. We know this can be difficult. Some colleges now require deposits of up to $500 to prevent a "melt" of matriculants. But it's foolish not to secure your place after all the hard work you've put into your high school career and applications. Of course, if the school does not require a deposit (as is the case at a few state colleges) say yes after asking for an extension, and see where else you get a nod.

Requesting Decisions before a College's Stated Notification Date

Let's assume you've applied to a college that offers scholarships based on merit. (This might be academic, athletic, or some other kind of merit.) You have applica-

WHAT THE DECLINE IN
COLLEGE-AGE POPULATION
MEANS TO YOU

If you're overwhelmed by the fact that yours is only one among thousands of college applications, cheer up. Mother Nature has a sort of revenge in store for many of today's admission officers.

Throughout the 1960s and 1970s colleges had the luxury of selecting students from a steadily growing pool of applicants. In response, almost all colleges expanded, some growing by leaps and bounds, while the prestige schools became increasingly choosy. But today these institutions face a "baby bust" that threatens to drive the less selective schools out of business.

Consider these facts. The population of college-age students hit a high of 3.2 million in 1976. This group will shrink to 2.7 million by 1990, and won't begin to increase in size again until 1994. By the 1990s, colleges will be drawing on a pool of high school seniors only three-fourths the size of the potential applicant group of the mid-1970s!

The ways that colleges respond to these shrinking markets will have a major impact on college admissions nationwide. Many colleges will increase recruiting in geographic areas from which they traditionally have received few applications. (All colleges draw their greatest number of applicants from surrounding states and communities.) Some schools will use sophisticated marketing strategies: students receiving high scores on the PSAT/NMSQT can expect to be the recipients of glossy viewbooks, friendly telephone calls, or other "personal contact" urging them to apply. Some students may even receive letters from the most desperate schools offering them automatic admission, and urging them to enroll! (Some colleges already use this ploy.)

Wealthier schools will probably begin offering more merit scholarships in order to attract top kids. Institutions in urban areas may expand continuing education programs, offering courses to adults to compensate for their shrinking teen applicant pool. In rarer instances, colleges may slowly shrink in size to match a decline in applications. Whatever schools do, the stark fact remains that there will not be enough students around to maintain current enrollment levels at every institution. Some schools will have to lose out in the scramble.

But for those 40 to 60 highly selective colleges, and the 10 "most selective" schools, the population shift may make admission tougher. With educational costs soaring, parents are becoming increasingly unwilling to drive themselves into debt only to have their children graduate from a "second-rate" private college, a college whose degree may have a market value (in terms of jobs or admission to professional school) no greater than the diploma from a much cheaper state school. As a result, students will apply to the "top" and "almost top" prestige schools while shunning the lesser-known private colleges.

In fact, some top schools are receiving record numbers of applications. In 1983, for instance, Brown University received over 13,000 applications, surpassing Harvard for the first time in sheer volume of applicants. Many of these top schools will, however, face a challenge of their own: how to maintain high academic standards *and* a diverse student body.

In sum, the "baby bust" will tend to make admission easier at almost all except the elite group of very selective colleges. At these schools, the level of selectivity will vary depending on a number of factors—demographics, the strength of the recruitment program, etc. What this means for you as an applicant is that your sure-admits and possibles may be easier to get into. Your reaches may be even more of a stretch. But this also means that it is more important than ever to do your homework for your application strategy. You will have to find out whether the colleges that interest you are getting more or less selective. Then you will have to apply that knowledge to your targeting of schools, as well as to positioning and packaging your application.

tions in at other selective colleges, and expect to hear from most in early or mid-April. Suddenly, in February, you are offered admission and a full scholarship from the merit college. But you have only two weeks to respond. And no extensions. What should you do?

1. If you can avoid it, never ask a college for a decision prematurely, however good your reasons. The fact of the matter is that, when pushed, a college is more likely to render a negative decision than a positive one. If the college is highly selective, it will be hesitant to offer someone a place in the class when it hasn't a feel for the remainder of the applicant pool.

If you *must* request an early decision from other colleges, then you must. But we strongly urge that you consider every other alternative before doing so, since by requesting action on your file prematurely, you will almost always lessen your chance of admission.

2. If you've won a full scholarship to a college, do not withdraw your applications to other schools. At least give yourself the luxury of an informed decision. Wait to hear from the other colleges. If you don't you may always wonder whether you would have been admitted to Harvard, Stanford, Notre Dame, or wherever. If you can walk away from an acceptance at those places knowing the full range of alternatives, great. But if you really don't know, you're doing yourself a disservice.

Dealing with Decisions and Rejections

Getting a rejection letter is seldom a positive experience (unless your parents have been pushing you to attend a college you absolutely detest, and the admission office saves you from battling Mom and Dad by rejecting you). If you're lucky, you will get in everywhere you apply. But if you've followed our advice in this book, there is a good chance that you won't get in *somewhere*. After all, you're supposed to be applying to at least one or two reaches.

Admission is a tricky business, and you won't know for sure whether or not you'll be admitted until you have the letters in hand. This brings up an important point: *the only bona fide, trustworthy communication confirming your admission is a letter from the Director of Admissions or an admission officer saying you've gotten in*. Promises, predictions, and verbal assurances from anyone else cannot be counted on. If a coach swears on Babe Ruth's grave that you will be admitted, wonderful! But the coach won't be making the ultimate decision. Neither will an alumnus who has taken a liking to you. Nor even an overeager admission officer. Until you get that letter from the admission office itself, don't count on anything. A telephone call or cable from an admission officer is legitimate; but we recommend you take no further action until you have written confirmation.

Another important point: *open all your mail*! A thin letter does not always mean a rejection. One applicant we spoke with had her heart set on attending a renowned Eastern college. Sally had visited the school numerous times, had friends there, and was convinced she wouldn't be happy unless she was a student there. But then disaster struck—she got a thin letter from the college, with the school's crest emblazoned on the outside. Sally was an emotional wreck. She was so upset she didn't open the envelope. She just *knew* they hadn't admitted her. After a crying jag that lasted almost two days, and a week spent in utter depression, Sally was convinced that she wouldn't survive the experience. She couldn't stop thinking about the place. Slowly, as her other acceptances came in, she began to adjust to the idea of enrolling at some distant second choice. But then a second envelope, a huge one, arrived from the school she would have killed for. Sally was shocked. What was this? Opening the envelope she found a packet of recruiting information and a card to return to the college in the event she wanted to enroll.

Sally was convinced it was a cruel mistake. Luckily, she had kept the first thin letter. Reaching into the corner of the room where she had thrown it, still stained with tears, she opened it. Of course, the letter congratulated her on acceptance, and said that a packet of materials was being mailed to her under separate cover. So—don't avoid the bad news. You may as well deal with it. And it may not actually be bad.

Those Rejection Letters

Let's assume you *have* opened your letters. Perhaps you have one or more rejections. We know it's difficult. But if you keep the following points in mind, you can make it easier for yourself and others around you.

1. No admission decision should lower your self-esteem. You're not a failure because you didn't get into a particular college. As we keep saying, admission into a particular college is determined by *who* that college wants that year and, more importantly, *who* applies in that year. Last year, you might have gotten in. The point is that no admission decision is a perfectly objective one. Your denial probably has more to do with the number of students clamoring for acceptance than whether or not you're qualified for that college. If you were realistic about your application strategy in the first place, you probably *are* qualified.

The school isn't rejecting you. It is denying you a place based on those twenty pieces of paper in your folder, and perhaps one or two meetings with you. That's not a foolproof way of making this important decision, but that's the way it's done. You're not a bad person because they said no, and they weren't saying no to you personally—just to their image of you as compared to the images of others applying.

2. You're not going to be dogged forever by not going to a given college. Most employment counselors agree that a degree from a prestige college can make a difference in getting a first job, and has some effect on graduate school admission. But ultimately, it's your performance in college that counts. A Phi Beta Kappa graduate of City College of New York may do better than a Harvard graduate with a B average when applying to grad schools. And once you're on the job, it won't matter much where you went to school. Being a Cornell or Princeton man means nothing if you're not doing the job.

3. You may be blowing the differences between two colleges out of proportion. Obviously, some colleges have more name value than others. But as we have pointed out, this sometimes does not relate to reality. When it comes down to the top thirty or forty schools in the country, the differences aren't all that great.

4. There's no point in complaining. It does you absolutely no good to say, "I wish I were at X College." Or, "If I were at X College, everything would be fine. My troubles would be over." Like most of your freshmen peers, until your first semester is over you'll probably be nervous about flunking out. Wherever you go, you'll have adjustments to make.

5. You will get a good education—if you want one. If you seek out the right professors and apply yourself, you'll excell. Success has a lot more to do with ambition, discipline, and direction than it does with where you go to school.

6. You can always leave if you really dislike the place you choose. There's always the possibility of transfer. But you'd be surprised—most students who go unwillingly to their second- and third-choice colleges, determined to transfer after their first year, find out they aren't so bad after all. And when they go back to visit their dream colleges after a year or two away, they are frequently happy they didn't wind up there.

Sorting Out Your Acceptances

Good work. You've felt like an indentured slave for years, and you've finally gotten the fruits of your labor. Maybe you were zapped at a couple of places. But on the other hand, you might even count a reach among your acceptances. You have a little time to decide. You may have a clear first choice, or you may not. Now what?

Talk to people. Even if you're absolutely positively sure that a given college is the place for you, talk it out. You should do this not only to get other peoples' opinions, but also to *hear yourself think*. You may not be as certain as you first thought. And if you're undecided, talking to others will help you clarify your own thoughts.

Talk with undergraduates at the various colleges. What do these people think of your choices? Are you misinformed? What do students from your high school who have attended these schools have to say? If you can afford it, telephone the undergraduates you

know. Are they enjoying their college experience? What don't they like about it? What about particulars? Intramural sports? Dance? The history department?

Visit the campuses. If you haven't seen them already and can afford to do so, *go*. Once you're there, talk to undergraduates, professors, and everyone else. Would you really be happy there?

Check the differences between the schools. What is available at each place? Is one stronger than another in a certain academic field? If you're an aspiring history major who wants an urban campus, you may be in the unenviable position of being admitted to a school that has a top-notch history department, but which happens to be located in the country. You may acquire brilliant insights into Thomas Jefferson, but be bored stiff on the weekends. You may also have gotten into another school in a large city, where you'll have an abundance of things to do but be faced with a second-rate department.

Dealing with Parents

We wish that there were some easy way to defuse the demands and unspoken expectations of parents. If you are lucky, yours support whatever decision you make about your college education. Then again, your father or mother may be convinced that Princeton (or some other college) is the *only* place for you. And if you don't get admitted there, you're a failure. Worse yet, let's say you *are* admitted. Mom or Dad willl insist that you attend, consider you a wastrel if you don't, and may even threaten to cut you off financially if you go elsewhere.

Unfortunately, some parents are more concerned about what your college choice might say about *them* than with what it will do for you. When April 15 rolls around, parents swap admission decisions at the office. The more places Junior is admitted to and the higher the caliber, the more prestige accrues to the proud parent. Neighbors inevitably compare notes on where so-and-so got in, and where he or she is going. These comparisons are a part of our society. Often the offenders haven't any idea how difficult it is to get into some schools, and just how traumatic the whole process is. It's bad enough that you have to get over your own disappointment at being denied your first-choice school. You shouldn't have to deal with your parents' disappointment as well.

Another problem is that parents frequently know less about colleges and the admission process than anyone else. Their notions about selective schools may be based on impressions made twenty or thirty years ago—information that might be totally outdated. They often have little understanding of the college decision-making process. Why weren't you admitted when Johnny next door was, even though his SAT scores weren't as good as yours? Usually, the frustration resulting from this kind of comparison turns into hostility toward the college—or toward you. In either case, the results can be disastrous: you don't want your parents writing complaining letters to the college, nor getting angry with you for not doing as well as your peers. Our suggestions for dealing with parents:

1. Above all, sit down with them and talk. For one thing, they will be helping you financially and emotionally; and they may help you define your own ideas if you're confused. At the very least they will feel you took them seriously, so that when you choose *your* college over theirs, they will feel they participated in your decision.

2. Listen to your own reasons for going to a certain college. Do they truly make sense? If they do, then they might convince your parents. Just organize your thoughts before you talk.

3. Get your ammunition together for your arguments. If you want to attend a private college over a state school because you believe you'll get a better education there, try to find some way to prove it— perhaps by digging up statistics on admission to graduate schools.

4. Be sure *you're* making the decision—the one you really want, not one you make just because it is in opposition to your parents' wishes. Consider alumni children. In most cases, they tend to have either very positive or very negative feelings about Mom or Dad's college—generally in direct proportion to the degree of the parent's enthusiasm and their respect for the parent. We've run into students who wouldn't dream of going to a parent's alma mater—just because they had heard about it all their lives and were completely bored with the idea of it. But in some cases it was far and away the best place they had been admitted to. Then again, there were others who blindly accepted their parents' choice as their own. Whatever your decision, make it *yours*.

5. If you're excited about a place and your parents are not, consider whether they might not become more enthusiastic after a visit there. (This requires some common sense, of course. There should be a reasonable likelihood they'll be impressed.) While on campus, see if you can't arrange to meet with an admission officer or faculty member. You could telephone (now that you're admitted, it's okay) or write to the admission office and explain your predicament: you want someone to impress your parents with the value of the educational experience at their school. Enlist the help of current undergraduates or others (relatives, alumni) who know the school.

6. If your parents are intractable, arrange for an impartial mediator—maybe your college counselor—to meet with them. Suggest that they talk alone; maybe the counselor can convince them. First ask your counselor whether he or she is willing to help you, of course.

7. Finally, be realistic. You will probably be depending on your parents for financial support. Most colleges do not recognize undergraduates as financially independent (and therefore eligible for full financial aid) unless their circumstances are extreme—say, they are orphans or wards of the state. You *won't* be considered financially independent because Dad refuses to foot the bill for college. You must come to some accommodation with your parents as to where you will go. At the very worst, if you can't talk them out of a college that is a second or third choice for you, enroll there, and then talk to your parents later about transferring.

Dealing with Other Students' Acceptances

Sometimes, life doesn't seem very fair—particularly when kids you think less deserving than yourself appear to have done better than you in the college sweepstakes. And you may be distressed when your friends get admitted to schools with big names, and you only get into Obscure U. You may feel additionally pained because you haven't been able to rejoice in your friends' successes. Don't. Envy is a natural human emotion. But what's done is done. Your task now is to try not to resent others or be angry at yourself, but rather to concentrate on making the best selection from the campuses open to you.

Appealing Decisions

Maybe after thinking things through, and ascertaining that you're not just dreaming, you come to the conclusion that you really should have been admitted to a certain college. We hear this all the time:

▶"They must have made a mistake!"

▶"The computer screwed up. If it hadn't, I'd have been admitted!"

▶"It's my teachers' fault. They didn't write strong enough recommendations."

▶"I just know they didn't get my latest SAT score, the one that went up twenty points. That really would have made the difference!"

Just how do you go about appealing a decision, and will it do you any good?

1. It's really not worth appealing a decision unless a school has a publicized procedure for doing so—such as the University of California at Berkeley. At other colleges, appeal processes are pro forma. Decisions will not be changed unless an erroneous credential was sent in, or very occasionally if an extremely positive credential was missing at the time of the decision. Even in these instances, selective colleges seldom if ever reverse their decisions. This is not only because doing so would create a dangerous precedent. The odds are still five to one against you—and may be even tougher because of the psychological weight against admitting someone with the class already filled.

2. If you still want to request a review of your folder, inquire politely whether this might be possible. Accentuate the positive, not the negative—that you feel very strongly about attending the college, that a review of your credentials might bring another decision, and that you will be willing to do almost anything to be admitted. If you have a factual rationale for the appeal, provide it: admission committees are much more likely to review their decisions if there is a compelling reason to do so.

3. Keep in mind that you're going through this for your own sanity, not with the hope of really getting in. It is unlikely that you will be admitted after an appeal, even at a college publicizing such procedures, and the odds against you at a school that has no appeal process are astronomical. But at least if you request reevaluation you will know that you've done everything you could to be admitted. You'll have done your best. In our opinion, however, unless the procedure is encouraged by the college, you'll be wasting time and energy.

Stuck on the Waiting List

As we explained earlier, many schools have waiting lists to ensure that the enrolling class meets the college's projections. Schools actually admit fewer students (generally anywhere from 10 to 100, depending on the size of the class) than needed so as not to oversubscribe the class if the yield rate unexpectedly goes up. Then they wait to see how many students respond to their offers of admission. Finally, they meet their targets by going to the waiting list.

Each college has a different waiting list procedure. The number who wind up on it and the number who are eventually admitted can vary from year to year. At Brown, for example, the waiting list has in the past been offered to as many as 400 students; generally, between 230 and 260 students elect to remain in the running. An average of 50 students have been admitted from the waiting list each year for the past several years. The actual number, however, has ranged from about 15 to over 100.

At Brown, no student is "ranked" on the list. Once the college learns how many additional applicants can be admitted from the list, it will review all folders to make an initial selection. Some are accepted, others denied, and another group is held over until the responses to the first batch of admission offers are in. Then the second selection is made. Students may hear as early as mid-May and as late as mid-June. When you receive a letter indicating you have been placed on a waiting list, remember that each college's procedure differs.

1. Return the card that asks whether you wish to remain under consideration on the waiting list. If the college doesn't hear from you, it may send another notice, but will eventually assume you're not interested.

2. We recommend that you send more than just the card. Write a letter outlining all the reasons that the college is on the top of your list. Emphasize that you'd be willing to come to the campus for an interview, provide further information about yourself, or do anything else that might help you to be admitted. Your tone should be pleasant and good-humored—not pushy or resentful. The college is, after all, saying that it might want to admit you a bit later on. It's not insulting you by putting you in limbo for the moment. Most colleges will not grant interviews to wait-list kids, feeling that they are unfair to other applicants who may not be able to get one. But try your best.

One student we know was pleasant but persistent about seeing her area admission officer. In her first letter, in which she expressed her desire to be kept on the waiting list, she asked for an interview. She sent another letter after receiving the usual "Sorry - but - we - don't - give - interviews - to - applicants - on - the-wait-list" response, stressing that she felt her personal qualities weren't coming through on paper. Finally she telephoned, and with grace and style convinced the admission officer to interview her—which he did.

To his surprise, the admission officer discovered she was right. She was charming, dynamic, and a critical thinker—none of which came across on paper. When the time rolled around for the final selection from the waiting list the girl was admitted. She spent four happy years at this Ivy campus and graduated with honors, once again confirming that admission committees make mistakes.

3. If you must send a deposit in to another college, do so. No matter what unofficial assurances you've been given about your eventual admission—even if you are told you're number one on the waiting list—do not withdraw from your other college. Most colleges have a "courtesy" wait-list. This is sent to students who the committee knows don't stand a chance of being admitted, but who for political or personal reasons need to be let down easily. Obnoxious valedictorians, not-too-bright alumni kids, the "nifty" kid who doesn't quite measure up to the college's standards, are all candidates for a courtesy wait-list.

In a few instances, this applicant may actually be admitted, if new information comes to light. But the point is that there's no sure way to know whether you'll be accepted from a waiting list.

4. Think about alternatives to simply waiting for a decision. Besides asking for an interview, you might indicate that you'd be willing to wait a semester or year before entering. Or live off-campus. The likelihood that you will be admitted under these conditions is *very* slim: remember that the selective schools want to see their whole class before admitting you, and they won't know what next year's class looks like until next

year. But if they don't respond to your suggestion positively, at the very least you will have communicated the depth of your interest. And that goes a long way toward a positive decision.

What to Do if You're Not Admitted Anywhere

Disaster! You've applied to eight colleges. You get eight rejections in response to your efforts. Of course, if you have carefully followed our suggestions, it's unlikely that you will have to face this. But there's always a remote chance that it will happen.

If it *does* happen, your first task should be to get over the shock of rejection. We know this isn't easy. Our best advice is that anyone with no immediate college to go to in the fall should concentrate on securing a place at *some* campus. Your second objective should be to discover why you were passed over at so many institutions. Were your sights set unrealistically high? Was there some part of your application that was unusually weak or unconvincing? How can you improve it on the next try? To formulate a strategy for an eleventh-hour application to a college that will accept you, or to plan some useful way to spend your time until you can reapply, we suggest the following steps:

Enlist the help of your counselor. First, your counselor can contact admission officers at the colleges to which you applied and find out which aspects of your application were weakest. By getting a fix on mistakes you may have made, you can remedy them when you reapply.

Second, admission officers at those colleges may be able to tell your counselor about selective colleges that are still looking for qualified applicants. Quite recently, two respected colleges—one a Midwestern liberal arts school, the other a well-regarded Eastern women's college—found themselves without enough matriculants to fill their freshman class. Their yield rates had dropped to an unusually low percentage, and as a result they had a smaller number of entering freshman than they had anticipated. These colleges contacted other selective colleges, asking that denied applicants with good credentials be redirected to them.

Once your counselor has found out about good colleges that are still accepting applications, he or she can contact them to arrange for applications forms and perhaps even an interview. If your odds look fairly good at a particular school, you may want to have your counselor emphasize that you are only applying there, or that you see it as your first choice among the alternatives open to you.

We recommend that your *counselor* do all of this because he or she is likely to have contacts on admission staffs, contacts that can be used to get this unofficial information. Your counselor is also likely to be taken more seriously and be given more "intelli-

STATE SCHOOLS GETTING TOUGHER

A recent survey conducted by the National Association of Secondary School Principals found that state universities and colleges had recently raised their admission standards. This seems to have occurred in part because the country's financial climate has brought the lower-priced public university more within the budget range of many families; and in part because state schools are simply continuing to improve. But the survey found that whatever the motivating reasons, 27 state systems had significantly raised their standards of admission over the past few years.

gence"—as a professional colleague—than you, as a denied applicant. But whatever your eventual plan, you should enlist the help of your counselor.

Find out about admission clearinghouses. It may be possible for you to find out more about openings at colleges in the spring by contacting an admission clearinghouse, or "matching service." Some educational consultants keep tabs on the colleges that are looking for qualified applicants after April or May. You might telephone a local consulting firm to find out whether they are aware of such openings and how much their services will cost you. (Check the Appendix for information on educational consultants near you.)

There is also a private clearinghouse that makes your academic credentials available to regionally accredited colleges. These colleges will then contact you and encourage you to apply if they are intrigued by your profile. This service costs $25. For more information, contact: College Placement Assistance Center, 318 4th Street, Union City, New Jersey 07087.

Look into local and state colleges. There are over 3,000 colleges in the United States. A good number of these are public institutions: state universities, community colleges, city colleges, junior colleges. Many of these tax-supported schools accept students until just before classes begin. Once again, have your counselor contact the campus that appeals to you. It may be a residential state college; it may even be a local or community college. We know these may not seem the most appealing alternatives. But you should view this fallback as just that: a fallback. You don't have to spend four years there, and can later transfer to a better-known college as a sophomore or junior. This suggests, of course, that you should take your studies at a fallback college as seriously as you would take them anywhere else: in order to transfer, you will have to present an impressive record. And this will require discipline and hard work on your part. For more information on two-year institutions, see *Barron's Guide to the Two Year Colleges*—Barron's Educational Series, Woodbury, New York: 1981.

Taking Time off

As you go through your senior year in high school, you may suspect that you aren't quite ready for college. A year spent working as a political aide, forest ranger, gasoline jockey, traveling, or studying abroad may help you prepare for campus life. Perhaps you haven't been accepted anywhere, and you're thinking about waiting another year before reapplying. Maybe a year spent out of school would somehow set you apart from other applicants and better your chances for admission. Maybe you don't really know why you're going to college, except that Mom and Dad think you should; and you want a better idea of what college will do for you before you commit yourself.

These are all legitimate concerns. The cost of a year at a residential college runs from $5,000 to $12,000. You will probably get much more from college and compile a better record if you have some notion of why you are there. If you dread the idea of more schooling or simply want some time to get your bearings, you should at least consider the possibility of taking a year off.

The important issue here is to make good use of your time. It makes very little sense to take a year off and hang around at home mowing lawns, washing cars, or doing some other job that you already handled as a high school senior. The key issue a college considers in your taking time off is whether you have *grown* because of the experience. And schools will want to see evidence of that growth, whether through recommendations, interviews, your essay, supplementary materials, or a combination of these elements. And if you decide to work before moving on to college, think about how that work will fit in with your positioning as an applicant.

Whatever you do, we recommend you keep a journal of your experiences—at least the more memorable ones. This material can be utilized later as you prepare your essays. As you work, think about what your job is doing for you—what you're learning, what you regret, what you would do differently, and what is most fulfilling. If you can articulate the value of what you've done and have gotten something worthwhile out of it, you'll not have wasted your time and energy.

Postgraduate Years

An increasing trend these days is for students — usually athletes—to do a postgraduate (P.G.) year at a private preparatory school before applying to colleges. P.G. years are said to allow for additional social and intellectual maturation before the freshman year. In reality, a good number of P.G. students are outstanding athletes who will excel in college athletic programs. This postgraduate time, enables them, many of whom come from undemanding public high schools, to get an exposure to a competitive academic environment, to be coached for the SATs, and gives them a chance to improve abysmal or mediocre academic records.

College admission professionals seem to be ambivalent about the value of P.G. years. For some students they can be extremely helpful. A student who has been bored by a less-than-top-notch high school program may come alive when challenged by demanding classes and good instructors. Students who may have had family problems may do better when they are allowed a year away from aggravations at home. Athletes enrolled in postgraduate programs often improve their academic skills to the point where they can survive a highly demanding college environment. And a young or immature student may be better "seasoned" after a transitional year at a preparatory school than he would be by leaping into his freshman year.

Postgraduate years are offered by a number of good preparatory schools, including Phillips-Andover Academy, Phillips-Exeter Academy, Northfield-Mt. Hermon School, and Lawrenceville Academy. Many other, schools, probably over 100, also offer this year. For more information on prep schools offering P.G. years, see *Lovejoy's Prep & Private School Guide* by Clarence E. Lovejoy, 5th ed., New York: Simon & Schuster, 1980, or *The Insider's Guide to Prep Schools* 1979–80, edited by J. Barnett and S. Goldfarb, New York: E.P. Dutton, 1979.

Is a P.G. year worth the time, money, and energy it requires? Unless you can get a scholarship—which is unlikely unless you're a blue-chip athlete—the expense may be almost as great as a year of college. In most instances, evidence of increased academic prowess or seriousness of purpose can be demonstrated just as well through a year at a local or less selective college—in addition to which, the course work will count for college credit. So unless you feel a bit young and unprepared for the emotional rigors of college life, we don't recommend this alternative.

Getting in through the Back Door

Let's suppose you very much want to attend a particular school. A strategy that is *occasionally* successful is the "back-door" entryway of part-time or nonmatriculant status. Every selective college has different rules for enrolling individuals who are not full-time students and who are not eligible for a degree. These part-time study programs exist for a number of reasons. In some cases, they have been established to fill the needs of working people who want to take one or two courses in their professional fields. Others have been designed to enroll high school students who are ready for college courses. These part-time students provide additional tuition income without increasing the full-time student population.

Occasionally, admission directors under pressure to admit the child of a noteworthy alumnus may use this sort of program to get the student on campus without obviously lowering admission standards. The student then has an opportunity to prove himself academically, and be admitted as full-time, matriculating undergraduate if he does get good grades. Occasionally a "deal" may be struck beforehand whereby the student is guaranteed a place in the class if he achieves particular grades in his courses.

The problem with this approach—if you want to use it to get a foot in the door and later apply as a full-time student once you have "proved yourself"—is that it is time-consuming and expensive. Few colleges offer financial aid to part-time nonmatriculating students. Moreover, housing is usually not available. And some colleges specifically prohibit special students from applying for full-time status in order to discourage just such strategies.

The advantage of this approach is that it does allow you to get known on campus. You can befriend professors and admission officers who will later act on your behalf. You can also show yourself capable of handling the academic work by doing well in classes. Remember, however, that your presence on campus will *not* guarantee admission.

But most importantly, your whole *attitude* will be wrong if you take this approach. Most of the students who have their hearts set on one and only one campus have not thoroughly investigated their options. They wrongly assume that everything will be perfect once they are students at that college. Too often, once students arrive at their dream schools (if they are "lucky" enough), they are thoroughly disappointed. Too often their insecurities, fears, unhappiness, and attitudes remain the same. Conversely, most students who are initially unhappy with their college choices eventually grow to like the college they select.

Given the expense, time, and risk involved in the part-time or special student strategy, we recommend against it. A far better approach is to transfer to another college if you are unhappy with your present situation.

Switching Tracks at Full Steam: Transfer

Frankly, we had doubts about including a section on transfer admission in a book written primarily for high school students. But both of us began our college educations at institutions that weren't particularly appropriate for us (largely because they were both so specialized). We hope that by having read this book and investigated colleges properly, you will avoid our mistakes. At the same time, we don't want to fuel students' dissatisfaction with their college choices and lead them to believe that by transferring, all their problems will be solved.

Too many students want to transfer for the wrong reasons. They may attribute their own lack of discipline to an "unstimulating" academic environment or "boring" professors. Some students think their emotional problems result from the unsociability of the campus or the pressures of academic life. Indeed, there are all kinds of illusions that you can sustain when you're unhappy.

There are basically two good reasons for transferring. The first has to do with academics, and the second with social or extracurricular life. Each is legitimate in its own right. But before you consider transferring, consider whether your motive is solid enough to justify the amount of time and energy you'll have to devote to the effort. (Yes, you have to work hard at transfer admission.)

Transferring should be taken seriously because for most students, the transition is not an easy one. To begin with, every transfer student is more a stranger to the community than an entering freshman. Many of the people transfer students befriend are freshmen—newcomers tend to stick together. But at the same time, the typical transfer student has already gone through the not-uncommon period of freshman angst, self-doubt, or acclimatization to freedom. So while the freshmen are wondering whether they'll survive academically, or are searching for their own identity among crowds of new faces, the transfer student just wants to settle down and enjoy his new surroundings.

Some transfer students never quite adjust to their new surroundings. They are, in essence, starting over as far as extracurricular activities go. As a result, they may not go quite as far in organizations and clubs as they could have had they remained where they were. And academically they may be thrown off-balance by the change.

On the other hand, some transfers do remarkably well. But we can't emphasize too strongly that transferring should be an alternative you consider carefully. Undertake it only after a thorough evaluation of your situation. Once you've decided, many of the basic principles and strategies in this book can be applied to transfer admission.

What Colleges are Looking for in Transfer Applicants

The most significant difference between freshman and transfer admission is that transfer applicants are selected to much greater degree on the basis of their academic *record*. (Freshman applicants are evaluated for their *potential*.) The reason for this is obvious: the college record is scrutinized because *it is there*. The attitude of most admission officers is, "If the information is there, why not use it?" The admission committee can only make an educated guess (some call it a prediction) about how well a freshman applicant will do if admitted. But with transfer prospects, a report of college-level work already exists. Why admit someone with poor grades? So transfer admission committees concentrate on the record. SATs and high school grade point averages are far less important in transfer admission. Some schools

even recommend against applying for transfer unless you have at least a B average in your college courses.

Second, transfer students must have a valid reason for wanting to transfer. Having a boyfriend or girlfriend on campus is *not* a legitimate reason. Neither is wanting to get out of a wintry climate, or even wanting to go to a college that sends a greater percentage of its premeds to medical school.

Consequently, the sorts of transfer applicants who are most appealing to admission committees are those who have a *distinct and compelling* reason for wanting to leave the college they presently attend and transfer to another: those at single-sex schools who want the more open environment of coeducation. Those at specialized schools (art schools, technical colleges, service academies) who want a broader range of courses and students. Those at liberal arts schools who want the specialization of an art school or technical college. Those who want a major not offered at their college. Or those who are deeply involved in some extracurricular endeavor that is not appreciated or supported at their present campus.

Of course, if you are applying for transfer, you have the advantage of knowing what college is like. You'll know what to look for in the campuses that interest you. And you can evaluate them dispassionately, without the starry-eyed enthusiasm of a typical high school senior. This doesn't mean, however, that you should neglect your research before you begin the application process.

Basic Things to Keep in Mind if You Are Considering Transferring

Selectivity. It's usually more difficult to predict the degree of selectivity at each college than it was when you were applying as a high school senior. At most institutions, the number of freshmen applicants and size of the freshman class remains stable from year to year. While you may not be able to ascertain who will get in, you can at least say that one out of so many applicants will be admitted. Transfer application pools, on the other hand, are far more volatile. The composition of the applicant group can differ from year to year, and the yield will vary accordingly.

More importantly, transfer openings are calculated on the basis of attrition, which can vary greatly from year to year. One semester, a much larger group of students may flunk out, or transfer, or take leave, or study abroad, than did last term. And the administration may choose to expand or shrink the overall size of the student body. This means that for one term, a school may be looking to fill 100 transfer slots; the next, it may only have 15.

Conventional wisdom has it that it is easier to be accepted as a transfer if one applies for the spring or summer term. While this may be true in some instances, no college accepts exactly the same number of transfers for each term: the number depends on the unpredictable factors discussed above.

Therefore, if you would like to transfer, you will have to plan carefully. You will have to utilize the same three clusters of reaches, possibles, and sure admits to ensure that you are admitted somewhere. And your strategy will have to be more intricate, since it's much harder to determine selectivity for each college.

Application procedures and eligibility. If there seems to be little regularity in freshman application procedures, there is almost none where transfer admission is concerned. Some colleges only accept transfers for the fall. Others admit them for every semester or quarter, including summer term. A few will only accept sophomore or junior transfers. Some will consider applications from anyone who has completed a semester of college work; others are interested only in those who have finished at least a year at college.

There is one requirement common to virtually every institution, however. After transferring, all students must be residents on campus for at least two years. This stipulation exists to ensure that every graduate receiving the college's degree will carry its intellectual and social stamp.

A word of caution: things change every year. You should not rely on outdated catalogs or word of mouth for information on transferring. Write for a bulletin and a current transfer application.

Your Transfer Application

Transfer application forms should be filled out as carefully as freshman forms. And your application strategy should be carefully thought out. Some general pointers which may be of use:

Contacting a dean or counselor at your present college.

Most colleges appoint a dean to assist students interested in transferring to another institution. You should treat this person as you would your high school counselor: cultivate him or her to work for you. If you have befriended an admission officer, ask that person to help you out as well. These people can give you their general impressions of colleges and their transfer admission policies. If you can't find any faculty member or administrator willing to help you, contact your high school counselor. Explain that you're not getting much counseling at your college. If you had any sort of positive relationship at all, the likelihood is that he or she will assist you.

Recommendations.

It is *absolutely essential* that you secure recommendations from your college instructors. If you have enrolled only in mammoth lecture classes and wouldn't even recognize your professor at close range, ask your graduate assistant (or proctor, tutor, fellow, or whatever the title is) to write the recommendation. Colleges will not take you very seriously as a transfer applicant if you cannot produce an evaluation of your college work from your instructors.

Always give your references to the instructor who knows you best. Follow our recommendations about substantive comments: it's far better to get a detailed, insightful comment from a graduate proctor than a general endorsement from a Nobel Prize-winning lecturer who scarcely knows your name or the quality of your work.

Writing the essay.

The same rules about high school essays apply here. Above all, avoid being tedious or repetitive. If the essay topic is open-ended, it may be wise to explain why you want to transfer. If you can work the essay into a useful positioning, do so. And keep in mind that your essay, packaging, and positioning will have less of an effect on your chances for admission than they did when you were in high school, since for transfer, a much greater weight is placed on the quality of your college record.

Activities.

The important issue here is not how busy you were in high school. Rather, it is how active you were *on campus*, and the degree to which your talents and experience will benefit the campus where you'd like to enroll. If you are applying to a school with higher academic standards and more rigorous classes, you must make a case for your ability to continue pursuing your activities in a more challenging environment. And, as with freshman admission, you should be aware of just what picture you are presenting. How are you positioning yourself, and packaging the information about you?

Interviews and campus visits.

Much of what we've already said about interviews applies to

transfer admission. The crucial difference is that in a transfer interview the conversation will focus to a large extent on your experiences at your present college and your desire to bail out. When addressing these issues, avoid too much complaining. Point out the positive aspects of your present college. But at the same time explain what you hope to get out of the new college that you don't presently have.

The interviewer will be listening for signs that you are a malcontent. Colleges don't want students who will be equally unhappy wherever they go. It's essential that your reasons for transfer sound thoughtful, plausible, and remediable.

A Final Word on Transfer

Transferring requires patience. In most cases, application deadlines are in the late spring for fall entrance, and late fall for winter entrance. But you may not hear from the admission office until days or even hours before the start of classes or orientation. Because the transfer selection process tends to be much less formalized than the freshman procedure, decisions aren't made as predictably. This ad hoc approach may work in your favor, since it tends to hold marginal candidates out for consideration until the last moment: admission is contingent on the number of spaces that become available as undergraduates choose not to return for that semester. If you *haven't* heard about your transfer application, you should assume that no news is good news. We know you may lose your deposit elsewhere. And you might have to make a fast move to another campus that may be half a continent away. But there really is nothing to do but wait.

CHAPTER EIGHT

FINANCIAL AID

These days, paying for college may seem a far more impossible task than getting admitted to a good school. In fact, the time spent waiting for word from your reaches can seem positively idyllic compared to the frustrating evenings you spend with your parents trying to make sense of financial aid applications. Unfortunately, this anxiety-ridden exercise is becoming more and more important as increasing numbers of college-bound students find themselves in need of some sort of financial aid.

College is expensive. Even at state universities, tuition, room, board, and incidental expenses for a single year can total over $8,000. And at private schools, yearly costs can easily exceed $16,000. Moreover, these figures continue to rise at a rate higher than that of inflation. Complicating the situation are the recent proposed cutbacks in federal aid to education.

But things aren't nearly as bad as they seem. Billions of dollars in public and private aid are still available to college students (over $16 billion for the 1985–86 academic year alone!). The difficult part is finding and obtaining those dollars.

This chapter cannot take the place of a good, comprehensive guide to financial aid. It will give you a considerable amount of information. But the field is a complicated and vast one, and a complete listing of scholarships and loans may run a thousand pages. Thus we recommend you consult one of the guides listed at the end of this chapter for more information.

Three Rules of Thumb

As you think about financial aid, you should keep these points in mind:

1. Your search will require footwork and research. What's the point of being admitted to your "dream" college if you haven't the resources to go there? Just as getting into the school of your choice required hard work, so will obtaining financial aid.

2. Make sure your financial aid information is up to date. Financial aid regulations change yearly. Utilize your school's college counseling center and get the latest information. Don't rely on outdated sources!

3. You should not rule out any college as too expensive. Most financial aid is based on need. Therefore, it may not cost you any more to attend a college charging $14,000 per year than it would to go to one charging $7,000. In each case, the amount of money your family would be expected to pay per year would be the same—what it could afford. The expensive college would make up the difference in aid. So don't rule out any school based on cost. See if you are admitted, see what sort of aid you get, then decide whether it's financially feasible to enroll.

If you can accept these three principles and put some effort into your financial aid strategy, you will find that the situation is not as discouraging as it may first seem. Your family does not have to be wealthy for you to attend a good college.

The Link Between Financial Aid and Admissions

A question that comes up in students' minds is: will I be hurting my chances of admission by applying for financial aid? Unfor-tunately, the answer to that question is—maybe.

Since the 1960s, most colleges have made their admission decisions without regard for the applicant's financial need. Only after the admission office admitted a candidate did the financial aid office analyze that student's financial need to determine how much he or she would "cost" the college. This policy was called need-blind admission.

But in 1982, Wesleyan University of Connecticut shocked the educational community by announcing that it could no longer guarantee need-blind admission. It would try not to link admission and financial aid, but if its fixed financial aid budget were exceeded, Wesleyan would consider rejecting applicants who requested financial aid. Wesleyan's announcement was especially troubling because the school had been perceived as wealthy, successful, and unlikely to face the financial difficulties confronting less prestigious "poorer" colleges.*

In fact, however, Wesleyan was only preaching what some colleges had practiced for years. Many colleges claimed to have "need-blind" admissions, but there was often a link between admission and financial aid. In some cases, borderline candidates were denied admission if their financial need was great. Or students would be admitted, yet not given the aid that would enable them to attend. Admission officers didn't always talk about this, but it was a reality.

---

* Wesleyan never had to use the policy in 1982; they wound up having enough money in their financial aid budget to cover the needs of all accepted students.

Since 1982 even well-endowed colleges have backed away from earlier pledges to keep admission and financial aid separate. Cornell University, for example, recently declared that it could no longer guarantee need-blind admissions. Other colleges have begun admitting students without meeting their demonstrated financial need, hoping that their families will make up the shortfall through belt-tightening or by taking out private loans. So, depending on the college you're applying to, you *may* be hurting your chances of admission by requesting aid if you are a marginal candidate and if the school is a definite reach for you. (Every college is willing to provide financial aid to attract a student it sees as a top prospect.)

Should you forego applying for financial aid at your reach schools in order to improve your chances of admission? This is a tough question to answer. It's very difficult to predict whether or not applying for aid will be a factor in admission. Generally, the better endowed the school, the better the chances that it will still practice need-blind admission.

Also, you have to decide whether you can really afford *not* to get aid. Of course, if you think you can make it without aid for a year, you can apply for aid as a sophomore. If you have done well, the college will probably want to keep you around, and will therefore grant you aid based on need. (Most private colleges do all they can to help their students once they have been admitted and enrolled.) But there is still the chance that you will not get aid in your second year—leaving

you stuck trying to raise thousands of dollars from work, parents, savings, and other sources. (Working your way through college is impossible these days.)

A second consideration is that you don't want to undermine your college experience by worrying constantly about finances. It's not fun to have to skimp on the most basic purchases—not to mention a few luxuries like a couple of beers on Saturday night or a ski trip. Nor is it a good idea to work so many hours a week that extracurriculars or studies suffer. (Financial aid offices expect students to work from 10 to 20 hours a week at a campus job; working more than 20 can have a serious effect on class performance.) You may finally decide that it's worth it to you to attend your second-choice school if you can get first-class financial aid from them.

A Word on the Current Federal Financial Aid Picture

There's been a lot of discussion lately about possible cuts in federal spending for financial aid. Indeed, in the spring of 1985 the Reagan administration proposed to slash the student assistance budget by 25 percent. Included were proposals for a family income ceiling of $32,500 on Guaranteed Student Loans, the mainstay of the program, and a cap of $4,000 annually on grants to needy students. (More on these programs later.) The implementation of these proposals would have meant the end of federal aid as we now know it.

The good news is that in July of

1985, Congress resoundingly rejected the administration's proposal. The outcome of the congressional budget resolution for fiscal 1986 assures that the student assistance program will be kept intact at least through 1988. As of this printing, in fact, the only cut in aid mandated by Congress is a spending decrease of $800 million over three years for the Guaranteed Student Loan program. But even this change will not cut substantially into loan benefits for students. Instead, the savings will probably be effected by streamlining the administration of the loan program, and by slightly increasing the interest rate for the GSL.

Other than that, there will be no changes in eligibility or assistance in the foreseeable future. Congress will eventually reevaluate the Higher Education Act, under which the student assistance program was established, but most educators are confident that no major changes will be made. Financial aid to college students is a bipartisan program which most legislators are loath to cut.

So, despite what you may have heard about cutbacks in financial aid, the money is available—and will continue to be available. And do not assume that because you come from a middle-class family you will be ineligible for financial aid. There's only one way to find out if you're going to get aid: you have to apply for it!

Colleges Up the Ante: Merit Scholarships

There's more good news about financial aid: An increasing number of colleges are offering merit scholarships. As we will explain later in this chapter, the bulk of financial aid available to students is based on need. In fact, since the mid-1960s most colleges have offered aid contingent solely on need. Few prestige schools awarded academic scholarships. Although some colleges (usually the less selective ones) did offer merit scholarships to attract "the best and the brightest," the traditional elite institutions disdained the practice as "buying students." With the decline in the college-age population, however, students are getting scarcer, and schools are getting more competitive about enrolling the brightest. (Colleges feel that bright students affirm their reputation for prestige, stimulate class discussion, and help to attract other bright students.) As a result, a number of schools have begun offering merit scholarships to lure top-notch scholars to their campuses.

This move away from totally need-based aid has not occurred without controversy. Smith and Mount Holyoke colleges announced in the spring of 1983 that they would offer cash grants to admitted students that were based only on merit. Their competition, the other women's colleges in the "Seven Sisters" league and other private selective colleges which still offered aid based largely on need, protested loudly that bodies were being bought. And although the grants amounted to only $300 or $400 per student, the furor was so great that in July 1983 Smith and Mount Holyoke dropped the plan.

Yet prestige colleges continue to create merit scholarship programs. This includes Brandeis, Duke and Case–Western Reserve, USC, and the University of Pittsburgh. Duke and Pittsburgh have a limited number of full-tuition grants; Case–Western Reserve goes as far as to offer 20 freshmen four-year scholarships for tuition *and* room and board.

Given that the college-age population will continue to decline until the mid-1990s, other colleges will probably follow the lead of these schools. But you should not overestimate the amount of merit-based aid available. According to financial aid administrators, less than 5 percent of the funds available to college students is actually merit-based. The remaining 95 percent is based on need.

Then there are what we call outside sources of aid—those other than the colleges and the federal government. Most of these are private sources, including corporations that sponsor scholarship programs for employees or hold national competitions, banks, credit unions, labor unions, and scholarship programs such as National Merit Scholarships. Finally, there are financial aid programs run by state governments.

The colleges. Without question, the college is the first and most important place for you to apply for financial aid. This is not only because each college has large sums of its own money marked for financial aid; your college's financial aid officer will be administering federal funds as well, and he will also certify you

for other federal and state programs.

Each college to which you are applying for admission will require you to fill out a financial aid application if you wish to be considered for aid. In most cases, financial aid from colleges is based primarily on need. In other words, the college will determine, after you fill out a needs-analysis form, how much money your family can afford to pay each year for your education. If you are admitted, the college will give you a sum of money that, when added to the amount they have determined your family can pay, will enable you to attend. Some colleges do offer scholarships based on academic ability or other talents, but for the most part, most selective schools continue to offer aid based on the student's need alone.

The college gets its money from its own sources—endowments, special funds—and from government aid programs called campus-based programs. These are administered through each college's financial aid office. Usually Uncle Sam gives a fixed amount of money to each college under these programs, to be given to students who qualify by virtue of need. College financial aid officers have a certain amount of discretion in assigning campus-based awards, subject to federal regulations. Since the sum of money is limited, not everyone who qualifies will get a campus-based award.

The federal government and state governments. Not all government aid programs are administered through colleges in

YOU MAY BE ELIGIBLE

In the early 1980s, applications for the government's Guaranteed Student Loan Program dropped sharply after a "needs test" was imposed on families with adjusted gross incomes of over $30,000. (Previously these loans had been available to all.) Reacting to the needs-test announcement, many families with incomes over $30,000 didn't bother to apply for GSLs. They simply assumed they weren't eligible. Today many families still make the same mistake. In fact, they *can* get loans. A student from a family with an income of over $40,000 per year may be eligible if he has brothers or sisters in college; even families with incomes of over $60,000 per year can qualify under the right circumstances.

campus-based programs. Sometimes you apply directly to the government and sometimes through the college aid office. Most of these are entitlement programs, meaning that if you apply and qualify on the basis of financial need, you will get an award; in other words, the budget for these programs is unlimited, unlike the campus-based federal aid programs. There are also some government loan programs for which you apply through a commercial lender such as a bank or credit union.

For state aid programs you will generally have to apply to the state agency running it.

Financial Aid: Where It Comes From

Billions of dollars in financial aid are available to college students each year. The bulk of that money comes from the federal government. But to confuse you, Uncle Sam funnels some of this money through the colleges themselves; parcels out more to commercial lenders like banks and credit unions; and allocates some to state governments. And for a few programs you sometimes have to apply directly to the federal government itself.

Colleges are the second biggest source of aid. Each college allocates its own funds to financial aid, supplementing the money in government aid programs.

Outside aid programs. There are many small scholarship and loan programs, most of them privately funded, to which you can apply once you have applied for college and government aid. These programs are run by a variety of private concerns, some of them profit-making (like those banks that give college loans—not federal loans administered through banks) and others nonprofit.

Where to look first

Now that you know where to apply for aid, you might ask, "Where should I go first?" Because most financial aid is based on need, you should first apply to college and government aid programs; only after you have exhausted those possibilities should you concentrate on outside aid programs. That's not to say you can't apply for outside scholarships at the same time you're applying to your college for aid; but your time will be better spent filling out the various forms required by colleges and Uncle Sam rather than writing an essay to win a big merit scholarship from a corporation.

Before you learn about applying for aid, you should be aware that there are three types of financial aid that you might receive, either individually or in combination:

1. Grants. These are outright awards of money. Unlike loans, they don't have to be repaid. A grant is also sometimes called a scholarship. In the past, scholarships were often merit-based. Today the term is generally used interchangeably with grant—which tends to mean a need-based award. For our purposes scholarship will mean awards made on the basis of achievement, not need.

2. Loans. These have to be repaid. Some government loan programs are channeled through commercial lenders like banks or credit unions. Others are offered through the colleges themselves, and administered by financial aid offices. Interest rates vary from a low 5 percent up to the current retail rate, depending on the particular loan program. Some federal programs even suspend interest payments entirely while you are in school. (Clearly you should try to get the loan with the lowest interest rate possible.)

3. Employment or work-study. Sometimes a campus job will be part of your financial aid award. Uncle Sam offers a special College Work-Study program that gives colleges funds to employ needy students in jobs related to their career plans. Work-study should not be confused with Cooperative Education, which is a private program enabling you to work your way through college by alternating full-time work and study.

How to Apply for Financial Aid

As we have said, most of the financial aid money available comes from colleges and the federal government. To get aid from either of these important sources, you must apply for it. And applying for aid is a multipart process.

First, you must fill out a needs-analysis form, which is used by the colleges and the government to determine how much money your family can contribute to your education, and how much money you will need to enroll at a given college or university. These forms are provided by certain scholarship services that then send financial analyses of your situation to the aid programs to which you are applying.

Second, you must fill out an aid application. In the case of college aid, it's the college's own financial aid application, which supplements the information contained in the needs-anlysis form. (Your college's financial aid officer will determine whether you are eligible for campus-based programs.) Finally, you must fill out a separate application for each federal loan program that is not campus-based.

The Needs-Analysis Form

The first step in securing financial aid is to file the needs-analysis form. The two needs-analysis forms most commonly required by colleges are:

▶ Financial Aid Form (FAF) of the College Scholarship Service (CSS)—a part of the College Entrance Examination Board, the same people who administer the SAT. The FAF is the form most commonly used by selective colleges. If the school to which you apply requests the SAT, chances are it will require the FAF. You can get the FAF from your college counselor, colleges, or by writing to the College Scholarship Service, CN-6300, Princeton, New Jersey 08541.

▶ Family Financial Statement (FFS) of the American College Testing Program. This form is generally used by the colleges that require you to submit ACT scores. Contact your counselor, colleges, or write to the Act Student Need Analysis Service, Box 1000, Iowa City, Iowa 52243.

Ask your counselor or read the college's literature to find out which form you should submit. If you use the FAF and your family has a business, you will have to fill out an additional form called the Business Form supplement.

By filling out either of these forms (and the college's aid application), you will be considered automatically for campus-based federal aid programs. In addition, by checking the appropriate boxes, you will be considered for other federal aid programs, and advised of your eligibility for those. Keep in mind that just filling out a needs-analysis is not the same as making out an application for aid.

Note: Uncle Sam has his own needs-analysis form, called the Application for Federal Student Aid (AFSA). It costs nothing to use it, but it is unnecessary if you are already using either the Financial Aid Form or the Family Financial Statement.

In many cases, you can apply for state aid through the FAF or FFS. You should check with your counselor, college financial aid officer, or state aid agency to ensure that this is the case. Some states require a particular version of the FAF or FFS. In other instances you may have to fill out a separate state aid application in addition to these forms. When you fill out the FAF or FFS, make sure that you have checked the appropriate box ensuring that your state agency will receive a report from the financial aid service involved.

Once you have determined which needs-analysis form you should use, you are faced with the formidable task of filling it out. (You may have to fill out both the FAF and the FFS, depending on which colleges you apply to.) Both these needs-analysis services charge fees. Be sure to indicate on the forms that you want to be considered for both federal and state aid—this will save you the trouble of filling out separate applications for each.

Be careful about deadlines—as with applications, they differ. For the Early-Version FAF, used when you are applying under an early notification plan like early decision, the deadline is February 15 of the year you wish to enter college; but it should be mailed as soon as possible after October 15. In addition, each college has its own deadlines, so you should fill out all forms as soon as you can. (Neither financial aid service, however, will process regular needs-analysis forms before January 1 of the year you plan to enter college.) The more you delay, the longer it will take you to get an aid award from a college—making it harder to decide where you should enroll, if the magnitude of your aid package at each school is an issue in your decision.

The needs-analysis forms will require a variety of data, including your own and your parents' income and assets; family size and educational expenses; debt; and unusual medical or other expenses. Before you and your parents fill out the form, you should gather together relevant financial information, including past income tax returns, W-2 forms, records of income from stocks or bonds, mortgage statements, medical records, etc. In most instances you will not be required to send your parents' tax returns along with your needs-analysis forms. However, on occasion you may be asked by the financial aid service or a college aid office to make tax returns available.

All this financial information will be kept confidential and will only be made available to the agencies you list on your needs-analysis form.

There is no quick and easy way to fill out these forms. Above all, you should be as accurate and open as possible. If you don't disclose requested information, it will delay the whole process of getting aid, or you may lose the aid altogether. If income tax returns are requested, *provide* them. In some instances, the needs-analysis form may be returned to you for further clarification.

Once you have filled out and mailed the forms, there will be a two- to six-week waiting period while they are processed. The financial aid service will make an estimate of your *expected family contribution*—essentially, the amount your family could reasonably be expected to pay for your first year of education. That information will be sent to the colleges in a needs-analysis report. You will also receive a report, called the FAF Acknowledgement by the CSS or the Student Financial Aid Report by the ACT. Each of these reports will contain a summary of the information you provided. *Check the report for accuracy.* Make sure it has represented your financial information fairly and sent reports to the colleges you requested. The reports will also indicate whether the colleges require any additional financial information. If you have checked boxes for state and federal aid, you should be contacted by the respective agencies involved.

For an additional fee, the ACT will send you a Comprehensive Financial Aid Report (CFAR), which is similar to the report sent to colleges. The CFAR gives you a step-by-step analysis of your expected family contribution; how it was calculated; information on the typical cost of attendance at a range of colleges; and what you'd be expected to pay at those colleges.

How Needs Are Analyzed

The mechanics of needs-analysis are complicated, but this is basically how it's done. Both the FAF and FFS utilize a needs-analysis system called the uniform methodology (U.M.), which takes into account many financial variables. The U.M. is designed to ensure consistency and fairness. A number of assumptions are made in its calculations: first, that parents have an obligation to pay for children's education to the extent that they are able, and that they *will* pay for that education; second, that the student should contribute to his or her own education; and third, that need should be based on the family's present financial status.

Now, you may ask, won't my need be different at a college costing $7,000 than at one costing $12,000? You're absolutely right. That's why the needs-analysis actually calculates your "expected family contribution"—what your family can reasonably contribute toward one year of college. That figure remains the same however much your college may charge.

The expected family contribution is calculated on the basis of

the following variables through the uniform methodology.

▶ Parents' income and assets, including home equity, stocks, bonds, and savings.

▶ The number of dependents in the family.

▶ Children's educational expenses.

▶ Number of children in college.

▶ Unusual expenses, such as medical care, theft and casualty losses.

The uniform methodology then deducts standard amounts for living expenses (the standard living allowance), an employment allowance, and the asset allowance, which takes into account the possiblity of retirement or loss of work and leaves a margin of cash for keeping a home or other asset. Of the remaining income and assets (discretionary income), the formula will take a percentage to arrive at the expected family contribution. This formula will also take into account your *own* assets and income, if you have any (estimated summer job earnings generally are included).

A tip regarding assets: savings will be expected to be used for paying college bills. According to Leo L. Kornfeld, W. L. Siegel and G. M. Siegel, aid experts whose book is listed at the end of this chapter, your family will be penalized if it saves more than $10,000 and is considered to be lower- or middle-income. Any savings over $10,000 will be factored more heavily into the formula for determining need-based aid. This means that you will receive less aid than you would had you not saved anything. Families may therefore want to consider shifting assets into less liquid forms.

The Aid Application

With your needs-analysis forms completed and mailed in, you must then proceed to fill out your aid applications. Your first step? Start with the colleges to which you're applying. They are important because most financial aid, whether private or government, is administered through them. Each college you apply to will have its own financial aid application. Fill it out and return it, keeping deadlines in mind.

At the same time, you should begin considering federal aid programs that are not campus-based. In some cases your college financial aid office will indicate whether you should apply for one of these programs and exactly what the procedure is. Do *not* overlook these programs, which include Pell Grants, direct sums of money (see page 153); Guaranteed Student Loans, low-interest student loans that are the best bet for middle-class students looking for federal assistance (see page 154); and Parent Loans for Undergraduate Students, which are higher-interest loans for parents (see page 155).

Finally, you should apply for outside sources of aid, including merit scholarship competitions, scholarships from employers, and loans from commercial lenders. In some instances, deadlines for these outside awards may coincide with deadlines for aid applications to colleges.

To make sure you don't miss your various deadlines, it's a good idea to make a chart listing each college to which you've applied. On the chart you should note (1) when the required needs-analysis form should be submitted; (2) when each college's aid application form must be returned; and (3) deadlines for any other action you will have to take, such as applying for a federal or outside aid program.

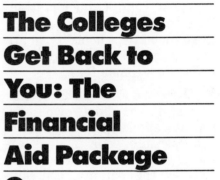

The Colleges Get Back to You: The Financial Aid Package

Once you have filled out the FAF or FFS and the college applications for aid, you will (we hope) get an offer of aid from each college to which you have been accepted. As we have said before, financial aid at most selective colleges is based on need alone. Certain colleges may provide merit scholarships (academic, athletic, debating, etc.) unrelated to financial need, but in most cases these scholarships are limited to a few thousand dollars. Despite the trend toward merit scholarships, not that many schools offer full-ride or full-tuition awards.

Instead, each college will usually offer a financial aid package, combining one or more elements of the financial aid triad: grants, loans, and employment. The work and loan portion are called the self-help component; the grant is termed gift aid. In most cases the total aid package will equal your *demonstrated need:* the amount of money you need to attend the institution without undue financial discomfort.

Your demonstrated need is calculated in the following fashion:

▶ The college determines your *educational expenses:* tuition, fees, room and board, educational costs such as books, incidental expenses, and transportation. (This usually includes two or three round trips home if you are a resident student, or daily travel if you are a commuter.)

▶ Using the FAF or FFS needs-analysis report and its own financial aid application, the college will calculate your family's *expected family contribution.* This includes the parents' contribution, based on income and assets, and the student's resources (your own assets and income).

▶ To arrive at your figure of need, the college subtracts your *expected family contribution* from your *educational expenses.*

Once your need has been established, the financial aid administrator will decide how your financial aid package is assembled. Different schools have different approaches, but generally there is a standardized packaging scheme that takes into account need *and* academic achievement. USC, for instance, uses a multi-tiered scheme whereby the first $1,000 of need is always given in gift aid, for example grants from both the government and the university. The next $2,000 to $2,700 is offered in self-help (loans and work). The remaining need is then divided between gift aid and self-help, with the ratio of gift aid to self-help depending on the academic achievement of the applicant. Almost all schools *do* take merit into consideration in awarding financial aid packages. They will increase the gift aid component—which is outright money in the pocket—and decrease the self-help portion for an outstanding prospect, to sweeten the overall aid package.

Once the various levels of self-help and grant aid are worked out, the financial aid office will determine your eligibility for federal and state grants or loans. Wherever possible, the school will attempt to get you federal or state aid, so that it will only have to allocate the smallest amount of its own funds to your award.

Ultimately, it is difficult to predict exactly how much your package will amount to, or what its components will be. When you receive a package it may contain the financial aid officer's estimate of how much federal funding you qualify for under a certain program. This amount will be subject to adjustment if Uncle Sam comes up with a different figure.

Once You've Gotten Your Aid Offer

Your offers of admission will usually be accompanied by offers of financial aid. Aid offers may, however, come in separate letters, and sometimes arrive later than decision letters. (If you haven't received a financial aid

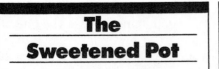

The
Sweetened Pot

Let's say there are two students with the same demonstrated need. They're called Mary and Harry, and Mary is the academic star of the two. They will receive the same total package from Elite University: $4,000. But the details of the two packages will be very different:

	HARRY	MARY
Elite U grant (gift aid)	$1,000	$3,100
Loans (self-help)	$2,100	$ 900
Work-study (self-help)	$ 900	$ 0
Total	$4,000	$4,000

The purpose of such sweetening, of course, is to attract the best prospects—like Mary—to the college, while enabling the average student like Harry to attend as well.

offer, that is a legitimate reason to request deferment of your reply to the college's offer of admission.) You should do the following things once you have received a financial aid offer.

1. Follow up on applications for federal or state programs, commercial loans, and merit scholarships. Are there any other forms you have to fill out? Has your college asked you to apply for a Guaranteed Student Loan or other federal program? Are you being considered for any merit scholarships that require addi-

tional forms or information? Do you need to provide additional documents to any other agency, or apply somewhere else? It is essential that you not get sloppy now.

2. Compare your financial aid offers. In considering what each school will cost you, you should take into account variations in the total aid and need picture. Although colleges calculate need based on total educational expenses, your aid letter will probably compare the total package against institutional expenses charged by the college itself: tuition, fees, room and board. Transportation costs and incidental expenses may vary greatly. If you have to fly across the continent to get to one college, and need only take a 50-mile bus ride to another, there will be a considerable difference in the cost of transportation. (You should count on three round trips per year.) Will you have greater incidental expenses at one college than another? (Different sorts of clothes can make a difference.) Are there any other factors to take into account?

Calculate your total expenses for each college by adding these factors to the cost of tuition, fees, and room and board. Then subtract your financial aid award from the total cost to see how much you will actually have to pay for each college experience.

You should also examine the *quality* of the aid package. Does one offer considerably more grant aid than another? Will one saddle you with a huge loan debt, while another allows you a little more financial breathing room once you have graduated? To get

Federal Aid in Your Package

If a college plans to give you a package something like this:

Grants	$2,000
Loans	$2,000
Work	$1,000
Total	$5,000

and you are eligible for a $1,000 Pell Grant, a $1,000 National Direct Student Loan, and $1,000 in College Work-Study funds, your aid package would look like this:

Pell Grant	$1,000
College Grant	$1,000
NDS Loan	$1,000
College Loan	$1,000
Work-Study	$1,000
Total	$5,000

If you did not qualify for a National Direct Student Loan, the school might ask you to get a Guaranteed Student Loan or some other loan from a commercial lender such as a local bank.

a sense of the figures involved, it might make sense to divide each package into self-help and gift components, to see how much you are contributing for each college.

Finally, take into account the interest rates charged by each loan. National Direct Student Loans, for instance, charge 5 percent per year, while PLUS loans charge 12 percent (see page 155). This is a considerable difference and could mean hundreds of dollars or more over four years of debt. When you have a choice between loans, choose the one offering the lower interest rate. If you have to assemble a total loan figure from two different programs, always take the full amount offered by the loan with lower interest, and make up the difference with the higher-interest loan.

3. Talk with your parents. Discuss how much they will be paying for each school. If your first-choice school has shortchanged you financially, you may have to convince your parents to make up the difference. Are the payments they will have to make realistic? Are there sources you have ignored or overlooked?

4. Consider alternatives if you can't swing the cost. If you're still caught short, think about alternatives to the standard financial aid package. Does the college offer a cooperative education program whereby you can work one semester and study full-time another? Is there any other way to assemble your budget? Can you defer admission for a year to raise some more money? Are there other loan programs you haven't applied for: Guaranteed Student Loans, Parents Loan for Undergraduate Students, bank loans? Can you skimp on certain expenses to make ends meet?

5. Consider bargaining with your financial aid officer. Once you have been admitted, you can afford to be a little more aggressive. Robert Leider was a financial aid expert who wrote a series of very comprehensive and aggressive guides to financial aid, now being updated by his daughter. He said that if the school to which you've been admitted seems really to have pursued you, you should attempt to negotiate with the financial aid officer. Writing in *Don't Miss Out: The Ambitious Student's Guide to Scholarships and Loans* (available for $4.00 from Octameron Associates, P.O. Box 3437, Alexandria, Virginia 22302), Mr. Leider suggests that your goal should be to increase the level of grant aid in your package and to decrease your loans. In some cases you may also convince the financial aid office to trade a loan for work or vice versa. This approach does, of course, require caution and common sense.

6. Make your decision. Weigh the variables: your parents' support, the extent you're willing to pay more for a "name" school, etc.; then decide. And congratulations!

Federal Aid Programs in Detail

As you consider federal aid programs, keep a few things in mind. First, government aid is based almost entirely on need. Only one loan program is open to all, irrespective of financial need. Second, remember that there's a lot more federal money available than the headlines about cutbacks would indicate. You can't get aid without applying—so apply! Third, keep in mind that Uncle Sam changes his regulations

every year. Make sure you get current information.

To be eligible for federal aid, you must meet the following requirements:

▶ You must be at least a half-time student.

▶ You must be a U.S. citizen, permanent resident with an I-151 or I-551 Alien Registration Card, or a resident of a U.S. Territory. (You cannot get federal aid if you are a foreign citizen on a student visa.)

▶ You must be making "satisfactory progress" toward your degree.

▶ You cannot be in default on a federal loan or owe money on a grant if you have been asked to refund part or all of it.

▶ If you are male, you must register for the draft.

Federal Aid You Apply for Directly

We will first examine the federal aid programs that you can apply to directly. (These are *not* campus-based programs, which are administered only through college financial aid offices.)

Pell Grants. The Pell Grant, formerly called the Basic Educational Opportunity Grant (BEOG), was renamed in honor of Senator Claiborne Pell of Rhode Island, who introduced the legislation that created the program. Pell Grants are available only to undergraduates. As they were originally intended for lower- and middle-income families, you may not qualify for them if you're considered affluent. Pell grants are an entitlement program, so if you qualify you'll get one, no matter how many other students apply.

Grants up to $2,100 per year are awarded, depending on need.

If you are applying for a Pell Grant as part of an overall aid package, you can do so by filling out a needs-analysis form and indicating that you want to be considered for federal aid. From either needs-analysis service you will receive a "Student Aid Index" indicating the amount of money you qualify for. By then submitting this to your college's financial aid office, you can receive payment. No separate application is necessary. However if the Pell Grant is the only financial aid for which you are applying, you need to submit a Pell Grant application and needs-analysis form. For more information on how the government determines eligibility, write for the *Formula Book*, Department DED-86, Pueblo, Colorado 81009. This booklet describes the formula for the Student Aid Index in detail.

Guaranteed Student Loan Program.

The GSL is a relatively low-interest loan (8 percent per year) issued by a commercial lender such as a bank, savings and loan, or credit union. It is for both undergrads and graduate students. The loan is guaranteed by Uncle Sam or your state guarantee agency; if you qualify, you should be able to find a lender. The GSL is the mainstay of the federal aid program. Over $3 billion is available in the 1983 budget. Most important, the GSL is an entitlement program—if you qualify, you'll get one.

Through this program, you can get up to $2,500 per year. In some states the amount may be lower.

The loan is repayable beginning six months after you graduate from or leave school. The lender must allow at least five years for pay-back, and some give you up to ten years. Deferments are available for military service, graduate studies, and under other circumstances. It should be noted that when you are issued a GSL, you must pay an origination fee of 5 percent of the amount borrowed. This subsidizes federal expenses.

You apply for a GSL by filling out a Federal GSL Application form. Get it from your college, a lender, or your state loan guarantee agency. Depending on state residency requirements, you may apply for this loan in your state of residence or in the state where you plan to attend college. After filling out the application, send it to the college where you plan to enroll. The college will attest to the fact that you are enrolled and provide financial information. Once the college has certified the application, you send it to a lender participating in the GSL program. Be aware that it will take you a minimum of four to six weeks to get the cash once the lender has approved the loan.

The federal government has established a needs test (known as the Remaining Needs Test) for students from families with an adjusted gross income of over $30,000 per year. If your family earns less than that amount, you will automatically be eligible; if not, you take the needs test.

For more information, contact your state loan guarantee agency (list begins on page 221) or see *The Student Guide: Five Federal Financial Aid Programs*, available free from the U.S. Department of Education.

PLUS Loans (Parents Loan for Undergraduate Students).

The PLUS program is meant to supplement other loan and aid programs. In essence, the program is structured in such a way that parents can pay for their children's college expenses much as they would for a home—through a long-term mortgage. Like GSLs, PLUS loans are made through commercial lenders and are guaranteed by the federal government. Unlike GSLs, the loans are made to *parents*, not students—unless the students are financially independent or graduate students.

Current interest rates are 12 percent per year, and the federal government does not furnish an interest subsidy to borrowers: the interest owed accrues both while you go to school and during deferments. So in relation to the GSL, this is a much more expensive program. Not all states offer PLUS loan programs, so check with your college aid office or state agency.

Parents can borrow up to $3,000 per year, to a maximum of $15,000 for each dependent student who attends college. As with the GSL, the PLUS loan ceiling calculation is made on the basis of need, minus other aid already available. There is an origination fee of 5 percent of the principal. Repayment by parents is monthly, and starts 60 days after the loan is issued. In other words, your parents begin paying back the loan while you're still in school. Independent students who receive PLUS loans are allowed deferrals of principal but not interest. A student with a PLUS loan will thus be paying back interest even as he studies.

On the other hand, you do not have to show need to qualify for a PLUS loan. To get a PLUS loan, get an application from your college or a state guarantee agency. Then find a lender. The lender will send your application to your college for certification and calculation of the amount you should receive. You may want to contact the financial aid office of a college near you to find out which lenders offer PLUSs. For more information, contact your college financial aid office or your state guarantee agency, which is listed in the appendix.

A Few More Federal Programs

These are additional federal programs that might be of interest to you in your search for college funds.

Nursing Student Loan Program.

This loan program is designed for nursing students. It is campus-based and available at all accredited public or non-profit nursing schools. If you qualify you can borrow up to $2,500 per year, with a total loan ceiling of $10,000. Interest charged is a low 6 percent per year, and student borrowers have up to ten years to repay.

Deferments are available, and portions of the loan amount can be repaid by working after graduation as a registered nurse in a non-profit or public institution. For each of the first three years worked in service agencies, 15 percent of the loan will be considered paid back; 20 percent of the loan will be waived for both the fourth and fifth years, up to a total of 85 percent. Check with your financial aid administrator for information.

Professional Nurse and Nurse-Practitioner Traineeships. This program will pay tuition as well as living expenses to those who qualify. For more information, write: Division of Nursing, Room 5C26, 5600 Fisher's Lane, Rockville, Maryland 20857.

G.I. Bill. Veterans benefits are still available, but only if you served in the military between January 31, 1935, and January 1, 1977. If you enlisted after January 1, 1977, you do not qualify. If you enlist today, you are eligible for the voluntary Veterans Educational Assistance Program. Under this scheme, Uncle Sam matches every dollar you save for school with two of his own, up to $8,100. Contact your local V.A. office or recruiter.

Federal Aid
through Colleges

The following are the campus-based programs offered by Uncle Sam through the financial aid offices of participating colleges. The amount of cash allotted to each campus-based program is limited, and you may not get a campus-based award even if you qualify. Each college receives a fixed amount from the Department of Education, and once funds are expended, that's it. You should be considered for these programs automatically if you fill out a needs-analysis form and college aid applications. Keep in mind that you have little say over whether you will get a campus-based award.

Supplementary Educational Opportunity Grant (SEOG). You can get up to $2,000 from this program depending on your need, the amount of SEOG funding at your college, and the other aid you are receiving. The SEOG is open only to undergraduates. For more information, contact your college aid office, or see *The Student Guide: Five Federal Financial Aid Programs.*

National Direct Student Loan (NDSL). This is a very low interest loan (5 percent per year) available to undergraduates and graduate students. Its low interest rate makes it very desirable, if you can get it—and your financial aid office decides whether you can. A number of factors go into this decision, including how your need compares with that of other aid applicants at the school. It is therefore possible to get an NDSL at one college and be denied at another. Repayment terms are very generous: pay-back starts six months after graduation, and you can take up to ten years to repay. While you are in school Uncle Sam picks up the interest cost. For more information, see *The Student Guide: Five Federal Fi-*

nancial Aid Programs or contact your college aid office.

College Work-Study Program (CW-S).

Under this program, you can earn money to contribute toward your educational expenses. Generally, you will make between $600 and $1,500 per year, depending on salary and number of hours worked per week. (Most work-study students put in between 10 and 20 hours a week.) Wages must be at least equivalent to the federal minimum wage. As a work-study student, you can only work for public or private non-profit employers, at a job considered to be "in the public interest." This program is a boon to colleges, as Uncle Sam pays 70 percent of work-study students' salaries and the employer—usually the college—picks up the other 30 percent. For more information, contact your aid officer.

Reserve Officer Training Corps (ROTC).

ROTC programs pay you a monthly subsistence allowance and education costs, in return for a certain number of years of military service as an officer after graduation. These programs can be very lucrative in terms of offsetting college costs, and there are a variety of them well worth investigating. The military services are very selective in choosing participants, however, and not all schools offer ROTC on campus. You should investigate these alternatives *early* in your senior year if you are at all interested.

For more information, contact a recruiter or the Air Force ROTC, Maxwell Air Force Base, Ala-bama 36112; the Army ROTC, P.O. Box 7000, Larchmont, New York 10538; the Marine Corps Commandant, Code MMRO-6 Hqs. USMC, Washington, D.C. 20380; or the Navy Recruiting Command, Code 314, 4015 Wilson Blvd., Arlington, Virginia 22203.

Bureau of Indian Affairs Higher Education Program.

Students who are at least one-quarter Native American and members of an Indian tribe may qualify for college aid from the Bureau of Indian Affairs. Grants and loans are available, plus special assistance in finding funds. Write the Indian Resource Center, P.O. Box 1788, Albuquerque, New Mexico 87013. There is also the Indian Fellowship Program for students in business, engineering, and natural resources; write to the OIE Fellowship Program, FOB-6, Department of Education, Washington, D.C. 20202.

State Aid Programs

In addition to Uncle Sam, all state governments run their own aid programs. A confusing number of these programs are available to college-bound students. It is impossible to describe them all here, but they provide over a billion dollars in aid every year and are well worth looking into.

Generally, you may apply for such assistance only in your state of residence, although occasionally you may be eligible for aid from the state where you will be attending college. Most states will allow you to spend their funds only at in-state colleges, but some have agreements with other state governments allowing funds to be used in either state. The states which currently allow you to spend their grant money in other "treaty" states include Alaska, Connecticut, Delaware, Maine, Maryland, Massachusetts, Minnesota, New Mexico, Ohio, Pennsylvania, Rhode Island, Texas, Vermont, Washington, West Virginia, and Wisconsin; and the District of Columbia.

One unfortunate spill-over from the growing role of states in the financial aid system is the tightening of residency requirements. Many legislatures will not grant resident status to out-of-state students unless their parents move within state boundaries. Being in the state for the purpose of education will not qualify you for residency. This means that you will continue to pay nonresident (higher) tuition throughout your college career. If you plan to attend a state university, you should check into residency regulations: they could cost you or save you money.

State aid, like federal aid, is based almost entirely on need. In certain states, however, academic ability is a factor. In California, for instance, Cal Grant recipients are selected on the basis of grade point average as well as need. New York Regents Scholarships are awarded on a similar basis. Maryland has a Distinguished Scholar Program award ($300 to $800 annually), based only on merit. Talk to your counselor, aid officer, or contact your state aid agency.

State assistance usually comes in four categories:

1. Loans.
2. Scholarships based on need, ability, or both.
3. Tuition grants predicated on need, and open to students attending private schools. These make up for the higher tuition charged by the school and are sometimes called "tuition equalization" programs.
4. Special programs for disadvantaged students.

For a good summary of state aid programs, see *Lovejoy's Guide to Financial Aid* by Robert Leider, which is listed in the appendix.

Merit Scholarships Offered by Colleges

Despite the near universality of need-based aid, some colleges do offer scholarships that are based on merit. These are of basically two types: academic and athletic.

Academic Scholarships. Many selective schools offer awards based on scholastic achievement to attract good prospects. As the population of college-bound students diminishes, an increasing number of schools are likely to offer them.

You should differentiate between types of academic scholarships. Some are awarded on the basis of merit; others, by virtue of merit *and* need. Those based on need are likely to be incorporated into your aid package, and will not diminish your family contribution. And you should not confuse academic scholarships with the "esoteric" college scholarships limited to students by their place of residence, name, academic interest, etc. These are not open to all applicants.

To be eligible for academic scholarships, you must usually be accepted or enrolled at the institution offering them. Each college administers its merit scholarships differently, and we haven't the space to list them all. We recommend you look at the following source: *The A's and B's: Your Guide to Academic Scholarships* by Robert Leider, available for $4.00 from Octameron Associates, P.O. Box 3437, Alexandria, Virginia 22302.

This is an excellent guide, with a comparative chart listing some 840 colleges that offer merit scholarships.

Athletic Scholarships. With the growth in popularity of sports and fitness, many students are finding themselves eligible for athletic scholarships. The money available is no longer limited to football, basketball, baseball, and hockey. Colleges now offer awards in tennis, soccer, water polo, swimming, field hockey, and other sports, for women as well as men. (At many selective colleges there are no such scholarships, but athletic ability is factored into the admission decision.)

If you think you might qualify for such a scholarship, you should talk to both your counselor and your coach. Find out which schools might be interested in

your athletic talent as well as your academic profile.

The *NCAA Guide for the College-Bound Student-Athlete* is free, available from NCAA, P.O. Box 1906, Shawnee Mission, Kansas 66222. It contains the rules established by the NCAA for recruitment of student athletes. Be aware, however, that as of this writing, the NCAA is tightening its regulations concerning participation in college sports: in short, you must be a decent student!

See the appendix for other listings of athletic scholarships.

Outside Sources of Aid and Loans

In addition to the grants and loans offered by colleges and federal and state governments, there is a considerable sum of outside, mostly private money available. As you consider these sources of aid, keep these points in mind:

1. Most selective colleges base their financial aid on need. If you win a scholarship from a source outside the college or government aid system, that outside money may be subtracted from the amount of aid the college was going to give you. Your expected family contribution would remain the same. (For more information on this, see page 148.

2. Contrary to popular opinion, millions of dollars of outside aid do not go begging each year. Most of these funds are part of highly restricted scholarship programs, and *need* is the primary criterion.

3. Outside scholarships seldom exceed $3,000 or $4,000 per year. Some are much smaller. While these sums can help you, you are still better off concentrating on government and colleges' need-based aid. Then you can investigate outside scholarships.

Competitive Merit Scholarships

If you're bright (and have the grades and tests to prove it), there are a number of organizations that sponsor scholarship competitions for college-bound students. Almost all of these programs require you to submit evidence of your academic ability, or to take competitive tests.

National Merit Scholarship Program. By taking the PSAT/NMSQT, you will be considered for National Merit Scholarships. If you are black, you also will be eligible for the National Achievement Scholarship Program for Outstanding Negro Students. Once you are designated a semifinalist (by achieving a score above 99.5 percent of the students in your state), you then compete for finalist status. Finalists are eligible for three types of scholarships: one-time awards of $10,000; college-sponsored, four-year awards of up to $2,000 per year, which are tied to need (you must choose a participating college; the college then decides whether you will be granted a scholarship); and four-year scholarships of up to $2,000 per year,

sponsored by corporations.

Competition is stiff. In all, 5,300 awards are offered each year. For a listing of the 240 colleges participating in Merit Scholarships, as well as all the corporations sponsoring the NMSC Program, write for *The Student Bulletin—National Merit Scholarship Corporation,* 1 American Plaza, Evanston, Illinois 60201.

National Honor Society. Two hundred and fifty scholarships of $1,000 are offered yearly to high school seniors belonging to the NHS. Contact your school's chapter for information.

Westinghouse Talent Search. Awards are offered to high school seniors who have completed an outstanding scientific project. Forty awards, ranging from $250 to $10,000, are made every year on the basis of academic achievement and a science project. Contact your school's science department, or write Westinghouse Science Talent Search, Science Service, 1719 N Street, N.W., Washington, D.C. 20036.

Harry S. Truman Scholarship Foundation. This is an essay competition for *college sophomores* geared to students dedicated to a career in public service. Awards can be as high as $5,000. Write to the Harry S. Truman Scholarship Foundation, 712 Jackson Place, N.W., Washington, D.C. 20006.

Century III Leaders Scholarship Program. The winner of this nationwide competition gets a whopping $11,500, while runners-up get $2,000, primary winners get $1,500, and state winners get $500. Write to the National Association of Secondary School Principals, 1904 Association Drive, Reston, Virginia 22091.

Senate Youth Program. One hundred and four scholarships (two per state) of $2,000 apiece are offered to elected officers of high school student governments. Write to The William Randolph Hearst Foundation, 690 Market Street, Suite 502, San Francisco, California 94104.

Esoteric Scholarships

By esoteric scholarships we mean award programs that are limited to certain students because of academic interest, place of residence, religion, ethnic origin, race, hobbies, extracurricular interests, parents' employer, parent's veteran's record, and a variety of other imaginative criteria. There are Danish Brotherhood in America scholarships for students of Danish ancestry. There is the National German Testing and Awards Program for students studying German. There is the Jacob's Pillow Dance Festival and School Scholarship for dancers. There are the JANGO (Junior Army-Navy Guild Organization, a World War II association) scholarships for offspring of JANGO members.

These scholarships are not difficult to win, if you meet the initial qualifications. Most awards are relatively small (from a few hundred to several thousand dollars), but may be worth looking into. Lesser-known prizes can sometimes go unclaimed.

Colleges also offer esoteric scholarships. Stanford University has a special scholarship program for Eagle Scouts from the Twelfth Scout Region. The University of Miami has a scholarship for Armenian students. Harvard has a scholarship program for students with the last name of Murphy. And colleges may offer scholarship prize competitions to students in a certain major.

Such "in-house" awards are usually awarded on the basis of merit or through competition, or included in financial aid packages. In most cases, a given scholarship is only available through the college offering it. Typically, the amount of the award will be incorporated into your financial aid package.

The best guide we have seen to such limited scholarships, ranging from the AAA National School Traffic Safety Poster Program to the Robert W. Woodruff Fellowship Program, is the *Financial Aids Catalogue for Higher Education* by Oreon Keeslar. For this and other books, see the financial aid list in the appendix.

Innovative Alternatives for Funding College

Colleges, institutional lenders, entrepreneurs, parents, and students have come up with many novel ways to fund the ever-growing cost of college education.

These are all alternatives of which you should be aware, since you may want to incorporate some of them into your financial aid strategy.

Tax-Exempt Bond Issues for Loans. A number of states are issuing tax-free bonds in order to raise money for student loans. Proceeds from these debentures are usually channeled to a state corporation that distributes the funds to in-state colleges, both private and public. The colleges then issue loans to students through their aid offices.

Borrowers must usually begin repaying interest on the loan immediately, but the principal can be paid off in 10 to 15 years. This makes such loans less attractive than federal ones, but in many cases families too affluent for federal assistance will qualify. Dartmouth College recently set aside $13 million in student loans from just such a tax-exempt bond offering. Check with your state financial assistance office to determine whether your state has such a program.

Middle-Income Loans. Some colleges are now dipping into their own pockets to offer loans to students who normally would not qualify for aid. Columbia University has allocated $4 million to subsidize loans with terms similar to federal loans. Hofstra University has a loan program specifically geared to middle-income families.

Low-Interest Loans. Many institutions are helping to defray the cost of education by lending money at low interest rates. Grin-

nell, Sarah Lawrence, and Lafayette colleges, plus Fairleigh-Dickinson and Lawrence universities (among others) offer these plans.

Pay As You Earn, or the "Yale Plan." This was first offered by Yale University—hence the name. Under this plan, the college postpones part or all of your tuition payments until after you've graduated and are in a position to make them.

"Moral Obligation" Scholarships. This plan, similar to the Yale Plan, was initiated by Beloit College of Wisconsin. In 1982 the college granted 240 such scholarships of $2,000 each. The recipient is expected to repay the scholarship (but is apparently not legally obligated to do so) in the form of donations to the college after graduation—taking into account the rate of inflation rather than interest rates. In essence, the college is gambling that students will be generous in their donations.

Prepaid Tuition Plans. Harvard, the University of Pennsylvania, USC, Washington University, and Brandeis University, among others, are trying this approach. The institution will allow students and their families to pay off their entire four-year tuition bill when they enter college. This ensures that students will avoid inevitable tuition increases. In most cases, the college will loan the cash necessary for this massive payment at competitive interest rates. (Brandeis's funds are obtained through the tax-exempt bonds issued through the

Massachusetts Higher Education Assistance Authority.)

Monthly Tuition Payment Plans. One of the major problems facing any family with a child in college is paying the large college bill twice a year—a cash flow problem. In response to this situation, many colleges offer installment payment plans, allowing parents to divide total fees into convenient monthly payments. Some colleges finance these time payments themselves; some work through a corporation specializing in such tuition plans. Others direct you to privately-financed tuition plans.

Tuition Finance Plans. If you are enrolled at a college that does *not* offer an installment payment plan, a number of privately-financed installment tuition payment plans are available. Generally, such plans will pay college bills directly to the institution, while parents in turn pay the company. The cash is loaned at competitive interest rates, with payback made over four to five years.

In most cases, these plans are adaptable to your family's needs, and repayment can be stretched over a longer period of time if necessary. Most loans contain insurance against parents' death or disability.

We suggest you examine each of these programs closely before choosing one. Among those of which we are aware are the Knight's Insured Tuition Payment Plan, Richard C. Knight Insurance Agency of Boston, 53 Beacon Street, Boston, Massachusetts 02108, (617) 742-3911.

There is also the Tuition Plan of New Hampshire, Donovan Street, Concord, New Hampshire 03301, (603) 228-1161.

Two companies offer tuition plans through participating colleges; contact them for a list of the institutions involved: Education Funds, Inc., 2700 Sanders Road, Prospect Heights, Illinois 60070, (312) 564-6242, is offered by some 200 colleges. Academic Management Services, 110 Central Avenue, Pawtucket, Rhode Island 02861, (800) 556-6684, is used by about 250 colleges.

Bank Loans. Many banks offer loans to pay for college education. These are usually unsecured and carry high interest rates. Another possibility is for your parents to take out a second home mortgage to obtain loan funds. Programs vary, so check with local banks for information.

Tax-Based Alternatives for Parents. Tax experts suggest two approaches to raising cash for children's college expenses. Both utilize the principle that the income tax bracket for children is significantly lower than that for parents. Setting up these financial instruments requires the advice of income tax experts, and a fair amount of discretionary income. If you feel you will qualify for need-based aid, you probably won't have the cash to exploit the tax laws. In addition, aid expert Robert Leider warns that these gambits can backfire, because children's assets are less protected under needs-analysis methodologies than parents'. If you don't feel you will qualify for aid, this is something to look into, but *only* after you have consulted tax and aid experts. The two plans are:

Clifford Trust. This involves a parent putting money into a child's trust fund for at least 10 years (the minimum trust period). Income from the trust goes into the child's bank account and is taxed at a lower rate. When the trust period is ended, the trust's assets revert to the parents, while the income accrued over the 10 years remains in the hands of the child, and can be used for college expenses. At least $10,000 is required to make the administrative costs of the trust pay off.

Income-Free Demand Loan. Under this approach, parents make an interest-free loan to a child. The money is invested in a lucrative instrument like a money market fund, and the interest accrued is taxed at the child's lower tax rate. The *demand* of the title means that the loan can be called in at any time the cash is needed, without having to wait for the end of a trust period.

Other Alternatives to Financial Aid

Cooperative Education. Over 1,000 colleges offer this form of work-study (not to be confused with the Federal College Work-Study program). This approach originated at the University of Cincinnati around the turn of the century. Cooperative education allows you to alternate full-time work, presumably related to career plans, with full-time study toward a degree. The advantage of this approach is that you will learn on the job, and defray the cost of your education with your earnings. Depending on the program, the student may alternate a semester of study with a semester of work, or work half the day and attend class half the day. Summer jobs are also a possibility.

The federal government is the single largest employer participating in cooperative education programs, contracting with 740 different colleges for such programs.

For a listing of over 1,000 colleges offering cooperative education, write: National Commission for Cooperative Education, 300 Huntington Avenue, Boston, Massachusetts 02115.

If you are interested in detailed information on co-op education, with special emphasis on the array of federal programs available, see *Earn & Learn—Cooperative Education Opportunities Offered by the Federal Government*, by Robert Leider. Send $3.00 to Octameron Associates, P.O. Box 3437, Alexandria, Virginia 22302.

Military Academies. The national military academies offer a "free" college education, all expenses paid, and a military commission. In return, they ask for a lot of hard work, discipline, and some five to six years of military service once you have graduated. You must make the decision as to whether it's worth it to bind yourself to Uncle Sam for about ten years. (You have a right to opt out of most academies until your third year, but after that, you're committed.)

To be considered for the three major service academies and the Merchant Marine Academy, you must secure an appointment from your Senator or Congressman. This puts you in the running, but there are additional admission procedures after that. You can apply directly to the Coast Guard Academy without such an appointment. For more information, contact the U.S. Military Academy, West Point, New York 10996 (Army); the U.S. Naval Academy, Annapolis, Maryland 21402 (Navy); the U.S. Air Force Academy, Colorado Springs, Colorado 80840 (Air Force); the U.S. Coast Guard Academy, New London, Connecticut 06320; and the U.S. Merchant Marine Academy, Kings Point, New York 11024.

Tuition-Free Schools. Two colleges of which we are aware offer full-tuition scholarships to every student admitted. They are both specialized, but worth looking into if you're heading into the areas they offer. They are Cooper Union, a New York City college offering degrees in art, architecture, and engineering; and Webb Institute of Naval Architecture, offering degrees in marine engineering and naval architecture. Write to Cooper Union, Office of Admissions, Cooper Square, New York, New York 10003, or Webb Institute for Naval Architecture, Crescent Beach Road, Glen Cove, New York 11542.

Financially Independent

Status. Some students believe that by declaring themselves to be financially independent, they can qualify for aid at no expense to their families. This is generally true, *if* you are considered truly independent. In such a situation, your needs-analysis will be made solely on the basis of your assets and income, regardless of your parents' financial condition.

However, a number of tests are imposed by colleges and the federal government to determine whether you are truly independent of Mom and Dad. The rules are still in a state of flux, but basically, to be considered financially independent by Uncle Sam for the 1985–86 school year:

▶ You must not have lived with your parents for more than six weeks in 1982 through 1985

▶ You must not have received more than $1,000 in assistance from your parents in 1982 through 1985.

▶ You must not have been claimed as a deduction on your parents' tax returns for 1982 through 1985.

College financial aid offices are even stricter about interpreting independent status. While colleges do recognize that there are legitimate circumstances under which a student may truly have severed all financial ties to his family, they also know that an increasing number of families and students engineer such independence artificially, to lower the cost of an education. The issue is a complex, vexing, and emotional one. Aid officers want to be fair to the genuinely independent without being fleeced. There is no nationwide standard for determining independence. In general, a number of criteria are used when aid officers evaluate independent status, corresponding roughly to federal guidelines:

▶ Whether or not the student has been claimed as a deduction by parents on their income tax returns.

▶ The degree to which the student has received financial support in the past few years from Mom and Dad.

▶ The length of time the student has lived on his or her own.

▶ The student's age.

You should, of course, check with each college to determine its criteria. And if you are considering trying to establish independent status to save yourself and your parents some money, keep these points in mind:

▶ Many schools impose extremely restrictive standards for independent status. You may still be asked to submit parental financial information, and that information may be calculated into your needs-analysis. Some schools refuse to recognize independence for graduating high school seniors altogether, unless they are orphans or wards of the state.

▶ Falsification of financial data on federal aid applications is a crime punishable by fine, imprisonment, or both. Misrepresentation on needs-analysis forms, if discovered, could be considered fraud and might deprive you of any aid.

▶ Your own assets will be assessed at a much higher rate than your parents' in a needs-analysis. This is in keeping with the philosophy that under these circumstances a student has the greatest responsibility to contribute to his or her education.

▶ If you are not applying to a school with truly need-blind admissions, you may be lowering your own chances of admission by showing a profile of much higher need than you would as a dependent student.

Alternatives That Can Save You Money

Advance Placement and CLEP. The college you are planning to attend may offer an advance placement program allowing you to gain college credits through exceptional work in high school. Through this program, you could save a semester or two of time and tuition. (We still advocate a full four-year college experience, but the choice is yours.) Another advancement program is the College Level Examination Program, through which you can obtain academic credit for work experience. This approach, considered a part of adult education, allows you to get credit through examination in some 40 fields. However, while most selective colleges will give credit or placement through the A. P. program, most do *not* recognize CLEP credits. For more information on either program, write the College Entrance Examination

Board, 888 Seventh Avenue, New York, New York 10019.

Community Colleges. Another possibility you may want to consider is to attend an inexpensive community college for one or two years, then attend a private selective college. In this way, you pay less for your first two years of college but still receive a "prestige" degree upon graduation. But there is some question as to how much money you actually save in this way, particularly if you qualify for aid, and whether two years is long enough to derive all the benefits you can from a selective college experience.

Financial Aid Matching Services

Capitalizing on the growing concern over the cost of college, a host of computerized matching services—almost all of them profit-making—have sprung up around the country. The owner of one such organization was featured in a *People* magazine article, attesting to the fact that the nation's financial aid experts have arrived, and stressing the country's growing obsession with outside sources of financial aid.

These services purport to match a student with potential private scholarships on the basis of the student's academic interests, religion, ethnic background, extracurricular interests, family employers, place of residence, and other factors.

Once you pay the fee (ranging from $19 to $49), you fill out a detailed questionnaire that is then compared against the matching service's data base. Through that comparison you receive a printout listing all the programs for which you might be eligible. You can then investigate and contact these sources for further information and applications. No service guarantees that it will find a scholarship for you, but most have made heady claims referring to the countless dollars ("millions," some say) in aid that go unclaimed each year. Most guarantee that if they do not turn up a certain number of scholarship "leads," they will refund the fee.

Are these services really worthwhile? According to aid professionals, probably not. Most financial aid administrators seem to feel a student will be better off keeping his money and doing his own research. These services might be useful to students without access to up-to-date sources of information. But a number of research services are under investigation by local and state governments after numerous subscriber complaints. And a recent study suggests that they are not worth spending money on at the present time.

In response to increasing questions from students about computerized aid services, the California Student Aid Commission formed a committee of aid administrators to look into the issue. In a two-phase study from 1981 to 1984, the committee sent 53 computer matching services questionnaires inquiring about the size and nature of their data base, their procedures, fees, deadlines, refunds, and whether the organizations were non-profit. In addition, the commission arranged for students to use the services and report the results.

The report issued by the committee turned up some interesting facts. First, virtually all the services were proprietary and profit-oriented. Of the 36 firms that responded, only 6 had their own data base. The others for the most part used information from one company, Academic Guidance Services, which as a "wholesaler" does not offer data directly to students. AGS licenses its information to as many as 100 search organizations and has about 3,800 sources in its data base. (Sources should be differentiated from leads, which are actual scholarships.) Data bases of other services ranged in size from 2,000 to 11,500 sources, with information on approximately 25,000 to 100,000 leads.

Most important, the study found that not one of the computer services surveyed was effective in actually *matching* students with aid resources. Few of the services asked detailed-enough questions or did sufficient follow-up to ensure that students were given scholarships for which they were truly eligible.

As part of its survey, the Student Aid Commission paid for 15 high school students to use two different data services—one with its own data base, the other subscribing to the AGS data pool. The results of this experiment were, to put it bluntly, dismal. Although each of the students got at least the promised number of scholarship "leads," the re-

quirements for these grants were so stringent that the students were ineligible for most of them. Of the 15 students in the survey, *not one* actually received a scholarship as a result of information received from the computer services.

In addition, the study found that:

▶ In almost every case, the match between student and lead was not good. One student was given 18 leads, 11 of which she was not eligible for.

▶ While refunds were promised to those who didn't receive the guaranteed number of scholarship leads, there was no assurance that users would be given leads to scholarships they were actually eligible for, nor that they would win them. No student attempted to get a refund because the *results* of the services were unsatisfactory.

▶ Many of the private aid sources provided were ones of which students and counselors were already aware, including National Merit, Bank of America, and Century III scholarships.

▶ In some cases the scholarships were no longer available, were inaccurately named, or were too narrowly defined to be of much use to students.

▶ While the services concentrated primarily on private aid sources, some students were given leads on federal or state aid programs of which they or their counselors were already aware.

▶ Since the services relied largely on the same data bases, students using more than one service frequently got identical information from each.

▶ Advertising claims about hundreds of dollars in unused aid were unsubstantiated, and there is little evidence, according to the study, that so much money goes unclaimed.

The study concluded that while it is *theoretically* desirable to use computer technology to match students and scholarships, at present none of the computer matching services seems to be doing that. In the future, things may change for the better. But even if proper matching can someday be accomplished, actually applying for and winning scholarships is a difficult task. Ultimately, a student must still fill out many applications, meet a multitude of deadlines, and *qualify* for the aid award.

Our conclusion? You're better off spending your money on up-to-date reference books, such as Oreon Keeslar's *Financial Aids Catalogue for Higher Education,* than on computer matching services. (Even where non-profit organizations have created such a service, the results have been discouraging. The University of Santa Clara surveyed results among 112 students who participated in its computerized matching program. Only two actually received grants through the service, and the combined scholarship funds amounted to $900. The program was discontinued.) A reference guide is a smarter investment because you are free to browse and determine the scholarships for which you might feasibly apply. Remember also that the bulk of financial aid is still need-based. Concentrate first on federal and state sources with the help of your counselor, *then* pursue merit scholarships.

If after reading this you decide to go ahead and use a computer matching service anyway, find out as much about it as you can. Ask your counselor whether he or she has heard of it. Once you contact the service, ask about the refund policy, and *get it in writing.* Ask about its data base. Ask whether you can have the names of local students who have used the service. Contact your local Better Business Bureau or government consumer agency and ask about complaints. And keep in mind that there is no quick fix for financial aid.

Investigating Financial Aid Policy

Here are some crucial questions to keep in mind as you read college pamphlets and talk to admission or financial aid officers. Address the more technical questions to a financial aid officer, once you've been admitted.

1. Are admissions really aid-blind? What you want to know, of course, is whether you will be denied admission on the basis of financial need if you appear to be a borderline admission prospect.

2. Are students who show demonstrated need ever admitted *without* having their need met? There's not much you can do about this, but at least you should know about it beforehand.

3. If you get an outside scholarship, will that be subtracted from your financial aid package? Your brilliance or athletic talent, when it gets you a merit scholarship from outside your college, will give you a little more financial breathing room, right? *Wrong!* In keeping with their policy of awarding aid entirely on the basis of need, many colleges will not allow you to use an outside scholarship as part of your expected family contribution. Instead, they will usually replace a part of the package—gift aid, self-help, or a combination—with the money you've "brought them." This releases the funds for another student's use, but doesn't do much for you. You may be no better off than before.

4. How much will you be able to earn with a campus job? Salaries range from minimum wage on up. If your job is funded by Uncle Sam's work-study program, the total you can earn may be limited to your demonstrated need.

5. Will you be able to get a job if you do not qualify for work-study? If you're not on aid, can you still get one? Many schools reserve campus jobs for recipients of financial aid. Once aided students are hired, the remaining jobs are opened to other students. If you're at an isolated campus where most jobs are tied to the college, need a job to help pay your expenses, and are not on aid, this could be a problem.

6. How much are you expected to earn in a job over the summer? Colleges will figure earnings from a summer job into your family contribution whether you work or not.

7. How do you apply for aid? When? Do you use the FAF, FFS, or any other forms? Is there a cut-off deadline beyond which you will not be considered for aid?

8. Will you still receive aid if you enroll in an off-campus program? Foreign study programs are the issue here. Are you limited to those sponsored by your university, or can you get aid while in other study-abroad programs?

9. How much grant aid is available from the college? Get a sense of how much money the school has.

10. What percentage of assets—especially savings—will you be expected to contribute? Get a sense of how assets are calculated into the needs-analysis formula of the college.

11. Is there a minimum need cut-off under which you will not get aid? Some colleges will not give aid to students whose need is less than $500–$800 a year.

12. Can the school suggest any other scholarship or aid sources to which you should apply? Financial aid offices may be able to suggest sources you may have overlooked.

13. Does the school offer any merit scholarships?

PART THREE

ANATOMY
OF A
DECISION

BEHIND THE SCENES

What kind of person goes into admission work? Who actually makes the decisions? All kinds of personalities, attitudes, and ideals comprise the admission community, but the people who stay in the field share one or more of the following attributes:

▶ They like young people and enjoy counseling them.

▶ They enjoy living in the college environment.

▶ They have a commitment to working in education.

▶ They have chosen, at least temporarily, to avoid the business world. And they believe that admission work will offer more variety than teaching.

▶ They enjoy traveling and speaking before groups.

Most A.O.'s, even at the most selective colleges, don't choose the field because they enjoy "a sense of power." In fact, admission people are usually looking for reasons to accept people, not reject them. Inevitably they do have to turn down a lot of applicants, but they don't enjoy that process. There are times when it's almost heartbreaking *not* to be able to say yes to students—especially those who have lively or lovely personalities.

Some admission people love interviews and see them not as a chance to trip people up, but instead as a marvelous opportunity to play counselor. One noted dean from a small, elite private college in the East admitted that he was a frustrated counselor. One of his greatest pleasures was sitting down with anxious, sweaty juniors, looking over their transcripts, suggesting ways they could better their record, and redirecting them to other good, private colleges, or even to prep school postgraduate programs if their statistics made their case hopeless.

To be an admission officer, you have to like people. You also have to be open-minded, see the world in grays and not absolutes, and possess a sense of humor.

Who Are Those Guys?

At any admission office, there are two basic kinds of people evaluating folders and making decisions: the professionals and the nonpros.

Professionals

The "lifers." These are people in the business to stay. Many have considerable experience with education and graduate degrees in related fields. Some of these lifers move from college to college, taking on new challenges and learning about new places to keep from going stale. Others stay at their jobs for years—even decades. They often have a sentimental attachment to their school, and can't imagine themselves going elsewhere and representing any other college. This group of admission professionals is particularly prevalent at elite private colleges.

Lifers are generally sensitive to the politics of their situation; most admission directors will admit that their jobs are very politicized—there's always someone complaining about a decision. Lifers tend to take fewer "flyers," or high-risk candidates. But they are the backbone of any admission office, providing a historical continuity of admission standards and administrative savvy.

The "young turks." You'd be surprised at how young some admission officers are. A survey of the average age of admissions staff members at the elite private colleges would probably turn up an average age below 30. (At Brown University, an informal survey made a few years ago showed the average age was 28.) This is because the demands of admission work generate a high degree of burnout. Many colleges recognize this, recruiting students just out of the graduating class to represent their alma mater. It is generally assumed that recent college graduates can relate to high school seniors better than most older groups. These young admission officers are often fired up with enthusiasm, having made the grade at a good college. What's more, they are now helping to shape the freshman class, and can be counted on to go out and beat the bushes trying to find the best prospects they can. They are also the most willing to burn the midnight oil while evaluating folders during the selection crunch.

The young turks are usually more liberal than the lifers, arguing for admission of high-risk candidates, or politically active students with mediocre academic statistics, or the "neat kid" who was so great in the interview. The lifers provide sage advice and perspective; the young turks provide passion and idealism, as well as a lot of energy.

While the lifers and young turks may seem to have different attitudes, they share a love of working with kids. Generally, every admission office represents a variety of academic backgrounds, personal histories, and personalities. As a result, admission decisions are balanced, with individual prejudices tending to cancel each other out. And if there's any area in which both lifers and young turks are in agreement, it's in believing that admission professionals have a broader perspective than both admission constituents and the nonprofessionals involved in the process.

Nonprofessionals

Every campus has nonprofessionals who contribute to admission decisions. Generally they do so by sitting on admission policy committees, by reading and evaluating folders, and by participating in selection committees. There are usually three types of nonprofessionals: students, faculty, and other administrators. Occasionally colleges will also elect alumni to their admission policy committees, and may seat them on the selection committee as well.

Each of these groups tends to have a different outlook on admission. Faculty members, first and foremost, are concerned with academic potential. After all, they have to teach these students, and want the most intellectually capable in their classes. They are concerned with the general standard of academic life on campus, and sometimes care little about the personal factors that admission professionals feel are so important.

If there is any point of conflict between the faculty and the pros, it's on this issue. Professors often have little sympathy for the student leader whose grades are below average, and may not be sensitive to the fact that a scholar may be antisocial or emotionally immature. That's why any selection committee that includes a great number of instructors will probably lean more toward the eggheads than the extracurricular whizzes. But some faculty, particularly those who have served for some time on selection committees, learn to recognize the nerds and to appreciate well-rounded candidates.

Students who sit on admission committees are much like the young turk professionals. They're passionate, more willing to take high-risk cases, and are especially concerned with admitting minorities and the underprivileged. Alumni are most apt to be concerned with admitting "legacies" (alumni offspring) and maintaining the athletic program. And other administrators, such as deans are usually bottom-line judges, assessing whether high-risk prospects will be able to survive their first semester on campus.

What Do They Look For

A lot of what admission committees are looking for is the *potential for growth*. They expect the college experience to nurture and change students. Therefore, admission officers must look between the lines of applications, seeking drive, diligence, initiative, humor, imagination, self-awareness, and a host of other qualities that indicate whether or not an applicant is really going to get something out of his college experience.

Colleges are also concerned with the match between a student and the campus: the degree to which the student will be happy with the college, and vice versa.

Looking for growth potential and the proper match of student to campus can't be accomplished without making subjective judgments. But simply because decisions are influenced by subjective assessments doesn't mean they're unfair. Admission people strive to be as evenhanded as possible in dealing with applicants. They will try to let opposing points of view on a folder come to light before making a decision; they will attempt to ensure that the standards of acceptance are applied uniformly throughout the process of selection. And they will make every attempt to solicit more information and additional staffers' opinions before sealing a denial in a controversial case. The time that admission officers lavish on some cases is remarkable, given that they may see thousands of folders per year. Finally, too, the very fact that the decisions are made by a group of individuals, each with slightly divergent attitudes and backgrounds, helps encourage a fair final judgment.

An In-Depth Look at a Selection Process

Brown University has one of the most thorough and sensitive admission procedures of any school its size. The legacy of the years when Brown was the smallest college in the Ivy League, its process stresses a very personal and individual look at each student whose application is on file. Let's look at this process by examining exactly what happens to an application.

Imagine that our applicant, Polly Smith, has sent an inquiry to Brown, visited the campus for an interview, or sent some other piece of information about herself before formally submitting an application. That document will be placed in a *correspondence folder*, which will hold all documents on Polly for the admission season—which runs, roughly, from spring to spring. That way, anything sent in prior to Polly's application won't be lost. When her application is submitted, it will be combined with all the material in her correspondence folder to start a *permanent folder*.

In the basement of the admission office are open bins that will contain, organized in alphabetical order, the 13,000 or so applications expected each season. In late August, these bins sit forlorn and nearly empty, save for a stray correspondence folder or transfer application. But soon—within four months, in fact—the very same bins will be overflowing with the 185,000 pieces of paper that come in every year.

By January 1, Polly will be required to submit her formal application, which contains basic information (family background, social security number, anticipated major) and application fee. Basic information from this application form is coded into a computer program to be used later in the office's housekeeping—keeping track of applicants, making sure that their folders are acted on, and ensuring that all of them receive decision letters. From this data base, the computer will later generate computer listings called *dockets*, which are used to organize meetings of the selection committee.

Polly's folder will be ready to be *read* (evaluated) when it contains the main application form, high school record, test scores (SAT and three Achievements, or the ACT), essay, and at least two teacher recommendations. Depending on whether or not she had an interview, submitted supplementary materials, or came to the attention of a university official, her folder may contain interview reports from staffers or alumni, additional references, departmental evaluations of artwork slides artwork or tapes of musical performances, and any other pieces of paper that represent her. In some cases, an A.O. may write a comment on a scrap of paper about a student met while visiting high schools or in group sessions at the college. Comments can vary from "nice"—with extensive elaboration—to "obnoxious, driven, most concerned with getting into medical school."

Actually, Polly will have two folders that comprise her file. One, the *permanent folder*, never leaves the file room and is a constant record of her candidacy. The other, the *reading folder*, contains all relevant documents and may be removed for evaluation and committee meetings.

Although all application materials are not due until January 15, many folders become complete before that date. By January 1, admission officers are deeply engrossed in the task of reading and evaluating. (They will have already made decisions on some 2,000 early action applicants.) As are the others, Polly's folder is assigned randomly by file room personnel to an admission officer or other reader. Generally, the only others who read folders are faculty members. Many admission officers read 50 folders per day; they are up until late in the evening to complete this task. In fact, the pressure of constant evaluation is relentless—missing your daily quota one day means having to do that many more folders the next.

Preparing the Folders

The first reader is supposed to *prepare* the folder—to give an overall summary of the applicant's highs and lows, point out any glaring inconsistencies, and recommend a general course of action if one seems apparent. A typical comment: "This is the best that Central High School has to offer. And though her tests are average, she's got her hand into everything—student government, drama, music. And she works summers as a publicist. Interview report is tops. Essay is incisive and well-organized—she writes about her school. Recommendations are effusive. Our alumnus interviewer adored her. We should overlook those tests; she's a winner. I don't know how the rest of the school looks, but I say we take her."

This reader will also give the application the first of a number of numerical ratings. These represent academic and nonacademic potential, often referred to as *academic over personal*, because the academic score comes first. The scale runs from 1 (low) to 6 (high). Thus Polly Pupil, as described above, might be given a 3/5 (3 academic, 5 nonacademic) or a 4/5. The rating will be entered in the computer file and will eventually reappear on the committee docket. The rating, however, will not be reprinted anywhere else on the folder so as not to unduly influence the thinking of the second reader.

The first reader may also code *distinctions* for the computer file, noting achievements in athletics, art, music, drama, student government, literature and writing, and so on. Once again, these are based on the reader's perceptions of the applicant, not on any hard and fast scale. There is also room on the "reader rating form" for handwritten notes on any pursuits or attributes that escape normal categorization.

The first reader will also decide whether to route the folder to another staffer who specializes in a certain sort of student. One A.O. may have an expertise in evaluating aspiring engineers. An ex-photographer may evaluate photographs, an ex-English major creative writing. The admission officer who sails may be asked to evaluate what certain regatta prizes mean for the preppy from Boston. Every folder will be read at least twice, if not three times, before it reaches the selection committee.

If a folder does not require additional expert readings, it will then go into the hands of the area admission officer. At Brown, recruitment and selection responsibilities are divided according to geographic areas. One admission officer may be assigned two or three of these areas, depending on his or her overall responsibilities and the number of applications received each year from those areas. (In all, Brown has 15 full-time admission professionals, about 25 support personnel, and a specialist in computers.)

The Student's Advocate

Now comes the hard part. The area admission officer must prepare applications from his or her area for presentation to the Board of Admission. The area officer, in effect, is the advocate for the students applying from that area. But while the officer may have the responsibility for representing them, the feeling is that his or her duty is not to "get in" as many as possible, but rather to suggest the decision that is best for Brown and the applicant. The mere fact that the A.O. has applicants, however, ensures that students get a fair shake. Inevitably, presenters come before the committee with more recommendations for acceptance than their colleagues will be prepared to accept.

The area officer first receives a bin of folders representing 100 to 125 students. Along with this comes a massive computer printout, the docket, listing the candidates in groups by high school. This allows them to organize the folders and keep track of the local school situation. Admission professionals, as we have said, are very sensitive to the reactions of high school officials, students, and parents to admission decisions.

The area officer will methodically begin to assess the school situation by looking over his computer docket. The docket will contain a listing, by high school, of each applicant, ranked by an average of combined reader ratings. (Someone with a first reader rating of 5/5 and a second of 5/4 will probably rank near the top of the bunch.) Reader ratings are not used for any other purpose than to get a quick scan on an applicant's relative position. They are not employed as cutoffs of any sort.

The officer may find a number of potential problems relating to the school situation. Perhaps the 700-testing valedictorian does nothing but study, while a number of applicants below him in rank are more appealing because they are good academic prospects and yet also have a lot to contribute on the nonacademic side. There may be a student with an extraordinarily impressive talent (athletic, creative, leadership) who does not have grades or tests as high as other students. And there may be alumni children to consider. Ultimately, a balance must be struck between the needs of the university and its desire to make decisions that will seem fair to the high schools.

The docket contains a number of significant pieces of information, not the least of which is a history of applications, acceptances, and enrollments from past years at each high school. This gives the admission officer an instant feeling for how the school's prospects have done in the past. The docket also contains SAT scores, class rank, the names of parents' colleges, any distinctions, the degree program to which each student is applying, and other data.

As he *preps* folders, the area admission officer writes a final comment in the folder and adds another "academic over personal" reader rating. He may even telephone teachers, guidance counselors, or alumni who have contributed references if something needs clarification. The comment in question might be positive but incomprehensible—"Polly was involved as head of the annual MORP—a sort of reverse prom for unsocial types." What does that mean? A call to the school turns up that "MORP" is prom in reverse, and that the event, rather than a protest against the school's traditional prom (which it once was in the late sixties) has evolved into a charity event with carnival activities and bands. Through a simple telephone call, a puzzle that contributed little to forming a picture of Polly, has been clarified.

The area admission officer probably traveled to "his" schools during the summer and fall, trying to interest prospects in Brown, and met with guidance counselors. He may know some of the applicants personally, and be aware of the academic quality of the high schools involved. If an officer doesn't know a school—and often some strange place pops out on the docket that no one has ever heard of before—he'll scan the school's summary of graduates, usually provided with the applicant's transcript. He may even call a local alumnus to find out about the school's reputation.

The area A.O. must then decide what action to recommend to the selection committee. There are three basic choices: *accept, deny,* and *hold over.* (An applicant who is put in the hold-over group will be considered in a final committee session at the end of the selection process. At this session, the applicant will be accepted, denied, or put on the waiting list.) While the A.O. does have a specific figure for how many students were accepted from the area in the past, he is not obligated to meet a specific target.

Finally, the area officer takes notes on each candidate for his oral presentation to the committee.

Once the folders are prepped, the A.O. is ready to present them to the Board of Admission, or the committee, as it is called. The schedule aims for decisions on 250 to 450 applicants per day, from February through April. The committee will meet day in and day out: morning, afternoon, and evenings, and on both Saturdays and Sundays.

Sitting in at a Meeting

Meetings of the Board of Admission at Brown take place in the admission building's conference area—a grand room with varnished wood trim, a large fireplace, and bay windows dating from the days when the edifice was a luxurious home. A leather-covered oval table occupies the room's center, and at it sits the area A.O., called the presenter, with his bin of over 100 folders representing applicants; Director of Admission James H. Rogers, who presides over every meeting of the board; and at least two or three other staff members. Often a faculty member of the Committee on Admission and Financial Aid is present to give the professors' viewpoint on applicants.

At the director's side are a series of depth charts for various men's and women's sports; listings of prospects from the University Development Office (a fund-raising department); listings of prospects from the Alumni Office, indicating applicants whose parents are prominent alumni; a rundown of musical prospects from the music department that includes the applicants' musical levels, instruments, and indications of how badly the band or orchestra needs them; listings from the art department, which has appraised the talent of students who submitted samples of their work; and others.

When the board is in session, the presenter stands and begins his or her oration on each applicant. In this instance, the schools being covered are in Ohio. We are looking at a large suburban high school in a major metropolitan center—a school that traditionally sends countless applications to selective colleges throughout the country, particularly in the Midwest and East.

The presenter begins with candidates from the bottom of the docket. (Remember, they were put there by combined reader ratings.) He will comment briefly on each: "This is John Sulka—a nice kid who wants to be a doctor but doesn't do much more than fly model airplanes and volunteer at the local hospital. His rank is in the third decile and his test scores are undistinguished: mid-500s. Achievements also in the low 500s. Form 7 (alumni interview) is unimpressed. Z." Z is the internal admission office designation for a denial—sometimes said "zip" or "zippo". A, of course, stands for acceptance, WL for waiting list. The process of sifting through the bottom group of the applicants from the high school moves quickly. Occasionally a committee member may demure and ask to see the folder, especially if the applicant in question has good academic ratings and low personal ones. The director, Jim Rogers, marks the committee decision on the outside of John Sulka's folder, and the decision is put into the computer file. He will also browse through the folder, looking for anything untoward or interesting.

As the presenter moves upward in the docket, the process slows down. On paper, at least, the kids begin to look more similar. There are a number of prospects with good Board scores and with ranks in the top fifth of the class. Some cases seem easy; others require a little more time. "Here's a likable lady. Her rank is good, top decile, she's taken a demanding set of courses, is extremely active as V. P. of the senior class, plays first violin in the school orchestra, and in fact has won a state prize for a violin competition.

"Recommenders see her as quiet and studious, but extremely pleasant. She's not a social butterfly but has a few close friends, and is respected. Her tests, however, are dismal—all in the low 400s. This may be because her parents are Lebanese immigrants and may not speak English at home. Dad's a doctor, Mom works in import-export. But she's a great girl, talented, and we ought to overlook her tests. I say we take her." As if to verify that is a difficult call, the presenter stands ready to give the folder to anyone who wants to read it.

"How bright is she, really?" someone asks. "Well, there's no question that she's limited in verbal areas," the presenter responds. "Her recommenders indicate that she's not the most brilliant in the school, but makes up for it by her inquisitive attitude and hard work." The committee agrees to postpone the decision for a few minutes while the folder is passed around the table.

In the meantime, another candidate is considered. About one-third of all applications are reread during the committee sessions. The discussion then returns to the lady violinist. "She's hard-working and a lovely personality," says one committee member, having just read the folder. "But she lacks a real zest. Her essay is pretty workmanlike; correct but not imaginative. I'd say that sums her up generally—correct but not imaginative." Someone checks the music department list. The candidate is on it, but far from the top prospect for violinists. "I don't know," someone else says. "They do like her at the school, but she doesn't really add anything that we don't already have. And it's not as if she's a real scholar."

"But the school support is strong," says the presenter.

"How about holding her over?" another person recommends. There is more discussion, and the committee decides that while the lady violinist deserves more than a denial, they can't really make a case for an acceptance. Rather than putting her in the hold-over group, they will put her on the waiting list now; it is certain she won't be admitted even from the hold-overs. And when the decision letter goes out it will signal to school officials that the admission office values their opinions, while letting the applicant and her peers know that Brown appreciates likable students with talent—even if their SAT scores are questionable.

The process continues, decisions always being made by consensus rather than by voting. If there is consistent opposition by one individual to a decision, the director will usually put his foot down on the side of majority opinion, but not before everyone tries to convince the recalcitrant party.

A Fair Shake

Implicit in this process is the recognition that there are very few absolutely right or wrong decisions, and that every applicant will get an education somewhere. But there is also a tacit agreement that everyone deserves a fair shot, and that the committee's job is to argue for the applicant who stands out or is special in some way, or the one who is uncommon to Brown's applicant group—a geo from a remote location, or a small-town New Englander; the inner-city minority kids; those whose parents aren't in the professions or business, or who aren't college-educated; the genuine scientists and mathematicians who may seem like nerds to their peers but who demonstrate brilliance in their fields and who will grow emotionally in college.

The presenter goes on to the next case. "Well, here's a charmer. Frank is described as pushy, driven, and is about as narrow as a yardstick. Law, law, law is all that comes out of his essay and recommendations. He'll make a great litigator, but he doesn't have much humanity. In fact, all through the folders there are consistent downchecks (meaning a conspicuous drop in objective grid ratings) for warmth and personality. He's totally egocentric. If you wanted to be nasty you could even say he's obnoxious. He'd do well here but would add nothing. Z."

Next is Polly Smith. "Every reader gave her a 5 for the personal side. There's genuine warmth in her recommendations, and every sign is that the school *and* other students love her. She's played lead roles in two school plays. She's a flutist. As president of the senior class, she led a successful effort to allow seniors off-campus privileges to work in internship programs. And get this—she landed a job as a publicist for a leading beauty salon! To cap it, she can write. Her essay is about the people who work in the salon, and it's hilarious." The committee accepts her.

"Next—Bruce Fielding. He's a brilliant mathematician and budding physicist. You can see that his test scores in math-science are all in the mid-700s. He did a National Science Foundation summer program at MIT and wound up writing a paper on relativity that his MIT physics teacher called 'brilliant.' He's taking a lot of A.P.'s at Shaker Heights High—a demanding school. But he's awfully thin on the personal side: Chess Club, Honor Society, and a lot of individual activities. I don't know. He doesn't have a lot to offer us except his academic talent. I'd say hold-over, maybe even Z."

A committee member who is an ex-engineer disagrees and asks to read the folder. While he does, the presenter goes on to the next case.

"This is Betsy Johnson. She's not a bad student, but she's pretty superficial—writes her essay on how she likes to lifeguard during the summer because she can enjoy the surf and sand."

"On Lake Erie?!" someone chimes in. The presenter goes on. "Other than lifeguarding, she doesn't have much to show for her time outside of class—candy striper at a local hospital, lots of travel with her parents. I don't think so. Z." Another committee member looks through the folder. "I agree." Since her reader ratings are average, there is little disagreement on Betsy Johnson. The committee then returns to Bruce Fielding, whose folder by this time has been read by the ex-engineer and another committee member.

"I really don't see how you can recommend anything but an A for Bruce Fielding. First of all, look at his physics Achievement Test—790! And it's not like he's a nerd—he plays pick-up basketball, goes on bicycle trips, and 'fiddles with photography,' in his words. But most importantly, he's a *real* physicist. He loves the subject, and I can't imagine he won't make some contribution to the field."

"He looks like a genuine scholar to me," the director notes as he reads through the folder. "What do you think?" he asks of the committee member who did a second reading.

"I still think he'd be better off at MIT," the presenter interjects.

"I think you're absolutely wrong on him," the second committee reader says. "He really does have broad interests, though he's not a big man on campus. The alumni interviewer said he was shy but very bright. I think he'll grow a lot as a *person* in college—he's probably too intelligent and eccentric to be accepted widely in high school. Sure he won't be a mover and shaker on campus, but he *will* contribute: can't you picture this guy explaining relativity to his unscientific friends during some late-night dormitory bull session about religion and the universe? I like him! Beside, why should every bright scientist go to MIT or Cal Tech? This kid should be exposed to a few poets, and vice versa."

"Anyway, it's hard to turn down a real scientist—which Bruce is," says the director.

"Okay. You convinced me," the presenter says. "Let's take him." Bruce Fielding gets accepted.

The process continues. "Moving on, here's a genuine geo who goes to high school in Bowling Green, Ohio. For those of you who don't know Ohio, Bowling Green is a little college town in the farm belt south of Toledo. The parents aren't farmers—they teach at the university—but they live in an old farmhouse. Fred likes the idea of farming. He's worked a couple of summers for a neighboring soybean grower, raises pigs for fun and profit, and grows his own corn. What's more, he was student body president at school and wants to go into politics. Tests are mediocre, but hell—it's not a very sophisticated place, Bowling Green."

"We don't see many like him. He sounds solid to me. But why did he apply here?" someone asks.

"He has an uncle who went to Providence College and recommended Brown. But he's applying to Eastern schools, he said in his essay, 'so I can be exposed to the rigors of an Eastern education.'"

A doubter chimes in. "But is he a *real* geo? After all, his parents are college professors."

"Just to prove that he's a geo, I saved the best for last," the presenter says. "Here is Fred's picture, which he sent in with his essay—Fred and his prize pig in front of his sty."

The picture is the hit of the committee session. Fred is admitted, and his photo is posted on a bulletin board over the committee room's mantle. On the board are various photos or supplementary application materials: an eight-by-ten glossy of a mountain climber rappeling against a sheer cliff face of granite; a mock school newspaper announcing a student's acceptance to Brown—in short, anything that sets students apart and gives them a special "handle" (or positioning) by which they are remembered.

The Final Sessions

Once all folders have been through the Board of Admission, there's a final series of committee sessions to decide on the 500 to 800 applicants in the hold-over group. The number that can be accepted will depend on the number of acceptances already granted. This number is subtracted from the office's target for acceptances (usually around 2,400 to 2,500) required to yield a freshman class of 1,300 or so. Many of the students with the most appealing personalities are in this group, as are the ones with special talents. Some holdovers are denied; others are accepted; and a few hundred are put on the waiting list.

In conjunction with the hold-over committee, there are a series of reviews for groups of applicants. The number of legacies admitted will be reviewed to make sure that the board hasn't been unduly tough on alumni children. Athletes, musicians, artists, and any other applicants rated by university faculty or officials are reviewed. Some minority students are reviewed by the Minority Review Committee, a group composed of students, faculty, and administration. Last but not least, there is a review to ensure that the university's financial aid budget has been kept within reasonable bounds.

Next there is the last-minute numerical count. Each year since the early seventies, Brown has seen a growth in its applicant pool. From 1977 to 1983, the number grew from 9,150 to 13,265 applications. While Brown's admission officers take pride in their school's booming popularity, they also know it means denying more qualified applicants than ever. And this prospect, though unavoidable, is not a happy one.

The committee's work proceeds from mid-February through early April. Daily decisions are coded into the computer file. A high-speed typewriter will dash off acceptance, denial, and waiting-list letters. Before being signed, each letter is checked against the applicant's folder to make sure that the decision being sent out is the correct one. Then, methodically and over days and days, Jim Rogers proceeds to hand-sign each letter—every one—to personalize the process somewhat. All 13,265 letters will be signed this way.

Finally, on a date agreed upon in the previous year by all the colleges in the Ivy League (usually April 15), the letters are delivered to the Post Office. At midnight, they go into the mail.

Brown's process, it should be said, stresses a number of factors. It is the composite picture of an applicant that determines whether he or she will be admitted, not one or two variables. Generally speaking, Brown isn't looking for any one type of student; it likes variety. It likes applicants who are a bit different, or those who have really excelled in some field, or those who take a real interest in their education, or those who have real zest and personality. But it also likes and looks for a variety of other applicants.

Brown's system—in which every student has a hearing, however brief, at the committee table, is attuned just as much to the person as to the "student." As every Brown admission officer will be quick to admit, the school could fill the class with students who have 700 board scores. But it has no interest in doing so. Brown wants ingenuity, imagination, or commitment to some field. It wants a truly well-rounded individual, and a balanced class. Tests are important, but not overwhelmingly so; grades are very important, but not the only consideration. It's the total picture that counts.

The ultimate question asked of every applicant is, "What will this person add to life at Brown? A great personality? A brilliant grasp of mathematics? Leadership? Warmth and tolerance?" If he or she has something to contribute and the academic picture is a good one, the answer will be yes.

Other Colleges' Approaches

What follows is a summary of a number of selection mechanisms. Keep in mind as you read that our intent is not to show you how you can get into these schools, but rather to enable you to better understand the range of admission systems nationwide. Each of the colleges selected for this survey represents, in a sense, the prototype of a variety of places. No summary can take the place of actually sitting in on the committee process; but if you understand the mechanisms of selection, you'll be better equipped to think about how you can improve your own chances.

The University of California at Berkeley
Berkeley, California

Along with the University of Michigan, Berkeley is regarded as one of the best state schools in the country. Every California resident who meets a certain academic standard is guaranteed a place on one of the University of California system's nine campuses. (Any resident with a grade point average of above 3.3, or combined SATs of above 1,100, or who meets a Freshman Eligibility Index combining grades and SATs will be admitted; similar but higher standards exist for nonresident applicants.) But Berkeley itself gets about 15,000 applications a year, and has room for only about 7,900 admissions. The rest of the applicants are redirected to other, less selective U.C. campuses. To complicate things further, standards may be different for each college or department within the university.

In general, admission begins with an evaluation of academic factors. To be admitted to Berkeley's College of Letters, Arts, and Sciences, applicants are arranged by order of GPA (which will be weighted by course difficulty beginning in 1983). The upper one-quarter of this ranking is admitted on the basis of GPA alone.

Another 20 percent of the final entering class will be admitted using a complex set of criteria, including their scores on objective tests. These folders are read by one of twenty admission staffers. Of this group of applicants, some will be admitted on the basis of test scores alone. (To be admitted in this way, the applicant must have a combined SAT score of 1,100 and at least 1,650 on three Achievement tests combined, with no individual test score below 500.) Admission officers will also recommend admission based on a number of factors, including residence in the San Francisco Bay area (local ties), GPA (those closest to the top 25 percent initially admitted), special-recruit status (athletes, disadvantaged students, special talents, etc.), or "hardship" (wanting a major that only Berkeley offers, etc.). The remaining 55 percent of the applicants are sent letters advising them that their application has been denied and "redirecting" them to other U.C. campuses.

There is, however, a Special Action committee that makes judgment calls. This committee includes faculty, students, and admission staffers. An admission officer can designate an application for special action for many reasons. The applicant may not be eligible for admission due to technical reasons, may be a worthwhile "risk" case, may have special talents and yet not meet admission criteria, or may be a member of an underrepresented minority. Each year about 800 folders, 5 percent of the total applicant group is seen by the committee, which admits about 200 applicants.

Clearly there are advantages and disadvantages to this sort of procedure. If you have good enough statistics, you're virtually guaranteed a place in the class. But since extracurriculars and teacher recommendations don't count very much, your ability to position yourself is limited. This reinforces our initial observation that grades (and then SAT scores) are usually the most important factors in admission decisions—and, at schools like Berkeley, generally the only criteria.

The University of Michigan at Ann Arbor
Ann Arbor, Michigan

Michigan is also a world-renowned state university, but its approach to admission is different from Berkeley's. Michigan is not under direct legislative control, although by agreement with the state it limits nonresidents to about 20 percent of each freshman class. Otherwise Michigan sees its main institutional objective as assembling "the best we can find." This goal includes all sorts of students, but the emphasis is on admitting the best. The balance, presumably, comes out "naturally" by taking the best.

Admissions are made on a rolling basis, and generally 80 percent of all applications are decided on the basis of one or two readings and sometimes a final evaluation by the director of admission. Generally, a Michigan resident will be admitted to the College of Literature, Arts and Sciences with a GPA of 3.4 and combined SATs of over 1,150; for nonresidents the figures are 3.6 GPA and SATs of 1,200. The staff of 18 admission professionals makes the bulk of the decisions, despite differing standards for each school within the university. Special applicants with lower than "normal" credentials (athletes, among others) may be encouraged to apply to the School of Education, which has lower admission criteria than most.

The remaining 20 percent of the applicants are sent to the review committee, which also makes rolling decisions. Folders are presented and organized into *good*, *better*, and *best* categories, then discussed and voted on. Essays are not required, and recommendations and interviews (which are not recommended) have little impact on admission. Out-of-class activity is figured into the decision, but ultimately academic honors and ability are more important. The school likes to say that it doesn't look for well-rounded students, but rather for academically able students who can excel in class and still participate in extracurriculars. Of approximately 13,000 applicants, some 8,100 are admitted.

Harvard University
Cambridge, Massachusetts

Harvard. There's no other school like it in terms of public image.

But its committee process is similar to that of many other schools. Each folder gets three readings by admission officers before going into a selection subcommittee. The area admission officer makes the first reading, the second is random, and the third is by the subcommittee chairman. These subcommittees are organized geographically, with the area admission officer presenting candidates from each high school as a group. Subcommittees include 6 to 10 members, including faculty members. (Harvard has 18 admission officers, and 12 faculty members take part in selection.) If no agreement is arrived at by consensus, a vote will be taken. Close calls are set aside for consideration by the full committee.

The full committee annually reviews about 3,000 to 3,500 cases, and everyone on the admission staff participates. Fifteen to 18 people may routinely be present, including faculty members and the dean of admission, who has selected the folders to be discussed in full committee from all the recommendations of subcommittee chairmen. Folders are presented to the full committee by subcommittee chairmen, and usually 10 to 20 percent of the group's decisions are reversals of previous decisions. The full committee exists to ensure that uniform standards are applied to all applicants, as well as to handle sensitive or high-risk cases.

While each subcommittee has a specific numerical target to meet, spaces are reserved for those accepted in the full committee's final review.

In general, Harvard likes achievers—either the top scholars, the academic superstars, or the "glue of the class"—the leaders and talented students who add variety to the college experience. Harvard recognizes that not everyone can be at the top of their college class academically. The school is therefore looking not only for achievers, but for achievers who will feel comfortable being at the middle or bottom of their class once they are in competition with all the other Harvard achievers.

Carleton College
Northfield, Minnesota

In keeping with its image as an intimate liberal arts college, Carleton has a small staff of six admission professionals. When a folder is complete, it will be read by two or sometimes three A.O.'s. To keep the admission readers from being influenced by past comments, evaluations are placed in a small envelope attached to the folder. Certain applicants are routed to specialists for evaluation. Faculty do not have a formal role in evaluation.

Roughly 60 to 70 percent of all applications are decided on after two or three readings, with a review of the folder by the dean of admission. The remaining folders go to the selection committee.

The order of business for the committee is predicated not on region or school, but rather on academic ability. A computer listing of applicants ranks them according to a formula balancing grades and test scores. The committee then deliberates from the top and bottom of the list, working toward the middle. In other words, the top 20 folders are decided on, than the bottom 20, and on to the next highest 20, the next lowest 20, until all the decisions are made. Although the computer makes up the order of consideration, the committee's decisions are made on the basis of a review of the applicant's folder. A presenter gives a profile of the candidate and his or her school, then summarizes the transcript, essay, recommendations, and other factors in the file. Decisions emerge from a great deal of discussion, and there generally is a consensus among staff members. (The committee is composed of the school's six professionals and the dean.) If no consensus is reached, a vote is taken.

Early decision applicants are given the benefit of the doubt, since they have indicated their desire to enroll at the college. The committee makes it a point to admit 60 to 70 "risks" per class—students who may not live up to formal requirements, but who because of background, special talents, or personality will make a contribution to the community. In terms of overall credentials, one negative factor will not necessarily bar an applicant from admission. The essay is important, as are recommendations.

In general, Carleton's admission office likes to resist the "well-rounded class" approach. Instead, it stresses what it calls the "courage quotient" in its students: that is, the extent to which applicants go the extra distance in personal and academic risk-taking. Carleton A.O.'s like applicants who ask questions without fear of losing face.

Pomona College
Claremont, California

Pomona College is a fine liberal arts institution that attracts students from all over the country. In fact, its name is probably better known in the prep schools of the East than in the high schools of Southern California. What makes Pomona's admission process unusual is that it relies on subcommittees that are organized not along geographic lines, but that correspond roughly to the school's many constituencies. Pomona's admission office has subcommittees for "tributes" (alumni offspring); athletes; minorities; development; languages and culture (international students or those with exotic backgrounds); fine arts majors; and a "take" committee for great kids who don't quite measure up academically; a "don't take" committee for bright grade-grubbers; and a "machine inappropriate" subcommittee that decides on applicants who don't fit into any other convenient category.

Completed applications are sent first to one of six area admission officers. The area staffer translates a student's academic record into a "Pomona formula," which predicts the student's grade point average in his first year. Then the area A.O. provides an evaluation of academic and personal qualities and decides which subcommittee the folder should go through. A second reading is provided by nonprofessional staff members—seven professors, two students, and an alumni representative. Roughly half the freshman class will be admitted on the strength of these two readings and final approval by the dean of admission. Admission readers look closely at an applicant's writing style; a good essay can overcome a low SAT.

Once a folder has been read two or three times, it is sent to an appropriate subcommittee. Each subcommittee is assigned a certain target of admits, formulated each year in response to past experience and institutional needs. Candidates are presented by the subcommittee chairman in alphabetical order. After discussion, a simple vote is taken. If a committee has a target of 17 students of a certain type (say, athletes) it may still advocate admission of a larger number to the full committee, where the final decisions are made.

Each subcommittee chairman must appear before the large committee, composed of faculty, students, the director of admission and admission officers. The subcommittee chairmen then act as advocates for "their" applicants, justifying decisions that were made. If, as we noted before, a subcommittee is assigned a target of 17 students and advocates admission of 20, the larger committee is responsible for deciding which 17 will be admitted. In this way, the larger committee is the forum of final selection. It is also a court of last resort, where subcommittee people can plead the cases of their favorite applicants. A final review ensures that consistent decisions have been made.

In general, Pomona puts a great deal of emphasis on academics and course-work. Extracurriculars are also important, however, and the school tends to favor students who show a real depth of interest in one or two fields, or "thoughtful participation"—getting involved in activities that are personally or socially meaningful. Pomona does look for a balanced class, and geographic origin is a significant factor in admission.

The University of Southern California Los Angeles, California

One of the largest private schools in the country, U.S.C has 15,500 undergraduates in a student body totalling 27,000. As you might expect, its size requires a large admission staff—over 30 admission officers, divided between those who visit and communicate with high schools, and those who evaluate folders, make admission decisions, and counsel students once they enroll. U.S.C. has rolling admission, so the earlier an applicant files, the better off he or she usually is.

Once an application is complete, an admission officer evaluates it. If the applicant meets certain prescribed academic criteria, he or she will be admitted. Students who do not meet the guidelines, however, cannot be denied by the first reader alone; the applicant must be routed to another admission officer.

Applications for certain schools (Cinema, Drama, Architecture, and Music, among others) will be sent to those schools for faculty evaluation. Some majors have higher requirements for admission than others. Applications are read successively until they reach the director or associate directors of admission, who are empowered to make a final decision.

Roughly 15 percent of all folders go to an admission subcommittee composed of admission professionals, students, and faculty. These tough cases are decided by a vote. In effect, this committee is the court of last resort for applications on which the director or associate director would prefer not to render a decision, or for students already denied who have requested an appeal.

Geographic origin is not taken into account to any large degree in admission decisions; it's felt that USC's draw is heterogenious enough to include a sufficient number of Easterners. Of all the factors considered, grades are by far the most significant.

USC's system is one that you'd expect to find in a school that processes over 15,000 undergraduate applications per year for some 16 undergraduate schools and colleges. It's highly selective only in about 10 academic majors—last year, Cinema accepted only 15 of 400 applications. Sixty-four percent of its applicants are admitted, and the yield is roughly 44 percent. Applicants who don't meet its standards (which the college does not release) may still be admitted on the basis of other factors, most notably extracurriculars, essays, and special talents.

Yale University
New Haven,
Connecticut

Yale basks in the glory of the Ivy League, and has a reputation for scholarly excellence. But its admission process is a bit different than most, for two reasons. First, the school has a strong feeling about faculty involvement in the selection process. This leads to more of an emphasis on academics in admission. Second, Yale has a rather dramatic committee process, which includes the use of a voting machine with a special "black cowl" to hide each member's vote.

Once a folder is complete, it is evaluated by an admission officer or faculty member. It is then sent to the area admission officer, who gives it a second reading. Tough cases or special interest applicants like athletes, minority students, or alumni children may receive a third reading. Once the folder has had a number of readings, it goes to the standing admission committee. The standing committee has about seven members present at all times, including the area officer, dean of admission, and at least two faculty members. Applicants are presented geographically, by high school, and in alphabetical order at each high school.

Although every folder goes through the committee, not every case is discussed; if two readers recommended admission, the committee will vote without discussing particulars. Many candidates, however, receive further consideration, and then a vote is taken. Certain rules apply to the voting: an applicant must have a strong majority of support (five votes) to be admitted. A single no vote may not mean denial; two such votes will usually seal the fate of the applicant. But it is the means by which the votes are actually taken that adds a touch of high drama to the proceedings.

Rather than simply raising a hand to make a vote known, each committee member has in front of him or her three electrical switches representing *accept*, *deny*, or *waiting list*. Shrouding the buttons is a black cowl. While this may seem like a superfluous and theatrical touch, the cowl is there for a good reason. Yale doesn't want one committee member to see how another is voting. Until recently, a simple flashcard system was used, but it was felt that when the vote was taken, too many members were hesitating and looking at each other's cards to see whether their vote accorded with others. With this new electronic system, only the dean of admission knows the final tally—and committee members votes in secret.

CHAPTER TEN

CASE STUDIES

Throughout this book, we have tried to provide some insight into how admission officers think.

The section that follows is unusual in that the admission staffs of seven selective colleges actually evaluated applications that we submitted to them. The five students we "created" are typical of many applicants. We had them "apply" to seven colleges: Brown, Carleton, Columbia, the University of Michigan, Notre Dame, the University of North Carolina at Chapel Hill, and Pomona.

The schools were selected because they represent a good cross-section of the types of selective colleges you probably will consider in your college search. Some are small, others large; some are public, others private. There are Eastern, Southern, Midwestern, and Western schools. Some emphasize academic grades and board scores, others personal qualities. They provided us with a fascinating variety of responses.

At the conclusion of the section are the responses from the admission offices at each of the participating schools. In addition to the decision on each candidate, the committees have provided comments on why they acted as they did. Note: The schools participating in this exercise knew that the "applicants" were not "real" people. Or not quite real. Some of the cases were thinly disguised individuals who had actually applied to several of the participating schools just a few years earlier. The colleges sometimes reacted differently to the cases than they had to the real people.

Each school was sent five full applications—one for each student. The applications were typed on each school's appropriate forms, and included family histories, references, transcripts, essays, and interview reports. As you will see, some of the essays have grammatical errors. These "mistakes" were intentional, and are reprinted as they were sent to the admission offices. (Unfortunately too many real students hurt their chances because of syntax or spelling errors in their application.)

All the colleges were sent the same set of essays and recommendations for each student. In other words, in each case we utilized a single positioning and packaging effort for all seven colleges. Moreover the colleges treated the "Alumni interview report" and the "Coach's report" as if it came from their respective alumni and coach.

Jack
Lawrence

Lynbrook High School
Lynbrook, New York

Class Standing: 70/320
SAT Scores: 590v/710m (April, Jr. yr.)
Achievement Test Scores:
660 Math Level II
620 Chemistry

Grades

9th Grade
English	88
Spanish	84
Algebra	97
Science	87
Social Studies	85

10th Grade
English	86
Spanish	82
Geometry	98
Biology	88
World History	84

11th Grade
English	85
Spanish	78
Trig./Adv. Algebra	95
A.P. Chemistry	87
American History	82
Mechanical Drawing	92

12th Grade
English
A.P. Calculus
A.P. Physics
Sociology/Economics
Adv. Arch. Design

Parents

Father: John; Textile worker, National Wool Co.
(No college)
Mother: Janet (deceased)
(No college)

Siblings:

William, 12

Activities

Student Council V. P. (sr.)
Student Council (soph., jr.)
Varsity Lacrosse (jr., sr.)
Private pilot's license
J.V. Lacrosse (fr., soph.)
J.V. Wrestling (fr.)
J.V. Football (fr., soph.)
National Honor Society (jr., sr.)

Work

Sophomore summer
TWA at JFK Airport
Airplane clean-up crew
50 hrs. per week
$2,500 earned that summer

Junior school year
Bounty Inn Restaurant
Busboy
15 hrs. per week during the school year
$3,000 earned during school year

Junior summer
TWA at JFK Airport
Baggage crew
50 hrs. per week
$3,000 earned that summer

Senior school year
Bounty Inn Restaurant
Waiter
Currently working approximately 20 hrs. per week

Awards

Freshman
Winner JHS Science Fair

Sophomore
Runner-up H.S. Science Fair

Junior
Winner School Science Fair
1st place Winner Northeast Regional Science Fair
National Runner-up—U.S. Air Force Science Fair

Degree program

Sc. B.
Aeronautical Engineering

Career goal:

Aeronautical Engineer

Essay

For most people about to fly on commercial airliners, the only thing as frightening as a crash is lost baggage. Working at Kennedy Airport the past two summers, I have heard dozens of people ask for "a safe seat" when checking in for their flights. Most seem to regard the request as a formality, with the unspoken recognition that no seat is particularly safe during an accident, and the whole matter is beyond their control in any event.

The subject of lost baggage, however, is quite another matter. Passengers never let their eyes roam from their suitcases, from the moment they set the bags on the scales to the instant they disappear down the conveyer chute into the unknown below. In fact, most people continue to watch the closed doors of the chute for several seconds after their luggage descends beyond their vision, in the apparent hope that their concern will translate into diligence by the unseen baggage handlers below.

Having spent two summers loading and unloading baggage for several airlines, I cannot understand why the major companies don't institute several basic reforms. It can't be economics, because the changes would cost very little. In fact, the reforms I proposed in my (winning) science fair project would seem to generate considerably more revenue than they would cost. This would occur because one of the principal reasons people switch airlines is lost baggage. This is particularly true of the most heavily traveled routes, the trunk routes, which have the largest number of airlines offering identical fares, services, and schedules. (A new definition of chutzpah could be an airline that brags about its food.)

The major reason bags get lost is that airlines use either (a) a mechanical sorting system, where one ramp is dedicated to one flight; (b) an electro-optical sorting system where designated bags are routed automatically; or (c) a manual sorting system. None of these systems are foolproof. Early- or late-loaded bags foul up the first system. Baggage left on its side confuses the electro-optical approach. And human error accounts for the third system's problems.

None of the systems take into consideration a sad fact of life: there is little incentive for baggage handlers to spot mistakes or correct them. The combination of these two factors—the mechanical and the human—led to my proposed BASH (Baggage Automated System Handling) design.

There are three basic elements to my BASH proposal:

1. An electronic sorter virtually identical to those found in supermarkets that use universal product case (UPC) cash registers.

2. Individual identification stamps worn by each baggage handler on his thumb.

3. A system of financial incentives that reward baggage handlers for minimizing errors.

BASH works simply. Each piece of luggage has its own destination tag, just as it does today. In addition to the three-letter destination code, each tag would also have a UPC code that would be optically read by an electronic scanner. Bags would then be diverted to the proper flight's bin. What makes BASH different is that before a bag is finally placed on the plane or in the containerized rack, the individual loading the bag would stamp the tag with his identifying number. By taking the extra second to double check the bag's destination, errors could be minimized. As an added incentive, baggage handlers would receive monthly bonuses for the fewest lost bags.

BASH still has many bugs that need to be eliminated before widespread adoption is possible. But only by recognizing that the lowest-level, most boring and repetitious jobs are often responsible for a company's most widespread problems can we hope to improve productivity. Incentives, responsibility, and accountability are the basis for improvement. We really shouldn't be satisfied with an attitude best reflected in a friend's description of his summer job: "I work for XYZ airlines. I send people to London and their bags to Paris."

We can do better.

Math Teacher Recommendation

Jack is a fascinating contradiction. He is obviously very bright, inquisitive, and self-disciplined in those areas that truly interest him. He can also be downright lazy in subjects that do not. I have been lucky enough to teach him in two courses in which he has a strong interest: freshman algebra and junior year trigonometry-advanced algebra (an AP Course).

In both of the math courses Jack has grasped complex topics quickly, participated in class vigorously, and prepared his homework assignments diligently. He was a pleasure to teach, and frequently helped other students who were having trouble with the material.

What I found more interesting and promising about Jack was his interest in pursuing knowledge outside his homework. In the past few years Jack has won several school and regional science fairs. For each of these competitions, Jack has explored an area that is obviously very important to him: airplane design. (In fact, he is totally fascinated by airplanes. His doodlings are detailed designs, his summer jobs have been at the airport, and I have heard that he has taken dates to a deserted road near the airport to watch the 747s land just a few feet away. True, this might be the 1982 version of watching the submarine races.)

As I mentioned, Jack's science fair projects motivated him to seek my assistance in exploring lift coefficients and drag resistance calculations. This is fairly heavy going, yet Jack managed to grasp it sufficiently to put together a rather impressive airplane design project for these fairs.

Personally, Jack is a very nice kid. He is quick, funny, and clearly "one of the guys." If there is a late-night party after a winning lacrosse game, you can be sure he's part of it. (Though he probably spent most of the game warming the bench, he does try.) If there is mischief in the school—such as the principal's Volkswagen on the roof—the odds are pretty good Jack was a part of it, if not behind it.

Jack should flourish in college. His home life has been a bit strained since his mother died, and he'll probably need considerable financial aid. But he's worth it, and should prove a real contribution to any college he attends. I recommend him highly.

American History
Teacher
Recommendation

At first I was a bit surprised that Jack asked me to write a recommendation for him, and thought of dissuading him from it. Then I was intrigued and finally honored. Jack is one of the more creative and interesting people I have come across, and it took me more than a minute to recognize his motivation and logic in asking me.

Jack was my student during junior year American History, a course in which he did very little, and then only mediocre work. I have also known Jack in my capacity as faculty advisor to the Student Council, of which Jack was recently elected vice-president. In that forum I have watched Jack exercise truly impressive leadership qualities. His ideas were often adopted, his arguments usually persuasive, his energy and enthusiasm contagious.

But Jack's mediocre performance in American History was not simply the result of little self discipline or lack of interest. Jack's mother became terminally ill, quite suddenly, and died during his junior year. While this certainly has a strong emotional effect on Jack, there were few other severe dislocations associated with the loss. Jack did drop out of several sports to take care of his younger brother.

Following his mother's death Jack threw himself into his one true academic love: airplane design. I have little doubt Jack could have done well in my course; he certainly has the ability. I am inclined to think he might even choose to take history—and English, economics, and sociology—courses once he reaches college. But he will do so voluntarily, and at his own pace; not because someone tells him to. "Requirements" are not something Jack lets go unchallenged. He is a questioner.

It is with a true sense of excitement that I recommend Jack Lawrence for college. I think he is a fine young man, and one who will blossom in the right environment.

School Report—
Guidance Counselor

Jack is one of the more interesting students graduating from Lynbrook this year. His grades are decidedly mixed, board scores good, and extracurricular achievements really quite special.

The most impressive of these achievements is his performance at local, regional, and national science fairs. Jack loves airplanes and his ambition is to be an aeronautical engineer. Starting in his freshman year Jack began designing airplanes. He read college texts, talked to professionals in the field, and even took a job as a busboy in a local restaurant in order to pay for flying lessons. Recently he got his private pilot's license. He even worked at Kennedy Airport loading luggage and cleaning airplanes just to be around them.

It was this summer work experience that led to his junior year science project, the one that won the regional science fair and the honorable mention in the national competition. Jack's project involved designing and building a working model for a new luggage loading/unloading system for airlines. It was truly impressive.

One other characteristic about Jack that should be noted. He epitomizes the words "school spirit." He gets involved, becomes a leader, and is a truly nice kid. He is not shy, but he is well-mannered. At times he can be very convincing. Last year Jack wanted to take the Mechanical Drawing course usually offered as a technical subject to students who do not pursue academic or college-bound courses. Despite his having to overload his schedule, Jack was certain the course was important to his science fair projects and aeronautical design efforts. He took the course, did very well, and was right: his science fair drawings were very well done.

Jack will make an important contribution to any college he attends, and I recommend him highly, without reservation.

Interview Report

Jack is one of those energetic, interesting kids who may not be the best student, but whom you know immediately is bright and good to have around.

In the hour we spent together, he showed me he had read about the college and knew what he was looking for.

We talked about his science fair projects, about his lousy grades in Spanish and history, and his explanations of both were articulate and well-reasoned. I now know why I lose my baggage when I fly overseas. With regard to the mediocre grades, Jack is fairly mature about it. He made no excuses but said he really wanted to pursue the airplane design project: "A conscious choice; hopefully the right one."

Bottom line: I liked the kid. Genuine, fun, interesting.

Christine Ellis

Lincoln School
Providence, R.I.

Class Standing: Top quarter of 60-girl class (no actual class ranking)
SAT Scores: 530v/480m
Achievement Test Scores:
800 French
680 English
780 History

Grades

9th Grade
English	B+
French	B+
Algebra	B−
General Science	C
Latin	B−
Art	B

10th Grade
English	B
French	B+
Geometry	B−
Biology	B
European History	A−
Art	B

11th Grade
In France: Awarded full credit for Junior year (no grades)
Courses: French Literature
Math
Chemistry/Physics
French History

12th Grade
English
AP French
AP American History
Art

Parents

Father: John; Architect; Self-Employed
College: RISD
Mother: Frances; Teacher, Classical High School
College: RISD

Siblings

John, 26, Brown University
Alicia, 22, Kirkland College
Mason, 15, Moses Brown

Activities

President, HOPE (Helping Other People Everywhere; fresh., soph., sr.)
Judicial Board (soph., sr.)
Horseback Riding (fresh., soph., jr., sr.)

Work

Summers
Babysitting
32 hrs. per week
$500 per summer

School year
Babysitting
10 hrs. per week
$400 saved

Awards

AFS Claiborne Pell Award in American History

Degree program

A.B.
Art History or History

Career goal

Unknown

Essay

Cliques, those tightknit groups of seemingly similar people, are as common in France as they are in Rhode Island. As someone who never fit easily into the jock clique, the "with-it" clique, or any of a half-dozen others, I was looking forward to the more homogeneous lifestyle of a French public school. What I found surprised me. For not only were cliques present in my French high school, but the similarities to American cliques were startling, and my approach to dealing with them virtually identical in the two countries.

Perhaps my expectations about France were naive, but I really believed that the cultural heritage, the historical perspective, and the classical education would limit the tendency of cliques to form and flourish. I was wrong. There were "punk" cliques, "Americanized" cliques, snooty cliques, and about a half-dozen others. At first, several groups seemed to take pleasure in excluding the "visiting American" or "the celebrity." Others wanted me simply for the "prestige" of having the foreigner as a part of their crowd.

My French sister Nicole, while wonderful, wasn't much help. She was a leader of the "classical" group—a small number of girls who prided themselves on their familiarity with art, classical music, and literature. Not that they were particularly better read than the others; they just enjoyed showing it off a bit more. Because my interests were very similar, I was invited to join them.

The thought of limiting my experiences during my year abroad to this single clique, however comfortable, was disturbing. I couldn't turn down or snub my French sister, yet I didn't want to be constrained.

The first few weeks were understandably the most difficult. I was a bit scared, certainly disoriented, and more than a little worried about doing what was "right." At first I traveled everywhere with Nicole and her friends. I knew I was being categorized by those girls outside her group, but really didn't have much choice. But after about a month, I realized I wanted to know more, to see more, and to experience so much more that was outside my French sister Nicole's circle. I only hoped that my solution would prove as successful in France as it had in America.

At Lincoln, I have never been particularly comfortable in any one clique. Yet somehow I have managed to be friendly with many people from a variety of cliques. My approach has always been to be friendly with everyone, but never to "bad mouth" or say nasty things about anyone. That doesn't mean I don't like to gossip; I truly do. But I try never to say anything mean about anyone. Maybe that is why I have felt comfortable dealing with many people at school from many different cliques.

When I approached Nicole with my dilemma, I was scared. I didn't want to alienate her or myself, yet I did want to meet other people. I explained the problem, and proposed the solution. I told her how much I valued her friendship, but that I wanted to meet people outside her clique. I also told her how similar the situation was at my high school in Rhode Island. But there I had years to develop the trust and confidence of people; in France, everything was passing by too quickly.

Nicole was wonderful; she understood perfectly. I was free to come and go with her group as I wished, but I could spend time with others as well.

During the year I met dozens of interesting and not-so-interesting people. I made close friends, and spent time with people whose names I can barely recall today. But all in all, it was wonderful. And Nicole even made some new friends outside her clique herself.

History Teacher
Recommendation

Christine is one of the finest young ladies I have ever had the pleasure of teaching. She is bright, levelheaded, even tempered, and very, very mature. She is a serious young woman whose abilities exceed her grades or test scores, and it has been a pleasure to have her in my class.

Chris is very well read. Not only has she completed her assigned readings diligently, but she has often gone beyond what is required of her. She voluntarily reads the classics, from mythology to the romantics, and has that unique ability to make connections and parallels between the ages. It is a rare and welcome discipline. In addition, her participation in class, while vocal and forthcoming, never makes her

classmates feel ill prepared. Somehow she manages to bring out the best in them.

Interestingly, Chris doesn't do particularly well on tests. It seems to make little difference if the exams are in class or SATs—she doesn't respond well to the pressure. She gets nervous and, to use a common expression, chokes. This is particularly interesting because she responds very well to the pressures of reading assignments or qualitative expectations. Traditional tests, however, seem to frighten her.

In short, Christine is a marvelous young lady! Intelligent, self-disciplined, incredibly nice and respectful. I am sure she will do marvelously in college, and recommend her without reservation.

French Teacher
Recommendation

I have had the pleasure of teaching Christine in three classes encompassing two languages, French and Latin. She is without question the most talented French student I have ever taught, and a very fine young lady. She grasps languages with an enviable ability, and manages to speak French like a Parisian. She is most impressive.

During her junior year, Christine studied in France, having been selected to represent Lincoln in the AFS program. Living with a French family, she took all her courses in French, and managed to do credibly in all of them. The reports we received from her French family and the school's teachers and administrators can make us all proud. Christine was a marvelous ambassador.

Christine's personal qualities are even more impressive than her academic credentials. She is sweet and considerate, the type of person who goes out of her way to help others. She is a bit shy but very mature, with sound judgment and a fine sense of responsibility. She is, in short, a terrific young lady.

It is with the highest regard that I recommend Christine Ellis to you. She will grow, flourish, and add significantly to your community. Enjoy her as much as we have.

School Report— Guidance Counseler

Chris Ellis hasn't received the highest grades in her class at Lincoln, but she has earned the highest regard of her teachers and classmates. Chris is one of those bright young people who do not test well, but her contributions in and out of class far exceed her grades.

Chris represented Lincoln in France during her junior year abroad as an AFS exchange student. Apparently she was as highly thought of there as she is here. Her school work and personal deportment were of the highest caliber. She seems to have made quite a good impression abroad, one of which we can all be proud.

Christine's participation in school activities is characteristically substantive but low key. She serves on the judicial board— having been selected by her fellow students—because of her good sense and fairness. Her performance there has been rather impressive, arguing for constructive alternatives to misbehavior rather than mere punishment.

Christine is very highly regarded by the faculty and students at Lincoln, and should be considered for admission along with students with much higher grades and SATs. We recommend her highly and without reservation.

Interview Report

Rarely is one treated to as pleasant an hour as I had with Christine Ellis. She is bright, articulate, attractive, a touch shy, and very nice. There is a sweetness that radiates from the kid.

We talked about her studies in France, her lousy grades, movies, art, current events, even some rather complicated business topics she admits to only half understanding. It was an animated conversation: fun, intelligent, comfortable.

Christine's principal academic interest is art history, though she hopes to pursue French, English, some Italian, and history. She seems very excited by the thought of college, and well prepared for it. The reservations I have about her grades and board scores are mitigated by her obvious intelligence. She may not be summa cum laude or Phi Beta Kappa, but I like her.

Arthur Perkins

Shaker Heights High School

Shaker Heights, Ohio

Class Standing: 5/500
SAT Scores:
  650v/680m (Jan. jr. year)
  690v/710m (April jr. year)
  720v/740m (Sept. sr. year)
Achievement Test Scores:
  700 Math Level I
  720 Math Level II
  680 History
  710 History (sr. year)
  670 French
  690 French (sr. year)

Grades

9th Grade

English	A
French	B+
Math-Algebra	A
Science	A
History	A-

10th Grade

English	A
French	B+
Math-Geometry	A
Biology	A
World History	B+

11th Grade

English	A+
French	A
Math-Trigometry	A-
Chemistry	A
American History	A-

12th Grade

English
French
Math
Physics
History

Parents

Father: James, Attorney
College: Yale; Columbia Law
  School
Mother: Alice; Housewife
College: Bryn Mawr

Siblings

Elizabeth, 12

Activities

National Honor Society (soph., jr.,
  sr.)
Mathletes (soph., jr., sr.)
J.V. Wrestling (soph., jr.)
Harvard Summer School (soph.
  summer)

Work

Junior summer
Paralegal, father's law firm
Earned $2,000 for summer

Degree Program

Pre-law, History, Political Science

Career Goal

Law

Essay

The law has always held a fasci-
nation for me. As the son of an
attorney and someone who as-
pires to the bar himself, I was
very lucky to have worked in a
law firm as a paralegal last summer. Although my responsibilities were limited to support services, I was able to observe a wide
range of legal abilities and problems.

The most interesting aspect for me was litigation—actual trial work. For several weeks the participating attorneys met with prospective witnesses, preparing testimony. I was able to accompany these lawyers, and helped file the resulting depositions. The most important lesson I learned was that unlike television shows where the opposing lawyer elicits surprise confessions from hostile witnesses, the best legal preparation involves "no surprises." When a witness, either friendly or hostile, takes the stand, a good lawyer will know *everything* the witness is about to say.

My additional responsibilities at the firm included Xeroxing, cataloging, and running errands. I cannot pretend that I received enormous legal training, but I did learn how to use the law library. This alone made the experience worthwhile.

My desire to become an attorney is even more certain, and I look forward to college to help me in my pre-legal education.

Math Teacher Recommendation

Arthur is one of the brightest people in the class. He is very hard working, determined to succeed, and extremely self-disciplined. He is always prepared for class and quick to volunteer an answer. His grasp of the material is excellent.

With regard to his personal characteristics, Arthur is a polite young man. He is a bit of a loner who should mature nicely in a college environment.

I am sure he will do very well in college.

English Teacher Recommendation

Arthur is one of Shaker Heights' most able students. I have had him in two classes and he has excelled in each of them. Arthur's writing ability is precise, his understanding of composition structure, excellent. He reads every assignment diligently and is not shy about "showing his stuff." He is not afraid of competition.

Unfortunately, Arthur's ability and his attitude have made him somewhat of an "outsider" at Shaker. He is not quite arrogant, but he is not particularly tolerant of other students' weaknesses.

In many ways Arthur's problem—and it is not a terribly serious problem—has been his parents. They are very forceful, very successful people who have been very strict with Arthur. There is a very keen "success quotient" operative in the Perkins family. As a result, Arthur is reserved, almost aloof, and not one to participate in many school activities.

Arthur should do well in college. He is highly recommended.

School Report— Guidance Counselor

Arthur Perkins is one of the top students at Shaker High. His grades are consistently excellent, his board scores outstanding. As a sophomore he was selected as a member of the National Honor Society, and he has performed well as a member of the Mathletes.

Arthur's father is a member of the City Council, and his mother the president of the PTA. It is a truly exceptional family.

Arthur will do very well wherever he goes, and is recommended without reservation.

Follow-up telephone call with Guidance Counselor

Guidance counselor, Mr. Carpenter, says Arthur is very smart but too much like the father: a pushy know-it-all. Arrogant, not very nice. The kid took the SATs three times, just to make sure his scores broke 700 on each exam. Arthur has few friends in school, but Carpenter is convinced the problem is 75 percent the parents and only 25 percent Arthur. But, he stresses, Arthur is *very* bright. He thinks that if we can get him away from the parents he will mature and grow nicely.

Interview Report

Obviously a bright kid; perhaps a little driven. We talked about the law—he wants to be an attorney like the father, who hovered outside the room like a vulture. Has done his homework about the college, but other than wanting to pursue the law, is not sure what he wants to study. Seemed pretty open to suggestions. When asked what his favorite book was, his eyes gleamed and he said, "Robert Caro's *The Power Broker*, the study of Robert Moses." The kid actually seemed to have read all 1,000 pages; I know because I barely got through the *New Yorker* excerpts. Not a bad kid, but a little too controlled, almost intense. Bright, but I'm not sure I'd want him dating my little sister.

David P. Mannheimer

Lincoln High School
Santa Monica, CA

Class Standing: 9/656
SAT Scores:
560v/780m (April jr.. year)
550v/750m (Oct. sr. year)
Achievement Test Scores:
750 Math I
800 Math II
550 Biology
720 Chemistry
500 Spanish

Grades

9th Grade
English	90
German	90
Intermediate Algebra, Honors	97
Biology, Honors	89
Social Studies	91

10th Grade
English	90
German	83
Math 10, Honors	94
Chemistry, Honors	95
World History	89

11th Grade
English	89
German	85
Math 12, Calculus, Honors	98
Physics, Honors	96
American History	88

12th Grade (first semester)
English	91
Calculus, UCLA	A
A.P. Physics 2	91
Computer Science, UCLA	A
Statistics	92

Parents

Father: Fred; Engineer, Hughes
  Aircraft
College: U.C., Berkeley, B. Sc.
Mother: Daisy, Housewife
College: UCLA, did not graduate

Siblings

Judy, 16

Activities

Computer Club (jr., sr.; treasurer,
  sr.)
Chess Club (jr., sr.)
Dungeons & Dragons (fresh.,
  soph.)
Model Airplanes (fresh., soph.)

Work

Summer
Computer Programmer
City of Santa Monica
30 hrs. per week
Earned $2,500

Awards

National Merit Semifinalist
N.S.F. Scholarship for summer
  program
State Math Competition Runner-
  up

Degree Program

Engineering/Computer Science

Career Goal

To own my own computer firm

Essay

One of the most important experiences that I have had is winning runner-up status in the State Mathematics Competition for high school students. I had the chance to compare my own abilities in math with some of the other students from California who also have a great aptitude in the subject. It was competition at its best.

Mathematics is probably the most important thing in my life right now. There is something definite and recognizable in figures. People are so indefinite, whenever they are together you never really know what they are thinking, no matter what they say. But the beauty of math and computers, as my father says, is that they are predictable. Equations and computer programs don't make mistakes, people do. When I figure out the solution to a problem or formulate a new program in the computer, I get a sense of accomplishment I do not feel in anything else. That is why someday I would like to have my own company. It would manufacture computers or video games. That is why I want to go to college, so I can get the knowledge I need to start my company. I would like to take some business courses also so I would be prepared that way.

School Report— Guidance Counselor

David is an old-fashioned kind of student we don't see very often these days. He has a fine mind, especially in mathematics and science, and puts it to good use in those areas. Unlike so many other of our kids, he is very cooperative, takes a great interest in his classes and studies, and isn't at all rowdy. I can't imagine that he does anything unwholesome. This attitude stems in part from his parents, who are conservative and very pro-education.

Because he is so different from the typical student today, David sticks to himself and might be described as a loner. I know that he would like to know more of his peers, but the fact that he is driven to excel in class and takes instruction well makes it difficult for him to be accepted by his contemporaries. Part of this may be because he is naturally shy and not terribly verbal.

David's real brilliance is in math, and if you're looking for a real computer and math whiz, he's your man. He is already taking college courses in the UCLA Honors Program in those areas, and I expect that he will do better than many of the full-time students there. I can imagine him going on to a first-class career in math, computers, or engineering. He's quiet and will stay in the background, but is a first-rate intellect in his areas of strength.

Math Teacher
Recommendation

David is a brilliant (in math), intellectual, mature, thorough kind of student. He takes instruction very well and isn't afraid to do extra work. He has an extraordinary mind for mathematics and should be very successful in that field. He is perhaps among the top five math students I have had in 10 years of teaching.

Personally, David is what you would call a "loner." He's not the type to make a lot of friends, I suppose some kids would call him a "nerd." But he is a teacher's dream. These days the kid or kids who takes class seriously is rare, which is why he probably isn't well-accepted by his peers. In college some of this problem will disappear, I can recommend him highly for college.

Physics Teacher
Recommendation

David is one of the best students I have had in physics. He took to the subject like a duck to water and did not hesitate to do extra work whenever it was possible. His comprehension of physical concepts is almost limitless, and his knack for theoretical discussion is good too. In every way, a first class if not original mind.

David is not the most popular kid in school because he is such a good student. His zealousness in pursuing his studies tends to turn off other students, and he isn't very helpful to other less able students in the class. They feel he "lords it over them," demonstrating his knowledge. In this sense he is a bit immature, but really is likable once you get past the serious facade. I think that once he is in a more accepting environment, with his own kind, he'll do better socially. Most of the time outside class he spends with his home computer. He's showed me some very interesting programs he's thought up.

I feel that David will be a tremendous intellectual addition to any campus. He won't be a BMOC, but might wind up winning the Nobel Prize someday.

Interview Report

David seemed reluctant to come to his interview, and in fact canceled the first appointment we had. When he showed up, I saw why; he's the sort of kid we used to call a "nerd" in our day. He had nothing to say for himself, at first, but when he finally opened up, it was about computers. He seems to have a real talent for math and computers; he did a National Science Foundation Program in it out at Cal Tech this summer. And he had a job last year programming computers for the Santa Monica City Hall. But when it came to out-of-class activities, the picture was sparse—Chess Club and Dungeons & Dragons, and some model airplane construction after junior high. David was withdrawn throughout our session and getting answers out of him was tough. That tendency runs in the family. I met David's father, who picked him up after our talk. Mr. Mannheimer is an engineer, too, and has all the precise little habits and abrupt manner you associate with the stereotype. I'm sure David has a home computer and works out interesting programs with Dad. I'm not trying to be snide; it's just that David was such a cipher. I can't imagine that he'll contribute much to campus life, though he might open up a little and become a real person in the more open environment of college. (I have a feeling he hasn't many friends.) If you're looking for a real math/computer whiz, David fits the bill. But I really think he'd be better off and happier at a place like MIT or Cal Tech.

Patrick Michael Mahoney

Hartwick High School
Hartwick, Iowa

Class Standing: 3/175
SAT Scores: 430v/470m (April jr. year)
Achievement Test Scores:
   470 English
   510 Math I
   470 American History

Grades

9th Grade
English	C
French	C –
Algebra 1, Honors	B
General Science	B
Social Studies	B

10th Grade
English	B
French	C –
Geometry, Honors	B –
Health	A
European History, Honors	B

11th Grade
English, Honors	C +
Algebra 2, Honors	B –
Biology	B –
American History	B

12th Grade (first semester)
English, Honors	B –
Trigonometry, Honors	B
Chemistry, Honors	A –
20th Century History	A –

Parents

Father: Michael; County Surveyor
(No college)

Mother: Betty; Homemaker;
  Prize Baker
(No college)

Siblings

Louise, 13
Ted, 10

Work

Hartwick City Gazette
Newspaper delivery (many
  years)
10–15 hrs. per week

Mr. Woody Franklin
Farm hand (summers since '79)
40 or more hrs. per week
Earned $500

Activities

Basketball (fresh, soph., jr., sr.)
Lettermen (soph., jr., sr.)
Wrestling (fresh., soph.)
4-H Club (fresh., soph., jr.)

Awards

National Honor Society, Vice
  President
All-State Basketball

Degree Program

American History or Political
  Science

Career Goal

Politics or law

Essay

I would like to discuss an issue
that is of personal *and* local concern to me. This is the U. S. Government grain embargo. I am
happy that President Reagan recently changed his position. Now
he will allow farmers to sell their
wheat and other grains to the Soviet Union. A grain embargo is
unfair because it singles out
farmers. Pepsi-Cola has a factory
in Russia. Other industries sell to
the Russians. Why should farmers be the only ones prohibited
from selling to the Soviet Union?

Grain is not a strategic product. The Russians have to pur-
chase it with hard cash. This
means that they cannot buy other
products with that cash because
they are spending it to feed their
people. If we do not sell grain to
them they will just buy it from
someone else. My feeling is,
therefore, that the president was
right to lift the embargo. Farmers should not be the only Americans who have to sacrifice for the
national security.

Math Teacher Recommendation

Patrick is a hard-working, self-di-
rected student. He is not the most
brilliant student I have en-
countered in my career (seven
years), but he is among the hardest working. I find him to be very
mature, especially in the way he
approaches setbacks and other
problems. At first in my course
this year he had difficulties in understanding some of the material
we covered. Rather than letting
the whole thing get him down, he
buckled down and really worked
hard, even coming to me for extra help. Now he is doing very
good work and is once again near
the top of the class. As a student
he is not overly creative, but always comes through in the pinch.

What might differentiate Patrick from other students is not only his size and athletic ability. It is his motivation and attitude, which are always top-notch.

History Department
Chairman
Recommendation

Patrick is not an intellectual, but he works extremely hard. He is highly motivated, mature, and his self-respect urges him to do as well as he can in every situation. He is fairly creative in his approach to History. I cannot speak to his originality since we stick to basics in my class. Patrick is not a student leader per se, but spends much time outside of class in athletics. By working hard at his studies as well as sports, he sets a good example for the rest of the school. He is popular with other students and faculty. He is also honest, enthusiastic, and participates avidly in anything that attracts him. Being a rural high school, we don't send many students to private colleges, or even state colleges. College will be a challenge for Pat. He always does well in the clutch, but I have to say that I wonder how well he will do against other students who have had a stronger college preparatory background.

School Report—
Guidance Counselor

Patrick is a top-notch young person with lots of potential. Not only is he quite a basketball player; he has succeeded in other fields as well. As a student he has a fine record and is very able at math. On a personal level Patrick is well-liked by teachers and students, due to his achievements and outgoing nature.

One of Patrick's best qualities is his sense of responsibility and duty. He is extremely hard-working, tenacious, and unwilling to let problems get the best of him. Last year he came to me at the start of the term asking to drop from the Honors class to a lower level of English. (The class was studying some very difficult prose and poetry.) I impressed on him the importance of taking Honors classes if he wanted to go to college. He came back a few weeks later to tell me that he had sought extra help, concentrated, and was doing fine. This is a good example of his persistence and enterprise.

Hartwick is a small town and Patrick is well-known here. He wants to achieve and do his best at all he can, and his parents are rightfully quite proud of him. He's not perfect, but his persistence and hard work should guarantee that he is a success at college— even at a competitive school like yours. He deserves a chance and I hope you give it to him.

Patrick's family gets along financially (his father is a county official) but is far from wealthy. He will need financial assistance. I'm sure, though, that he'll pitch in, since when he is not studying or playing ball he is usually working delivering papers in the summer for a farmer outside of town.

Athletic Rating Form

Coach's comment
A local alumnus who once played

for me has seen him play many times. Patrick and I have talked on the telephone every week since October.

Patrick is a very good player. He has been coached poorly so far, but has almost limitless potential. He may even be a pro prospect.
Rating of ability (1–10; 10 high): 9+

Interview Report

I had a hard time getting in touch with Patrick. Finally after a few false starts we got together. Pat is quite a basketball player and we had a good conversation about this. He was recently voted League MVP. He has other interests also, many related to athletics. Personally, he was likable and mature. I got the feeling that he is quite ambitious and wants success, yet he isn't quite as good a student as other applicants I have seen. His academic strengths seem to be in math and science rather than "soft" subjects. Still, I think that despite the challenge of college work, he is the sort of person who will do satisfactorily in class. If the basketball coach really needs him, you should give him a chance. You won't find many midwestern kids from farm towns in your applicant group this year, I think.

The College Decisions

The comments below are summaries of those made by the following people, and sometimes reflect comments made by other admission officers at the colleges. Where the comments are not verbatim, they summarize the substance of what was said.

Brown: James H. Rogers, Director of Admission

Carleton: Richard Steele, Dean of Admissions

Columbia: James McMenamin, Director of Admissions

University of Michigan: Cliff Sjogren, Director of Admission

University of North Carolina at Chapel Hill: Richard Cashwell, Director Undergraduate Admission

Notre Dame: Kevin Rooney, Assistant Director of Admissions

Pomona: R. Fred Zucker, Dean of Admissions

Jack Lawrence

Brown. An interesting kid, but there's a problem: Brown doesn't offer a degree in Aerospace Engineering. In addition, the Math II Achievement test score is low for someone so strong in math. The essay was amusing, but we'd be concerned about accepting a person so committed to a field not offered by the college. We might accept Jack and send him a letter explaining that Aerospace Engineering is not a formal major offered at Brown, but that an independent major could be devised to fulfill some of his interests.

(Note: The real "Jack Lawrence" never applied to Brown during his high school senior year because he didn't know about the independent major option, but more importantly because he didn't think he would get in. Ultimately he transferred to Brown, switched majors, and graduated.)

Carleton. Jack's application generated considerable discussion. Mixed record with flair, creativity; inconsistent grades. Some question whether he really wants liberal arts and engineering, and whether he'd be willing to take distribution requirements. The sort of person Carleton can really do a lot for. A risk of sorts, but one of the profs would enjoy bringing him along. Accept.

(Note: The Dean's concern about Jack's willingness to take distribution requirements was right on target. It was Jack's unhappiness about distribution requirements that led to his transfer to Brown, which has no distribution requirements.)

Columbia. An interesting case: studied aeronautical design; private pilot's license, leader in school, science fair winner, athlete, well written, funny essay. Wish his academic record was stronger. A good kid but deny.

University of Michigan. An inconsistent record; nothing outstanding. Strong extracurricu-

lars, but not very impressed with the personal statement's originality. Delay for grades, then probably postpone; in sum: deny. We would probably accept him into LS & A (liberal arts), but his grades are too low for engineering.

(Note: The real "Jack Lawrence" applied to Michigan in 1969 and was accepted. Dean Sjorgren noted that engineering is a stronger program today, and that its admission standards are tougher. Interestingly, in 1969, LS & A was the stronger program of the two, and Jack would have been rejected had he applied to it.)

University of North Carolina. His grades simply aren't strong enough and there was an error in his essay. Deny.

Notre Dame. A considerable amount of disagreement about this case. Good academic potential, but performance varied from course to course. The committee enjoyed his essay—particularly those who do a lot of flying—and the acronym BASH. One small factor is that Jack is Jewish, and not many Jewish students apply to Notre Dame. The few who have attended Notre Dame seem to have made real personal contributions to the place, as well as doing very well academically. Jack was one of the 10 to 15 percent of applicants who triggered a full committee review. Accept.

(Note: Notre Dame asks the religion of its applicants.)

Pomona. Some concern about him being lazy, and his interest in an engineering program that Pomona doesn't offer. No special interests that make him fall into a specific category in the committee, but his personal appeal—and decent academics—would result in an acceptance.

Christine Ellis

Brown. There is strong personal appeal here, but unfortunately, the community and school involvement don't sufficiently offset her tests and grades. Her Achievements appear unrealistic in view of her very low SAT's, and we would phone the school to find out why. Unless she were a "local big deal", Brown would not accept her.

(Note: The real "Christine Ellis" actually applied to Brown in 1972 with the same record shown. At that time she was wait listed and then accepted. The difference? Since 1972, the number of applicants to Brown has almost doubled. P.S. She attended and graduated from Brown.)

Carleton. Mature, level-headed, and well-respected. A really big heart. She hungers for growth, but can she take the pressure of college? She'd be a great dorm person. Carleton will be good for her. Admit.

Columbia. She obviously makes an impression on those who know her well: a real humanist. Sensitive, somewhat shy, but forthright. Grades O.K. but poor SATs. A wait list, but it hangs on her senior year performance and the overall competitive picture.

University of Michigan. Disappointing SATs but impressive achievements. Her personal statement is very good and she has taken a very demanding course load. And the quality of her school helps her case. Admit.

University of North Carolina. Low grades, no significant extracurricular involvement. Deny.

Notre Dame. Her academics were just not strong enough, and we're not that interested in the France experience. We have lots of people who have been abroad. There just isn't anything there to allow us to take her. One other factor: we have room on campus only for about 500 women (compared to 1,200 men) a year. She would just be buried in the applicant pool. Deny.

Pomona. One of those rare altruistic people who everybody responds to very positively. Good essay, but not a strong candidate academically. But because of her personal qualities, she deserves a second look by the committee. Wait list, but a probable deny.

Arthur Perkins

Brown. This is a kid we see a great deal of, a typical 5 over 2—bright academically, but without a lot going for him on the personal side. He would be denied.

Carleton. Certainly he could do the work here, but there are flags out: arrogant, driven. It will be good for him to get away from his parents; a "missionary" case. Kids who are at all inclined towards arrogance get brought up short here in a hurry. Probably not a bad kid. Admit.

Columbia. A classic case: a bright kid who deserves a top-notch school, but who is not very active in the community; who's somewhat pushy, narrow, and predictable. He's not only pre-law, he's pre-trial lawyer! The warning signs are out; he needs to be humanized. Columbia can do something for him. Accept.

University of Michigan. A super-tester with poor recommendations who's pushy. We don't really care about the arrogance; most Nobel Prize winners are and this kid has enormous potential. There is very little a counselor could say to keep us from admitting him. We have no hesitation in accepting him.

University of North Carolina. We'll accept him, but we're not too happy about it. His activities are not very impressive.

Notre Dame. While there may be a heavy amount of parental pressure, it could be overcome as he matures in college. For one reason or another we have an incredibly large number of really nice personalities on campus, so an arrogant type doesn't faze us too much; the rough edges will be rounded off. There is so much academic talent there, he might end up being a great lawyer someday. We'll accept him.

Pomona. It's hard to decide about him; there are so many negatives. And the counselor's phone call is a problem. It's probably true that his parents have created a lot of the problems he seems to have. He won't get in on the first cut; we'll wait list him, and he's a possible admit.

David Mannheimer

Brown. This kid would have to have beaten up little old ladies, to get the personal qualities marks he did on the recommendations. Well-balanced academically, but seemingly too much of a loner for Brown to take him. Deny.

(Note: Jim Rogers felt that this case study was exaggerated and unrealistic.)

Carleton. Good grades and board scores, but a loner, narrow, immature. Not very active, and an unimpressive essay. He may bloom here, but who'd want to room with him? He'd probably be better off elsewhere. Wait list.

Columbia. David wants predictability and sees beauty in math and computers. He's not so sure about people. Activities are not focused, and he's a loner. Not someone to be excited about despite math and science talents. Deny.

University of Michigan. Very impressed with this kid. Good, strong grades and SATs. Well defined personal goals, and we'd like 100 kids like him. With regard to the negative alumnus interview: we'd encourage the alumnus not to do any more interviews for us. Accept.

University of North Carolina. No significant leadership or extracurricular activity. Wait list.

Notre Dame. We reacted very strongly and positively. (There are no interviews in our process, so the negative alumnus comments should be discounted.) David would probably be offered some sort of academic merit scholarship. Accept.

Pomona. He is perhaps the prototypical nerd. We are somewhat concerned about the alumnus interview, the matter-of-fact, not-at-all-compelling personal essay. David is not the kind of guy you'd want to sit next to on a long plane ride. But there was nothing in the folder that was *that* negative. He could actually make a real contribution as a scientist or mathematician. Accept.

Patrick Mahoney

Brown. It depends on the depth chart—and he seems to be at the very top. Academically he's not as strong as some of the other athletes Brown and the rest of the Ivy League see. Since he was at the very top of the coach's list, he'd probably be accepted. Otherwise the prospects wouldn't be good for his admission, despite his small town background.

Carleton. A nice kid with a good attitude, but Carleton will be a real challenge to him. The big question: can he succeed academically here and still play basketball? He would really help the team. A sappy essay, but we like his persistence, and he seems very "coachable." In sum, we'd be doing him a disservice both athletically and scholastically. A small college won't give him the experience and exposure he needs for pro ball. And he might not make it academically. Deny.

Columbia. As our alumnus interviewer said, we don't see many like him at Columbia: midwestern farmer. Good athlete, nice kid. What else can we ask someone to do in one's own environment? True his tests are low, but I would bet on his personal strengths to get him through our demands. I'm in his corner. Admit.

University of Michigan. Good class rank, low SATs, respectable achievements. Good, strong recommendations. A little concerned about his personal statement. A good kid, but Michigan may be too tough for him. If the coach is really high on him, we could ask Patrick to take the ACTs, hope he does well, and discuss the possibility of the Education school option with him. We would delay for senior grades then postpone; i.e., wait list then deny.

University of North Carolina. Unless he is an incredible athlete, deny.

Notre Dame. A reasonably good curriculum and grades for a small-town kid. The SATs aren't really a major concern. The coach's interest in Patrick qualifies him for a grant-in-aid. In an average year about three or four grants-in-aid are awarded for men's basketball, and about the same number for women's. These are independent of need, and for basketball are generally a full ride. Accept.

Pomona. Patrick's ability to compete in a selective college atmosphere doesn't bother us very much. We have found that students who do well in high school almost anywhere will continue to do well in college. Although his SAT scores are low, they're not disastrously low. And his achievements indicate the ability to do the level of work necessary to keep him in school. His basketball prowess would *not* lead to his being admitted outright. The geographical factor would be a consideration—accept.

A Final Note

The "applications" presented here are only five among hundreds of thousands received by selective colleges every year. They were formulated to illustrate certain "dilemmas" to which admission officers must typically react. You should not view them as *summarizing* in any way the admission decisions at the colleges involved. However, this chapter should provide some insights into the concerns that admission officers have when they evaluate an application—insights that you can put to use as you complete your own application.

Summer Programs for High School Students

The following is a partial listing of summer programs. Remember that not every program is conducted every year, so it is best to check. In addition, competition is usually rather intense, and it sometimes helps to apply early in the year.

Academy of Art College
540 Powell Street
San Francisco, CA 94108
General art courses

American Field Service
313 East 43rd Street
New York, NY 10017
Study abroad

American Institute of
   Foreign Study
102 Greenwich Avenue
Greenwich, CT 06830
*4 week travel/study,
summer abroad*

Amherst Summer Session
Amherst, MA 01002
For able students who have completed their junior year

Andover Summer Session
See Phillips Academy

Barat College
Lake Forest, IL 60045
*Psychology, theatre, music,
religion*

Berklee College of Music
1140 Boylston Street
Boston, MA 92215
General music classes

Brigham Young University
C-356 ASB
Provo, UT 84601
*General program and sports
camps for high school graduates.*

Carnegie-Mellon University
5000 Forbes Avenue
Pittsburgh, PA 15213
*Fine arts, math, writing, and
philosophy*

Choate-Rosemary Hall School
% Mr. W. Wingerd
Box 50, Summer Session
Wallingford, CT 06492
*Enrichment and basic high school
courses*

Career Discovery at Harvard
Harvard University
20 Garden Street
Cambridge, MA 02138
*Introduction to college life and
living*

Colgate University
Hamilton, NY 11346
A.P. program for juniors

Cornell University
Ithaca, NY 14853
A.P. program for juniors

Experiment in International
   Living
Admissions Director
E. I. L.
Brattleboro, VT 95301
Summer abroad, partial scholarships

Catlin Gabel Summer Theatre
8825 S.W. Barnes Rd.
Portland, OR 97225
Complete study of production plus performing

George Washington University
Washington, DC 20052
For math and English honor students

Georgetown University
Washington, DC 20057
General studies for able students

Harvard University Summer
   Session
Cambridge, MA 02138
Academically able students in 10th and 11th grades

Israel Summer programs
Jewish Federation Council
   of Los Angeles
6505 Wilshire Boulevard
Los Angeles, CA 90048
Summer study and tour programs

Menlo College
Director of Admissions
Menlo Park, CA 94025

Program for juniors and seniors only

New Dimensions School
9250 W. Olympic Blvd.
Beverly Hills, CA 90212
College preparatory school

Northwestern University
Evanston, Illinois 60201
Summer high school music program and national high school institute

Occidental College
1600 Campus Road
Los Angeles, CA 90041
Summer term in Wash., D.C. or general courses in L.A.

Phillips Andover Academy
Andover, MA 19810
For able students grades 10–12

Phillips Exeter Academy
Exeter, NH 03833
English and science grades 9–12

Punahou School
Mr. M. Dougherty
Assistant Director
5010 Stephora
Covina, CA 91724
All high school students

Skidmore College
Saratoga Springs, NY 12866
College level programs for high school students

Stanford University
Office of Admissions
Palo Alto, CA 94305
For able students grades 10–12

Thatcher School
Ojai, California 93023
Summer science program

University of California
Berkeley, CA
Summer program

University of California
Davis, CA 95616
Summer workshop scholarship in agricultural sciences for students completing junior year

University of California
Santa Cruz, CA 94720
Summer language institute

University of North Colorado
Greeley, CO 80639
General summer program

University of Redlands
Director of Summer Session
Redlands, CA 92373
General program for high school grads

University of Southern California
University Park
Los Angeles, CA 90007
High school honor students entering 12th grade—radio and TV and continuing education

Wellesley College
124 High Rock Lane
Westwood, MA 02090
Exploration summer program

Westlake School
Summer program
700 N. Faring Road
Los Angeles, CA 90024
Grades 4–12 general program

Youth for Understanding
2015 Washtenaw Avenue
Ann Arbor, MI 48104
Student exchange programs in Europe. Scholarships available

Special Studies

Fernald at UCLA
Dept. of Psychology
UCLA
Los Angeles, CA 90024
213-825-2140
For learning problems and remedial programs

Outdoor Studies

Biking Tours
Blyth & Co.
93 Bloor Street W.
Toronto M5S 1M1

California Conservation Corps.
1530 Capital Ave.
Sacramento, CA 95814
California residents. Work in California forests, wildlife, and water areas

California Mountaineering &
Technical Rock Climbing School
P.O. Box 1099
Joshua Tree, CA 92252
All facets of climbing

Earthwatch
68 Leonard Street, Box 127
Belmont, MA 02178
Research expedition in U.S., Europe and Mid-East

Seacamp Association
Route 1 Box 170
Big Pine Key, FL 33045
Marine science program for ages 12–17 years

Educational Consultants

The Independent Educational Counselors Association (IECA) is a non-profit professional organization. Its members specialize in college-bound counseling, placement and matching.

For a list of educational consultants who are members of the IECA, contact them at: IECA, Cove Road, P.O. Box 125, Forestdale, Massachusetts 02644, (617) 447-2127.

Books on Financial Aid

Octameron Associates publishes a very good series of "college money" booklets. They are straightforward, aggressive, and amusing to read:

Don't Miss Out; general information on financial aid: $4.00
The A's & B's: Your Guide to Academic Scholarships; information on merit scholarships. $4.00
College Grants from Uncle Sam. $2.00
Colleges Loans from Uncle Sam. $2.00
Earn & Learn. $3.00
Financial Aid Officers: What They Do to You and for You. $2.50
Octameron also offers an aid update service to supplement these books. Include $0.75 per book for shipping. Write: Octameron Associates, P.O. Box 3437, Alexandria, VA 22302.

How to Beat the High Cost of Learning, by Leo L. Kornfeld, G. M. Siegel and W. L. Siegel. New York: Rawson, Wade Publishers, Inc., 1981. Provides much information, especially on federal aid programs. $7.95

Financial Aids Catalogue for Higher Education, Oreon Keeslar, Editor. Dubuque: William C. Brown Publishers, 1983. This volume has descriptions of over 4,000 scholarship programs, ranging from well-known to extremely esoteric. It includes a checklist of categories for you to consider when looking for aid. Order from the publisher at 2460 Kerper Boulevard, P.O. Box 539, Dubuque, Iowa 52004-0539. $28.95

Financial Aid for College-Bound Athletes, by Marlene and Dr. Stephen H. Lazar. New York: Arco Publishing, 1982. Contains detailed information for would-be student-athletes. $8.95 paperback

The Student Guide: Five Federal Financial Aid Programs, U.S. Government Printing Office, Washington, D.C., 1985. Information on Uncle Sam's main programs. Write to Department of Education, 400 Maryland Avenue, S.W., Room 1059, Washington, D.C. 20202. Free

Need a Lift?, The American Legion, Indianapolis. Source listings of scholarship and loan information, with special attention to programs for veterans and their children. Write to American Legion, P.O. Box 1055, Indianapolis, Indiana 46206. $1.00

The College Blue Book: Scholarships, Fellowships, Grants and Loans, Nineteenth Edition, New York: Macmillan Publishing, 1983. This is a library volume listing a variety of assistance programs.

Lovejoy's Guide to Financial Aid, by Robert Leider. New York: Monarch Press, 1985. A very good and lucidly written general guide by the author of the Octameron series. $9.95

Guaranteed Student Loans and State Student Aid*

The following is a list of sources of information.

Alabama
Alabama Commission on Higher Education
1 Court Square, Suite 221
Montgomery, AL 36197
(205) 832-3790
GSL and State Aid

Alaska
Alaska Commission On Postsecondary Education
400 Willoughby Avenue
Pouch FP
Juneau, AK 99801
(907) 465-2962

Arizona
GSL: Arizona Educational Loan Program

301 East Virginia Avenue
Phoenix, AZ 85004
(602) 252-5793

State Aid: Arizona Commission for Postsecondary Education
1937 West Jefferson
Phoenix, AZ 85009
(602) 255-3109

Arkansas
GSL: Student Loan Guarantee Foundations of Arkansas
1515 West Seventh Street, Suite 515
Little Rock, AR 72202
(501) 371-2634

State Aid: Department of Higher Education
1301 West Seventh Street
Little Rock, AR 72201
(501) 371-1441, Ext. 56

California
California Student Aid Commission
1410 Fifth Street
Sacramento, CA 95814
GSL: (916) 323-0435
State Aid: (916) 445-0880

Colorado
GSL: Colorado Guaranteed Student Loan Program
1990 Grant, Suite 500
Northglenn, CO 80233
(303) 866-2748

State Aid: Colorado Commission on Higher Education
1300 Broadway, 2nd Floor
Denver, CO 80203
(303) 866-2748

Connecticut
GSL: Connecticut Student Loan Foundation
25 Pratt Street

*From *The Student Guide—Five Federal Financial Aid Programs*, 1985–86. Government Printing Office, Publication no. E-81-15001.

Hartford, CT 06103
(203) 547-1510

State Aid: Connecticut Board of
Higher Education
61 Woodland Street
Hartford, CT 06105
(203) 566-2618

Delaware
GSL: Delaware Higher Education Loan Program
c/o Brandywine College
P.O. Box 7139
Wilmington, DE 19803
(302) 478-3000 Ext. 210

State Aid: Delaware Postsecondary Education Commission
Carvel State Office Building
820 North French Street
Wilmington, DE 19801
(302) 571-3240

District of Columbia
GSL: Higher Education Assistance Foundation Higher Education Loan Program (HELP) of
D.C., Inc.
1030 Fifteenth Street, N.W.
Suite 1050
Washington, DC 20005
(202) 289-4500

State Aid: Office of Post-
Secondary Research and Assistance
D.C. Dept. of Human Services
1331 H Street, N.W., Suite 600
Washington, DC 20005
(202) 727-3688

Florida
Florida Student Financial Assis-
tance Commission
Knott Building
Tallahassee, FL 32301
GSL: (904) 488-8093
Student Aid: (904) 488-6181

Georgia
Georgia Student Finance Com
mission
9 La Vista Perimeter Park
2082 E. Exchange Place
Suite 200
Tucker, GA 30084
GSL: (404) 493-5468
State Aid: (404) 493-5444

Hawaii
GSL: Hawaii Education Loan
Program
1314 South King Street, Suite
962
Honolulu, HI 96814
(808) 536-3731

State Aid: State Postsecondary
Education Commission
124F Bachman Hall, University
of Hawaii
2444 Dole Street
Honolulu, HI 96822
(808) 948-6862

Idaho
GSL: Student Loan Fund of
Idaho, Inc.
Processing Center
P.O. Box 730
Fruitland, ID 83619
(208) 452-4058

State Aid: Office of State Board
of Education
650 West State Street, Room 307
Boise, ID 83720
(208) 334-2270

Illinois
GSL: Illinois Guaranteed Loan
Program
102 Wilmot Road
Deerfield, IL 60015
(312) 948-8550

State Aid: Illinois State Scholarship Commission

102 Wilmot Road
Deerfield, IL 60015
(312) 948-8550

Indiana

State Student Assistance Commission of Indiana
964 North Pennsylvania Avenue
Indianapolis, IN 46204
GSL: (317) 236-2366
State Aid: (317) 232-2351

Iowa

Iowa College Aid Commission
201 Jewett Building
9th and Grand
Des Moines, IA 50309
GSL: (515) 281-8537
State Aid: (515) 281-3501

Kansas

GSL: Higher Education Assistance Foundation
34 Corporate Woods
10950 Grand View Drive
Overland Park, KS 66210
(913) 648-4255

State Aid: Board of Regents—
State of Kansas
1416 Merchants National Bank
Topeka, KS 66612
(913) 296-3421

Kentucky

Kentucky Higher Education Assistance Authority
1050 U.S. 127 South
West Frankfort Office Complex
Frankfort, KY 40601
(502) 564-7990
GSL and State Aid

Louisiana

Governor's Special Commission on Education Services
4637 Jamestown Street
P.O. Box 44127
Baton Rouge, LA 70804

(504) 925-3630
GSL and State Aid

Maine

State Department of Educational and Cultural Services
Division of Higher Education Services
State House Station 23
Augusta, ME 04333
(207) 289-2183

Maryland

GSL: Maryland Higher Education Loan Corporation
2100 Guilford Avenue
Baltimore, MD 21218
(301) 659-6555

State Aid: Maryland State Scholarship Board
2100 Guilford Avenue
Baltimore, MD 21218
(301) 659-6420

Massachussetts

GSL: Massachusetts Higher Education Assistance Corporation
330 Stuart Street
Boston, MA 02116
(617) 426-9796

State Aid: Massachusetts Board of Regents of Higher Education
330 Stuart Street
Boston, MA 02116
(617) 727-9420

Michigan

GSL: Michigan Department of Education
Guaranteed Student Loan Program
Box 30047
Lansing, MI 48909
(517) 373-0760

State Aid: Michigan Department of Education

P.O. Box 3008
Lansing, MI 48909
(517) 373-3394

Minnesota

GSL: Higher Education Assistance Foundation
1600 American National Bank Building
Fifth and Minnesota Streets
St. Paul, MN 55101
(612) 227-7661

State Aid: Minnesota Higher Education Coordinating Board
400 Capitol Square
550 Cedar Street
St. Paul, MN 55101
(612) 296-3974

Mississippi

GSL: Mississippi GSL Agency
3825 Ridgewood Road
P.O. Box 342
Jackson, MS 39025-2336
(601) 982-6663

State Aid: Mississippi Postsecondary Education Financial Assistance Board
P.O. Box 2336
Jackson, MS 39205
(601) 982-6168

Missouri

Coordinating Board for Higher Education
P.O. Box 1438
Jefferson City, MO 65102
(314) 751-3940

Montana

Montana University System
33 South Last Chance Gulch
Helena, MT 59601
(406) 449-3024
GSL and State Aid

Nebraska

GSL: Cornhusker Bank Building
11th and Cornhusker Highway, Suite 304
Lincoln, NE 68521
(402) 476-9129

State Aid: Nebraska Coordinating Commission for Postsecondary Education
301 Centennial Mall South
P.O. Box 95005
Lincoln, NE 68509
(402) 471-2847

Nevada

GSL: Nevada State Department of Education
400 West King Street
Carson City, NV 89710
(702) 885-3107

State Aid: Financial Aid Office
University of Nevada, Reno
405 Marsh Avenue, Room 200 TSSC
Reno, NV 89557
(702) 784-4666

New Hampshire

GSL: New Hampshire Higher Education Assistance Foundation
44 Warren Street
Concord, NH 03301
(603) 225-6612

State Aid: New Hampshire Postsecondary Education Commission
61 South Spring Street
Concord, NH 03301
(603) 271-2555

New Jersey

GSL: New Jersey Higher Education Assistance Authority,
C.N. 543

Trenton, NJ 08625
(609) 292-3906

State Aid: Department of Higher
  Education
Office of Student Assistance
Number 4 Quakerbridge Plaza,
C.N. 540
Trenton, NJ 08625
(609) 292-4646

New Mexico
GSL: New Mexico Educational
  Assistance Foundation
2301 Yale S.E., Building F
Albuquerque, NM 87106
(505) 277-6304

State Aid: Board of Education
  Finance
1068 Cerrillos Road
Santa Fe, NM 87503
(505) 827-5017

New York
New York State Higher Educa-
tion Services Corporation
99 Washington Avenue
Albany, NY 12255
GSL: (518) 473-1574
State Aid: (518) 474-5642

North Carolina
North Carolina State Education
  Assistance Authority
P.O. Box 2688
Chapel Hill, NC 27515
GSL and State Aid: (919) 549-
8614

North Dakota
GSL: Bank of North Dakota
Student Loan Department
700 Main Street
Drawer 1657
Bismarck, ND 58501
(701) 224-5656

State Aid: North Dakota Student

Financial Assistance Program
10th Floor, State Capitol
Bismarck, ND 58505
(601) 224-4114

Ohio
GSL: Ohio Student Loan Com-
mission
P.O. Box 16610
Columbus, OH 43216
(614) 466-3091

State Aid: Ohio Board of Regents
3600 State Office Tower
30 East Broad Street
Columbus, OH 43215
(614) 466-7420

Oklahoma
Oklahoma State Regents for
  Higher Education
500 Education Building
State Capitol Complex
Oklahoma City, OK 73105
(405) 521-8262
GSL and State Aid

Oregon
Oregon State Scholarship Com-
mission
1445 Wilamette Street
Eugene, OR 97401
GSL: (800) 452-8807 (within OR)
(503) 686-3200
State Aid: (503) 686-4166

Pennsylvania
Pennsylvania Higher Education
  Assistance Agency
660 Boas Street
Harrisburg, PA 17102
GSL: (800) 692-7392 (within PA),
(717) 787-1932
State Aid: (800) 692-7435 (within
  PA),
(717) 787-1937

Rhode Island
Rhode Island Higher Education

Assistance Agency
274 Weybosset Street
Providence, RI 02903
(401) 277-2050
GSL and State Aid

South Carolina
GSL: South Carolina Student
  Loan Corporation
Interstate Center, Suite 210
P.O. Box 21337
Columbia, SC 29221
(803) 798-0916

State Aid: Higher Education Tuition Grants Agency
411 Keenan Building, Box 11638
Columbia, SC 29211
(803) 758-7070

South Dakota
GSL: South Dakota Education
  Assistance Corporation
115 First Avenue, SW
Aberdeen, SD 57401
(605) 225-6423

State Aid: Department of Education and Cultural Affairs
Richard F. Kneip Building
Pierre, SD 57501
(605) 773-3134

Tennessee
Tennessee Student Assistance
  Corporation
B-3 Capitol Towers, Suite 9
Nashville, TN 37219
(800) 342-1663 (within TN),
(615) 741-1346
GSL and State Aid

Texas
GSL: Texas Guaranteed Student
  Loan Corporation
P.O. Box 15996
Austin, TX 78761
(512) 835-1900

State Aid: Coordinating Board
  Texas College and University
  System
P.O. Box 12788,
Capitol Station
Austin, TX 78711
(512) 475-8169

Utah
GSL: Servicing Corp. of Utah
1706 Major Street
Salt Lake City, UT 84115
(801) 487-4448

State Aid: Utah State Board of
  Regents
3 Triad Center, Suite 550
Salt Lake City, UT 84180-1205
(801) 533-5617

Vermont
Vermont Student Assistance
  Corporation
Champlain Mill
P.O. Box 2000
Winnooski, VT 05404
(800) 642-3177 (within VT),
(802) 655-9602
GSL and Student Aid

Virginia
GSL: Virginia State Education
  Assistance Authority
6 North Sixth Street
Suite 400
Richmond, VA 23219
(804) 786-2035

State Aid: State Council of
  Higher Education for Virginia
James Monroe Building
1010 N. 14th Street
Richmond, VA 23219
(804) 225-2141

Washington
GSL: Washington Student Loan
  Guaranty Association
500 Colman Building

811 First Avenue
Seattle, WA 98104
(206) 625-1030

State Aid: Council for Postsecondary Education
980 East Fifth Avenue
Olympia, WA 98504
(206) 753-3571

West Virginia
GSL: Higher Education Assistance Foundation Higher Education Loan Program of West Virginia, Inc.
P.O. Box 591
Union Building, Suite 900
723 Kanawha Boulevard East
Charleston, WV 25322
(304) 345 7211

State Aid: West Virginia Board of Regents
950 Kanawha Boulevard East
Charleston, WV 25301
(304) 348-0112

Wisconsin
GSL: Wisconsin Higher Education Corporation
137 East Wilson Street
Madison, WI 53702
(608) 266-2897

State Aid: Wisconsin Higher Educational Aids Board
P.O. Box 7858
Madison, WI 53707
(608) 266-2897

Wyoming
GSL: Higher Education Assistance Foundation
American National Bank Building
20 Street at Capitol, Suite 320
Cheyenne, WY 82001
(307) 635-3259

State Aid: Wyoming Community College Commission
2301 Central Ave.
Barrett Building, Third Floor
Cheyenne, WY 82002
(307) 777-7763

American Samoa
GSL: Pacific Islands Educational Loan Program/United Student Aid Funds, Inc.
1314 S. King Street
Suite 962
Honolulu, HI 96814
(808) 536-3731

State Aid: American Samoa Community College
P.O. Box 2609
Pago Pago, American Samoa 96799
(684) 699-9155

Commonwealth of the Northern Mariana Islands
GSL: See American Samoa
State Aid: Northern Marianas College Board of Regents
P.O. Box 1250
Saipan, CM 96950
(Saipan) 7312

Guam
GSL: See American Samoa
State Aid: University of Guam
UOG Station
Mangilao, Guam 96913
(671) 734-2921

Puerto Rico
GSL: Higher Education Assistance Corp.
P.O. Box 42001
Minillas Station
Santurce, PR 00940
(809) 726-2525

State Aid: Council on Higher Education

Box F—UPR Station
Rio Piedras, PR 00931
(809) 751-5082/1136

Trust Territory of the Pacific Islands and Wake Island
GSL: See American Samoa
State Aid: Community College of
  Micronesia
P.O. Box 159
Kolonia, Ponape, FSM 96941
(Ponape) 480 or 479

Micronesian Occupational College
P.O. Box 9
Koror, Palau 96940
(Palau) 471

Virgin Islands
Board of Education
P.O. Box 11900
St. Thomas, VI 00801
(809) 774-4546
GSL and State Aid

USAF, Inc.
United Student Aid Funds Processing Center
P.O. Box 50827
Indianapolis, IN 46250
(800) 382-4506 (IN)
(800) 428-9250 (all other states)

Financial Aid Computer Matching Services

The following is a partial list of financial aid computer matching services. The companies and organizations listed responded to a survey administered by the California Student Aid Commission. This list is reprinted with their permission. Please note, however, that a group's inclusion in this list is *not* an endorsement. Investigate each group you are interested in before you invest your time, money, or hopes.

Key to Chart

Type I. Organizations that offer a computer search service for students and maintain their own data base.
Type II. Organizations that maintain a data base only.
Type III. Organizations that offer a computer search service for students utilizing another organization's data base (See Type II):
  III-A: Academic Guidance Services
  III-B: Student Financial Services
  III-C: Diversified Financial Corporation (the committee was unable to determine an address for this organization so it was not included in this survey)
Mail returned. This implies that a wrong address was used or that the service was out of business; (see below for Q#1 and Q#2).
No response. Means that the financial aid service did not respond to:
Q#1: The initial questionnaire sent out by the committee requesting general information on the services.
Q#2: The second questionnaire, which asked the extent to which services actually tried to match students to scholarship sources on the basis of sex, race, heritage, extracurriculars, career goals, etc.

Name of Organization	Mail Returned		No Response		Fee	Type
	Q#1	Q#2	Q#1	Q#2		
Academic Directions, Inc. New York, NY	X	N/A				
Academic Guidance Services Marlton, NJ					–	II
Academic Research and Marketing Corp. Ltd. Benton, IL				X		
Allstate Scholarship Guidance Service Beverly Hills, CA					$45	III-A
American Scholarship Council San Jose, CA					$38	I
Avila International Academic Financial Aid Division Hacienda Heights, CA				X		
Bexar County Scholarship Clearing House San Antonio, TX			X	N/A		
Career Dynamics Bellflower, CA				X	$45	III-A
CASHE (Computer Assist. Scholarships for Higher Education) College Student Financial Services, Inc. Gaithersburg, MD				X	$40	I
College Money Locator Encino, CA		X			$39	III-A
College Scholarship Service Elizabeth, NJ				X		
Darr Financial Services Lawndale, CA				X		
EducAid Atlanta, GA					$42.95	III-A

Name of Organization	Mail Returned		No Response		Fee	Type
	Q#1	Q#2	Q#1	Q#2		
Education Assistance Researchers Minneapolis, MN			X	N/A		
Educational Funding Services Tacoma, WA		X			$29.95	III-A
Educational & Training Services San Diego, CA				X	$49	III-B
F.A.C.T.S./Barry A. Fullerton Melbourne, FL			X	N/A		
Financial Aid Scholarship Service Burbank, CA			X	N/A		
Financial Aid Services Peterson's Guide Princeton, NJ					$45	I
Financial Aid Finder Fairfield, IA					$29	III-A
Great Lakes College Scholarship Services Toledo, OH					$19–$49	III-A
Guidance Information System (GIS) Time Share Corporation Avon, CT					—	II*
H.E.L.P., Inc. Lincoln Park, MI	X	N/A				
Just Scholarship, LTD Los Angeles, CA			X	N/A		
National Scholarship Service (NSRS) and International Scholarship Research Service (ISRS) San Rafael, CA					$35	I

*GIS is purchased by approximately 4,500 schools, colleges, and counseling centers nationwide who make the information available to students (usually at no charge). GIS indicated that their data base contains 600 sources.

Name of Organization	Mail Returned		No Response		Fee	Type
	Q#1	Q#2	Q#1	Q#2		
Nation-wide Promotions Student Scholarship Program Manchester Center, VT			X	N/A		
Nationwide Scholarship Services Tarzana, CA				X	$45	III-A
Private Loans San Diego, CA				X	$45	III-C
Scholarfund Redlands, CA			X	N/A		
Scholarship Bank Los Angeles, CA				X	$35–$45	I
Scholarship Clearing House Los Angeles, CA					$39	III-A
Scholarship Computer Center Seattle, WA			X	N/A		
Scholarship Finders Chicago, IL		X			$45	III-A
Scholarship Guidance Service Van Nuys, CA				X	$39	III-A
Scholarship Information Research Service Coral Springs, FL					$25	I
Scholarship Information Services San Diego, CA				X	$45	
Scholarship Match Citizen's Scholarship Foundation of America Concord, NH				X	–	II
Scholarship Matching Service America's Outstanding Names and Faces Andover, MA				X	$40	III-A

Name of Organization	Mail Returned		No Response		Fee	Type
	Q#1	Q#2	Q#1	Q#2		
Scholarship Matching Service Oak Park, IL				X	Not Given	III-A
Scholarship Referral Service Somerville, NJ				X		
Scholarship Research Tampa, FL			X	N/A		
Scholarship Research Consultants Henry Allen Company Northridge, CA				X	$45	III-A
Scholarship Research Service St. Paul, MN	X	N/A				
Scholarship Search New York, NY			X	N/A		
Scholarship Sources Student Financial Aid Search Los Angeles, CA			X	N/A		
Scholarships Unlimited Phoenix, AZ		X			$32.95 $49.95	III-A
Sources of Financial Aid Sacramento, CA				X	$39– $45	III-A
Student College Aid Houston, TX					$45	III-A
Student Financial Services Alpine, CA			X	N/A		II
Student Guidance Service Manchester, MO					$20– $49	III-A
Student Scholarship Services La Habra, CA			X	N/A		
Toleco Distributions Woodland Hills, CA				X	$39	III-A
Universal Student Aid Service Philadelphia, PA			X	N/A		

INDEX